The Journey of Humanity

ODED GALOR

The Journey of Humanity

Humanity

The Origins of Wealth and Inequality

DUTTON

DUTTON

An imprint of Penguin Random House LLC
penguinrandomhouse.com

First published in the United States of America by Dutton, an imprint of
Penguin Random House LLC, 2022.
Adapted from *The Journey of Humanity*, first published in Hebrew in Israel by Kinneret
Zmora-Bitan Dvir, Israel, in 2020. *The Journey of Humanity* copyright © 2020 by Oded Galor.

This book is based on numerous contributions of the author to unified growth theory and
to the exploration of the role of deep rotes of comparative development. An earlier version
of this book was written jointly in Hebrew, with Dr. Ori Katz, and was translated to
English by Eylon Levy, before being modified.

Figures designed by Darren Bennett.

LIBRARY OF CONGRESS CATALOGING-IN-PUBLICATION DATA
has been applied for.

ISBN 9780593185995 (hardcover)
ISBN 9780593186015 (ebook)

Printed in the United States of America
1st Printing

To Erica

Contents

II THE ORIGINS OF WEALTH
AND INEQUALITY

The Journey of Humanity

Mysteries of the Human Journey

A squirrel scurries along the windowsill of a Venetian Gothic structure at Brown University. It pauses for a moment and takes a curious peek at a peculiar human being who is spending his time writing a book, rather than devoting his energy – as he should – to foraging for food. This squirrel is a descendant of those who scampered through North America's virgin forests thousands of years ago. Like its distant ancestors and contemporaries around the world, the squirrel spends most of its time gathering food, evading predators, searching for mates and seeking shelter from precarious weather conditions.

And in fact for most of human existence, from the emergence of *Homo sapiens* as a distinct species nearly 300,000 years ago, the basic thrust of human life was remarkably similar to that of a squirrel, defined by the pursuit of survival and reproduction. Living standards bordered on the subsistence level and scarcely varied over the millennia or across the globe. But perplexingly, over the past few centuries, our mode of existence has been drastically transformed. From a historical standpoint, humankind has experienced a dramatic and unprecedented improvement in the quality of life virtually overnight.

Imagine if some residents of Jerusalem in the time of Jesus, 2,000 years ago, were to step into a time machine and travel to the Ottoman-ruled Jerusalem of 1800. They would undoubtedly be impressed by the magnificent new city wall, the considerable population growth and the adoption of new innovations. But although nineteenth-century Jerusalem was quite different from its Roman predecessor, our time travellers would adjust with relative ease to their new surroundings. Admittedly, they would have to adapt their behaviour to the new cultural norms, but they would be able to maintain the trades they had practised at the dawn of the first century and sustain themselves easily enough, since the knowledge and skills acquired in ancient Jerusalem would still be pertinent at the turn of the nineteenth century. They would also find themselves vulnerable to similar perils, illnesses and natural hazards as those endured in the Roman period, and their life expectancies would hardly alter.

Envision, however, the experience of our time travellers if they were whisked away in our time machine again, just another two hundred years ahead, to early-twenty-first-century Jerusalem. They would be utterly astounded. Their skills would now be obsolete, formal education would be a prerequisite for most occupations, and technologies that might seem like witchcraft would be daily necessities. Furthermore, as numerous fatal diseases of the past would have been eradicated, their life expectancy would instantly double, requiring an entirely different mindset and longer-term approach to life.

The gulf between these eras makes it difficult to conceive the world we left behind not so long ago. As the seventeenth-century English philosopher Thomas Hobbes put it bluntly, human life was *nasty, brutish, and short.*[1] At the time, a quarter of newborns died of cold, hunger and assorted illnesses before reaching their first birthday, women often perished during childbirth, and life expectancy rarely exceeded forty. It was a world engulfed in darkness after the disappearance of the sun over the horizon, a place where women, men and children devoted long hours to ferrying water to their homes, washed infrequently, and spent the winter months in smoke-filled homes. A time period in which most people lived in far-flung rural villages, rarely ventured from their birthplace, survived on paltry and monotonous diets, and could neither read nor write. A dismal era when an economic crisis did not simply demand belt-tightening, but rather led to mass starvation and death. Many of the daily hurdles that concern individuals in the present day pale in comparison to the hardships and tragedies faced by our not-so-distant forebears.

It has long been the prevailing wisdom that living standards have risen incrementally over the entire course of human history. This is a distortion. While the evolution of technology has indeed been a largely gradual process, accelerating over time, it has not resulted in a corresponding improvement in living conditions. The astounding ascent in the quality of life in the past centuries has in fact been the product of an abrupt transformation.

Most people of a few centuries ago led lives comparable to those of their remote ancestors – and most other individuals around the globe – millennia ago, rather than to those of their current descendants. The living conditions of an English farmer at the turn of the sixteenth century were similar to those of an eleventh-century Chinese serf, a Mayan peasant fifteen hundred years ago, a fourth-century BCE Greek herder, an Egyptian farmer 5,000 years ago, or a shepherd in Jericho 11,000 years ago. But since the dawn of the nineteenth century, a split second compared to the span of human existence, life expectancy has more than doubled, and per capita incomes have soared twenty-fold in the most developed regions of the world, and fourteen-fold on Planet Earth as a whole (Fig. 1).[2]

This continuing improvement has been so radical, in fact, that we often lose sight of just how exceptional this period is in relation to the rest of our history. What explains this *Mystery of Growth* – the scarcely conceivable transformation in the quality of life of the last few centuries, in terms of health, wealth and education, which dwarf any other changes in these dimensions since the emergence of *Homo sapiens*?

In 1798, the English scholar Thomas Malthus offered a plausible theory for the mechanism that had caused living standards to remain stagnant, effectively trapping societies in poverty, since time immemorial. He argued that whenever societies managed

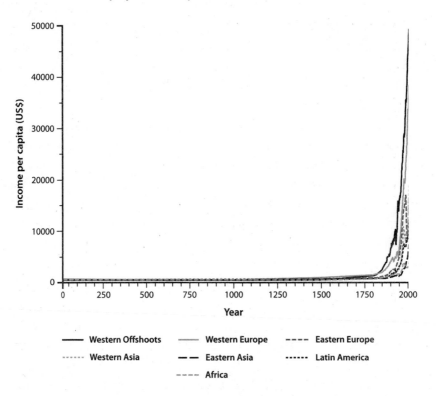

Figure 1. The Mystery of Growth

The dramatic spike in income per capita across world regions over the past two centuries follows thousands of years of stagnation.[3]

to bring about a food surplus through technological innovation, the resulting boost in living standards could only ever be temporary as it would lead inevitably to a corresponding rise in birth rates and a reduction in mortality rates. It was just a matter of time, therefore, before the ensuing population growth would deplete the food surpluses, and thus living conditions would revert to subsistence levels, leaving societies as poor as they had been before the innovation.

Indeed, during the period known as the Malthusian epoch – which is to say, the entirety of human history up until the recent dramatic leap forward – the fruits of technological advancements were channelled primarily towards larger and denser populations and had only a glacial impact on their long-term prosperity. Populations grew while living conditions stagnated and remained near subsistence. Variations between regions in terms of the sophistication of their technology and the productivity of their land were reflected in differing population densities, but the effects they had on living conditions were largely transitory. Ironically, however, just as Malthus completed his treatise and pronounced that this 'poverty trap' would endure indefinitely, the mechanism that he had identified suddenly subsided and the metamorphosis from stagnation to growth took place.

How did the human species break out of this poverty trap? What were the underlying causes of the extent of this epoch of stagnation? Might the forces that governed both the protracted economic ice age and our escape from it foster our understanding of why current living conditions are so unequal across the globe?

Fuelled by the conviction, and the evidence, that in order to understand the causes of the vast inequality in the wealth of nations we would have to identify the principal driving forces behind the process of development as a whole, I have developed a unified theory that seeks to encompass the journey of humanity in its entirety.[4] In shedding light on the forces that governed the transition from an epoch of stagnation to an era of sustained growth in living standards, it reveals the fingerprints of the distant past in the fate of nations.

In the first part of our voyage, we will explore the Mystery of Growth, focusing on the mechanism that confined the human species to a subsistence-orientated existence for most of history, and the forces that ultimately enabled some societies to break out of this trap and realise the unprecedented levels of prosperity enjoyed by many of the world's inhabitants today. Our voyage begins at the point of departure of humanity itself – the emergence of *Homo sapiens* in East Africa nearly 300,000 years ago – and traces the key milestones of the journey of humanity:

the migration of *Homo sapiens* from Africa tens of thousands of years ago, the scattering of people across the continents, the subsequent transition of societies from hunter-gatherer tribes to sedentary agricultural communities, and more recently the Industrial Revolution and the Demographic Transition.[5]

Human history is rich with countless and fascinating details: mighty civilisations that rose and fell; charismatic emperors who led armies to massive conquests and defeats; artists who created enchanting cultural treasures; philosophers and scientists who advanced our understanding of the universe, as well as the numerous societies and billions of lives lived away from the spotlight. It is easy to become adrift in this ocean of details, buffeted by the waves and unaware of the mighty currents underneath.

Instead, this book explores and identifies these undercurrents: the forces that have governed the development process. It demonstrates how these forces operated relentlessly, if invisibly, throughout the course of human history, and its long economic ice age, gathering pace until, at last, technological advancements in the course of the Industrial Revolution accelerated beyond a tipping point, where rudimentary education became essential for the ability of individuals to adapt to the changing technological environment. Fertility rates started to decline and the growth in living standards was liberated from the counterbalancing effects of population growth, ushering in long-term prosperity that continues to soar in the present day.

At the centre of this exploration is the question of the sustainability of our species on Planet Earth. During the Malthusian epoch, adverse climatic conditions and epidemics contributed to devastating decimations of the human population. Today, the impact of the growth process on environmental degradation and climate change raises significant concerns as to how our species might live sustainably and avert the catastrophic demographic outcomes of the past. The journey of humanity provides a hopeful outlook: the tipping point that the world has recently reached, resulting in a persistent decline in fertility rates and the acceleration of 'human capital' formation and technological innovation, could enable humanity to mitigate these detrimental effects and will be central for the sustainability of our species in the long run.

Intriguingly, when prosperity skyrocketed in recent centuries, it did so only in some parts of the world, triggering a second major transformation unique to our species: the emergence of immense inequality across societies. One might suppose that this phenomenon occurred primarily because the escape from the epoch of stagnation has occurred at different times across the globe. Western European countries and some of their offshoots in North America and Oceania experienced the remarkable leap in living conditions as early as the nineteenth century, while this ascent was delayed in most regions of Asia, Africa and Latin America until the latter half of the twentieth century (Fig. 2). But what accounts for some parts of the world undergoing this transformation earlier than others?

Disentangling the Mystery of Growth will enable us to grapple, in the second part of our voyage, with the *Mystery of Inequality* – the roots of the differences in development paths between societies and the momentous expansion of the gap in living standards among nations in the past two hundred years. Uncovering the deep-rooted factors behind this global disparity leads us to reverse the course of our journey and to take major sequential steps far back in history, ultimately reverting to the place where it all began – the exodus of *Homo sapiens* from Africa tens of thousands of years ago.

We shall consider institutional, cultural, geographical and societal factors that emerged in the ancient past and propelled societies on their distinct historical trajectories, influencing the timing of their escape from the epoch of stagnation, and inducing the gap in the wealth of nations. Institutional reforms, at random critical junctures in the course of history, occasionally placed countries on different paths and contributed to their divergence over time. Likewise, the proliferation of distinct cultural norms contributed to the variation in the movement of the great cogs of history across the globe.[6]

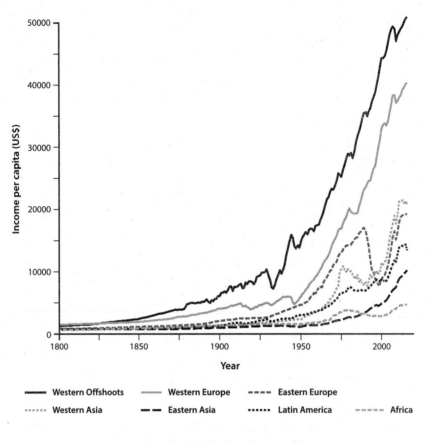

Figure 2. The Mystery of Inequality

The divergence in per capita income across world regions in the past two centuries.[7]

Yet, deeper factors, rooted in the distant past, often underpinned the emergence of cultural norms, political institutions and technological shifts, governing the ability of societies to flourish and prosper. Geographical factors, such as favourable soil and climatic characteristics, fostered the progression of growth-enhancing cultural traits – cooperation, trust, gender equality and future-oriented mindset. Land suitability for large plantations contributed to exploitation and slavery, and to the emergence and persistence of extractive political institutions. The disease environment adversely affected agricultural and labour productivity, investment in education and long-run prosperity.

And biodiversity that invigorated the transition to sedentary agricultural communities had beneficial effects on the process of development in the pre-industrial era, although these favourable forces have dissipated as societies transitioned to the modern era.

But there is an additional factor lurking behind modern-day institutional and cultural characteristics that joins geography as a fundamental driver of economic development – the degree of diversity within each society, its beneficial effects on innovation and its adverse implications for social cohesiveness. Our exploration of the role of geographical characteristics will take us 12,000 years back in time to the dawn of the Agricultural Revolution. The examination of the causes and consequences of diversity will lead us tens of thousands of years further back to the first strides of our species out of Africa.

This is not the first attempt to describe the core thrust of human history. Great thinkers such as Plato, Hegel and Marx argued that history unfolds according to inescapable universal laws, often disregarding the role of societies in shaping their own destinies.[8] This book, by contrast, neither posits an inexorable march of humanity towards utopia or dystopia, nor purports to derive moral insights about the desirability of the direction of this journey and its consequences. Suffice to say, the modern era of sustained improvement in living standards is hardly equivalent to a Garden of Eden, where social and political strife are absent. Massive inequities and injustices persist.

Instead, in order to understand and help mitigate the ultimate causes of the immeasurable inequality in the wealth of nations, this book is designed to faithfully present an interdisciplinary, scientifically based narrative of the evolution of societies since the emergence of *Homo sapiens*. In accordance with the cultural tradition that views technological development as progress,[9] the outlook derived from this exploration can be described as fundamentally hopeful, in terms of the overarching trajectory of societies across the globe.

In focusing on the grand arc of the journey of humanity, I do not intend to diminish the importance of the vast inequality within and across societies, but rather to empower us all with an understanding of the actions that could alleviate poverty and injustice and contribute to the prosperity of our species as a whole. As will be established, while the great forces underlying the journey of humanity continue to operate relentlessly, education, tolerance and greater gender equality hold the keys to our species' flourishing in the decades and centuries to come.

I

The Human Odyssey

1

First Steps

Climbing the winding path towards the Mount Carmel Caves in modern-day Israel, it is possible to envision the majestic environment that would have surrounded this site in prehistoric times. The Mediterranean climate would have been pleasant across the seasons, with moderate temperature fluctuations. The creek snaking through the mountains in the adjacent verdant valley would have been a source of potable water. The forests beside the mountain range would have been suitable for hunting deer, gazelles, rhinoceroses and boar, and out in the wild, in the open areas abutting the narrow coastal plain and the Samarian mountains, there would have grown prehistoric species of cereals and fruit trees. The warm climate, ecological diversity and raw materials surrounding the Mount Carmel Caves would have made them ideal homes for numerous bands of hunter-gatherers over the millennia. Indeed, remains unearthed in these ancient caves, now a UNESCO World Heritage Site of human evolution, attest to a sequence of prehistoric settlements over hundreds of thousands of years, as well as tantalising potential encounters between *Homo sapiens* and the Neanderthals.[1]

Archaeological findings from this and other sites across the globe indicate that archaic and early modern humans slowly but steadily acquired new skills, mastered the use of fire, developed increasingly sophisticated blades, handaxes, and flint and limestone tools, and created artworks.[2] A key driver of these cultural and technological advancements, which came to define humankind and set us apart from other species, was the evolution of the human brain.

Genesis

The human brain is extraordinary: large, compressed and more complex than the brain of any other species. It has tripled in size over the last six million years, with most of this transformation occurring 200,000–800,000 years ago, largely before the emergence of *Homo sapiens*.

Why have the capabilities of the human brain expanded so significantly over the course of the history of the human species? At first glance, the answer might appear self-evident: having an advanced brain has clearly allowed us to achieve levels of security and prosperity that no other species on Earth has managed to attain. Yet the reality is considerably more intricate. If a brain resembling the human one is indeed so unambiguously beneficial for survival, why has no other species developed a similar brain over billions of years of evolution?

Consider this distinction for a moment. Eyes, for example, developed independently along several evolutionary tracks. They evolved among vertebrates (amphibians, birds, fish, mammals and reptiles), cephalopods (including cuttlefish, octopuses and squid), as well as in a simpler form – ocelli – in invertebrates such as bees, spiders, jellyfish and sea stars. The distant ancestor of all these species, which lived more than 500 million years ago, seems to have had only basic light receptors, capable of distinguishing light from dark.[3] Nevertheless, since accurate vision has provided a distinct survival advantage in different environments, complex eyes evolved independently in some of these different groups, uniquely adapted in each case to the individual species' habitat.

This phenomenon, whereby similar traits evolved independently in different species rather than emerging from an existing trait in a common ancestor, is known as *convergent evolution.* There are numerous other examples, such as the development of wings among insects, birds and bats, and the comparable body shape that evolved in fish (shark) and marine mammals (dolphins) to suit life underwater. Evidently, various species have acquired similar beneficial traits by independent means – but not brains capable of crafting literary, philosophical and artistic masterpieces, or inventing the plough, the wheel, the compass, the printing press, the steam engine, the telegraph, the aeroplane and the internet. Such a brain has only evolved once – in humans. Why is such a powerful brain so rare in nature, despite its apparent advantages?

The resolution of this puzzle partly lies in the brain's two major drawbacks. First, our brain exhausts enormous amounts of energy. It consists of only 2 per cent of the body's weight while consuming 20 per cent of its energy. Second, its large size makes it difficult for a baby's head to pass through the birth canal. Consequently, the human brain is more compressed or 'folded' than other species' brains, and human babies are born with 'half-baked' brains that need years of fine-tuning to reach maturity. Human infants are therefore helpless: while the young of many other species can walk by themselves shortly after being born, and are rapidly able to acquire their own food, humans need a couple of years before they can walk by themselves in a stable fashion, and many more before they can reach material self-sufficiency.

Given these drawbacks, what led to the development of the human brain in the first place? Researchers have argued that several forces may have contributed jointly to this process. The *ecological hypothesis* suggests that the human brain evolved as a result of the exposure of our species to environmental challenges. As the climate fluctuated and nearby animal populations adapted accordingly, prehistoric humans with more advanced brains would have been better able to identify new food sources, devise hunting and gathering strategies, and develop cooking and storage technologies that allowed them to survive and thrive in the shifting ecological conditions of their local habitat.[4]

The *social hypothesis*, in contrast, maintains that the growing need to cooperate, compete and trade within complex social structures gave a more sophisticated brain, with its better ability to understand the motives of others and anticipate their reactions, an evolutionary advantage.[5] Likewise, being able to persuade, manipulate, flatter, recount and amuse – all of which would benefit one's social standing, as well as conferring advantages in themselves – spurred the development of the brain and the capacity for speech and discourse.

The *cultural hypothesis*, meanwhile, highlights the ability of the human brain to assimilate and store information, allowing it to be passed from one generation to the next. According to this viewpoint, one of the unique advantages of the human brain is its capacity to learn efficiently from the experiences of others, facilitating the acquisition of habits and preferences that boost survival in diverse settings without relying on the far slower process of biological adaptation.[6] In other words, human babies may be physically helpless but their brains are equipped with unique learning capacities, including the ability to grasp and retain the behavioural norms – the culture – that enabled their ancestors to survive and will help their descendants to prosper.

One mechanism that may have further contributed to the development of the brain is *sexual selection*. It could be that humans developed a preference for mates with more advanced brains, even in the absence of overt evolutionary advantages of the brain itself.[7] Perhaps these intricate brains attested to invisible qualities that were important for protecting and raising children, and potential mates were able to infer these qualities from perceptible attributes such as wisdom, articulation, quick thinking or a sense of humour.

The evolution of the human brain was the main impetus for the unique advancement of humanity, not least because it helped bring about *technological progress* – ever more sophisticated ways to turn the natural materials and resources around us to our advantage. These advancements, in turn, shaped future evolutionary processes, enabling human beings to adapt more successfully to their shifting environments and to further advance and utilise new technologies – an iterative and intensifying mechanism that has led to ever greater technological strides being made.

In particular, it is thought that developments in the mastery of fire, which allowed early humans to begin cooking their food, spurred additional growth of the brain by reducing the energy required to chew and digest, thus making calories more accessible and freeing space in the cranium previously occupied by jaw bones and muscles.[8] This reinforcing cycle may have fostered further innovation in cooking technologies, which may have led to further growth of the brain.

Yet our brain is not the only organ that sets us apart from other mammals. The human hand is another. In conjunction with our brains, our hands too evolved partly in response to technology, specifically the benefits of creating and utilising hunting tools, needles and cooking gear.[9] In particular, when the human species mastered the technology to carve stones and make wooden spears, the survival prospects of those who could use them forcefully and accurately improved. Better hunters could support their families more reliably, and therefore raise more children to adulthood. The intergenerational transmission of these skills increased the share of proficient hunters in the population, and the advantages of further innovations, such as sturdier spears and, later, stronger bows and sharper arrows, contributed to the evolutionary advantage of these hunting skills.

Positive feedback loops of a similar nature have emerged throughout our history: environmental changes and technological innovations enabled population growth and triggered the adaptation of humans to their changing habitat and their new tools; in turn, these adaptations enhanced our ability to manipulate the environment and to create new technologies. As will become apparent, this cycle is central to understanding the journey of humanity and to resolving the Mystery of Growth.

Exodus from the Cradle of Humankind

For hundreds of thousands of years, the human species roamed in small bands of hunter-gatherers in Africa, developing complex technological, social and cognitive capabilities along the way.[10] As prehistoric humans became ever better hunters and gatherers, their population in the fertile regions of Africa increased significantly, ultimately reducing the living space and natural resources available to each of them. Thus, once climatic conditions permitted, humans started branching out to other continents in search of additional fertile grounds.

Homo erectus, arguably the first hunter-gatherer species of human, spread out to Eurasia nearly two million years ago. To date, the oldest fossils of early *Homo sapiens* to have been discovered outside of Africa are 210,000 years old (uncovered in Greece), and 177,000–194,000 years old (found on Mount Carmel in northern Israel).[11] Yet it appears that the descendants of these first modern humans to leave Africa became extinct or retreated into Africa due to adverse climatic conditions during the glacial period.[12]

It was in Africa, then, about 150,000 years ago that the most recent (matrilineal) ancestor of all living humans, Mitochondrial Eve, emerged. Although there were of course numerous women in Africa at the time, their lineages ultimately became extinct. All humans on Planet Earth today are descended from this one African woman.[13]

The widely accepted 'Out of Africa' hypothesis suggests that the current population of anatomically modern humans across the globe descends predominantly from a more significant migration of *Homo sapiens* from Africa as early as 60,000–90,000 years ago.[14] Humanity flocked to Asia via two routes: the northern via the Nile Delta and the Sinai Peninsula to the eastern

Mediterranean region known as the Levant, and the southern one via the Bab-el-Mandeb Strait at the mouth of the Red Sea into the Arabian Peninsula (Fig. 3).[15] The first modern humans reached South East Asia more than 70,000 years ago,[16] Australia 47,000–65,000 years ago,[17] and Europe nearly 45,000 years ago.[18] They settled Beringia approximately 25,000 years ago, crossing the land bridge over the Bering Strait during several periods of the Pleistocene Ice Age, and entered deeper into the Americas 14,000–23,000 years ago.[19]

These waves of migrations out of Africa contributed to the size and the diversity of the human population across Planet Earth. As prehistoric humans settled new ecological niches, they enjoyed access to new grounds for hunting and gathering and started to multiply more rapidly. Meanwhile, their adaptation to diverse new environments led to greater human and technological diversity, fostering the spread and cross-pollination of innovations, and leading to further population growth.

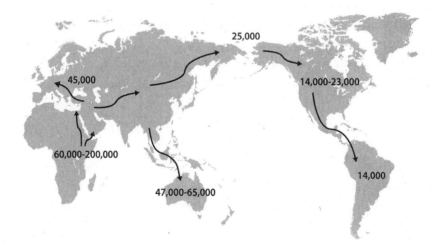

Figure 3. The Migration of *Homo sapiens* out of Africa

The estimated migration routes of *Homo sapiens* and their approximate years before the present. (Frequently revised in light of new discoveries.)

Ultimately, however, population growth led to the same scarcity of fertile land and resources that had spurred the migration from Africa in the first place. Despite their new tools and techniques, humans' living standards gradually reverted towards the subsistence level. The inability to sustain the growing population, as well as climatic changes, eventually induced humanity to explore an alternative mode of subsistence – agriculture.

Early Settlement

Nearly 12,000 years ago, as the climate gradually warmed in the aftermath of the latest glacial period, *Homo sapiens* experienced a dramatic transformation. Across the world, people gradually swapped their nomadic wandering for sedentary lifestyles, and began to make great strides in art, science, writing and technology.

Evidence from the Natufian culture (13,000–9500 BCE), which flourished in the Levant, suggests that in some places the transition to permanent dwellings predated the onset of agriculture. Despite being predominantly hunter-gatherers, the Natufians lived in stable residences, made typically of a drystone foundation with brushwood superstructure. Each settlement contained up to a few hundred people, who ventured out for hunting expeditions and for gathering native wild crops.[20] But for the majority of the world's human population at the time, it was the transition to agriculture that was the primary inducement to sedentism.

The Agricultural Revolution, also known as the Neolithic Revolution, first emerged in the Fertile Crescent – a lush region along the Tigris and Euphrates rivers, down the eastern Mediterranean coast, and around Egypt's Nile Delta – which was abundant in a wide variety of domesticable species of plants and animals. Agriculture emerged independently, about 10,000 years ago, in South East Asia, and from these distinct locations it spread swiftly across the Eurasian land mass. The rapid diffusion of agricultural practices within this vast region was enabled by the east–west orientation of these continents and the feasibility of the dispersal of plants, animals and technologies along similar lines of latitude without encountering major natural obstacles.

In contrast, as argued by the American geographer and historian Jared Diamond in his Pulitzer Prize-winning book *Guns, Germs and Steel*, sub-Saharan Africa and the Americas, which contained far fewer domesticable species of plants and animals, experienced the transition to agriculture significantly later.[21] Despite an early onset of agriculture in Meso-America and in some regions of Africa, the diffusion of agricultural practices was slower within these areas because the north–south orientation of these continents created major differences in climate and soil between regions. Moreover, the Sahara and the largely impassable tropical rainforests in Central America served as natural barriers to this diffusion process.

Nonetheless, after hundreds of thousands of years of painfully slow technological and social change, this process – the transition from hunter-gatherer tribes to agricultural societies, and from nomadic lifestyle to sedentary living – spread within a few thousand years to most of humanity. During the Neolithic Revolution, humans domesticated a wide range of wild plants and animals around the world. Wheat, barley, peas, chickpeas, olives, figs and date palms, as well as sheep, goats, pigs and pigeons, were first domesticated in the Fertile Crescent. Grapes and pomegranates in the nearby Transcaucasian region. Rice, buffalo and silkworms were domesticated in China, and ducks in South East Asia. Sesame, aubergines and zebus in the Indian subcontinent. Sorghum, yams, coffee and donkeys in Africa. Sugar cane and bananas in New Guinea, and maize, beans, squash and potatoes, as well as turkeys, llamas and alpacas, in the Americas.[22]

Central for our story, agricultural societies benefited from significant technological advantages, which persisted for thousands of years. Unlike hunting and gathering tribes, these communities generated significantly larger output, which supported a growing population. Bigger and better equipped than hunter-gatherer tribes, agricultural societies ultimately displaced and absorbed non-agricultural groups as they proliferated across continents.

Meanwhile, the intensification of trade within each agricultural community freed individuals to specialise in a particular occupation, as a farmer, potter, weaver, toolmaker, merchant or artisan, for example. Gradually this led to the emergence of distinct social strata including, of particular importance, a non-food-producing class who were dedicated instead to knowledge creation. Taken together, the subsequent advancements in art, science, writing and technology herald the onset of civilisation.

The Dawn of Civilisation

Most agricultural societies initially maintained the social frameworks that had prevailed prior to the Neolithic Revolution. The cohesiveness of these small-scale, tribal societies with their densely interwoven kinship ties facilitated cooperation and the mitigation of disputes. Tribal leadership enforced the community's rules and fostered cooperation, but significant social strata rarely emerged, and nearly all individuals engaged in agricultural or pastoral activities.

But as settlements grew in size, as their populations became denser, and as people's occupations became more various, there arose a need for more widespread cooperation, beyond the capabilities of the kinship framework. The complex political and religious institutions that emerged to serve this need allowed our ancestors to collaborate on a much larger scale, enabling them to build vast irrigation systems, mighty temples, intimidating fortresses and formidable armies.[23] Entirely new social layers were born, including rulers, noblemen, priests, artists, tradesmen and soldiers.

Jericho, one of the earliest continuous settlements in the

world, began to expand around 9000 BCE and lasted well into the biblical period. It consisted of a dense warren of houses, abundant in tools and ritual objects, that were home to 1,000–2,000 people, and was surrounded by a stone wall 3.6 metres high, featuring an 8.5-metre-high tower.[24] A second important settlement in the Fertile Crescent – Çatalhöyük (7100–5700 BCE) – was a regional trading centre for pottery, flint and obsidian tools, and luxury goods. This site, located in Anatolia, in present-day Turkey, contained rows of decorated mud-brick houses built right up against each other, accommodating at its peak approximately 3,000–10,000 people who farmed wheat, barley, legumes, sesame, almonds and pistachios, and raised domesticated livestock including sheep, goats and cattle.

Most of the great cities of the ancient world sprung up initially on the banks of the Euphrates, Tigris and Nile rivers, 4,000–6,000 years ago. They included the ancient centres of the Sumerian and Akkadian civilisations, Uruk and Ur, which reached nearly 100,000 inhabitants during this period, and Memphis in ancient Egypt.[25] Cities in China – and subsequently India and Greece – approached the same size as that of the dominant settlements in the Fertile Crescent about 3,300 years ago, while Carthage, in North Africa, reached this stature a thousand years later. Intriguingly, it was not until 2,000 years ago that a European city – Rome – topped the rankings of the world's largest cities, and it was not until the twentieth century that a city in the Americas – New York – was crowned the most populous worldwide.

Once again, this transitional moment in the journey of humanity was spurred by and led to technological advancement. A sudden acceleration of innovation at this time enabled further domestication of plants and animals, and improved cultivation, storage, communication and transportation. Methods of cultivation that were gradually introduced included the use of hoes, hand- and ultimately animal-drawn ploughs, irrigation systems and eventually terraced farming. Societies mastered the use of fire in the processing of clay and metal, and used these materials along with cement for the construction of dwellings, tools and grain storage. They learned to utilise water energy to grind grain; saddled domesticated horses, donkeys and camels to carry them across land; and harnessed the wind's power to sweep them over oceans and seas. Five and a half thousand years after the people of Jericho constructed their fearsome 8.5-metre-high watchtowers, the Egyptians built the Great Pyramid of Giza, soaring initially to a height of 146.5 metres.

In addition, the technology of writing first appeared in Sumer in southern Mesopotamia 5,500 years ago. It emerged largely independently in Egypt 5,200 years ago, in China 3,300 years ago, and autonomously in Meso-America as early as 2,500 years ago. Writing was developed initially for accounting and recording purposes, and subsequently for funerary inscription. Yet it also, importantly, allowed societies to store useful knowledge, pass it on to future generations, and solidify unifying myths.

As did earlier periods of technological change, the Neolithic Revolution not only transformed the lifestyle and tools of human beings, but in doing so it also stimulated biological adaptations to their new environments. The co-evolution of genes and culture is perhaps best exemplified by an adaptation brought about by the domestication of animals – lactase persistence. Lactase is an enzyme that is essential for the digestion of lactose – a sugar found in dairy products. Like other mammals, prehistoric humans only generated lactase in infancy. But mutations that emerged in Western Asia, Europe and East Africa as early as 6,000–10,000 years ago permitted the persistence of lactase generation and thus milk consumption beyond infancy.[26] Specifically, among the societies of cattle herders and shepherds that inhabited these regions, adults who happened to be able to produce lactase could use their animals as a portable and renewable source of food. The evolutionary advantage this conferred led to greater prevalence of this trait in these populations over time. As a result, over 90 per cent of adults in the British Isles and Scandinavia are lactose-tolerant, whereas the proportion plummets to under 10 per cent in East Asian communities – where the economy was not traditionally based on sheep and cattle.[27]

Animal milk was not the only natural product that we evolved to consume. Similar mutations enabled the digestion of starch, allowing humans to integrate bread into their diets. Nor were our adaptations limited to an expanding diet. The rise in population density and the domestication of animals led to greater prevalence and thus resistance to infectious diseases and contributed in some societies to an innate immunity to malaria.[28]

Thus, the Agricultural Revolution set the stage for a cycle of mutual reinforcement between technological change and human adaptation. Triggered by population growth and climate change, and shaped by geography, a technological transformation took place – a change in our material relationship with our environment, involving greater use of domesticable plants and animals. It resulted in social and biological adaptations that both enabled this technological transformation and intensified our dependence on it. Ultimately, it was this cycle, an underlying force that has continued ever since, that generated significant growth in the human population and its control over its living environment, transforming *Homo sapiens* into the dominant species on Planet Earth.

Yet as noted at the outset, despite these enormous advances in knowledge and technology, quite mysteriously human living standards, measured in terms of lifespan, quality of life and our degree of material comfort and prosperity, remained largely stagnant. To resolve this mystery, we have to delve deeper into the origins of this stagnation: the poverty trap.

2

Lost in Stagnation

The eighteenth-century cleric Thomas Malthus was raised in a wealthy family among England's social elite. An influential scholar, he deplored the utopianism of contemporary philosophers such as William Godwin and Nicolas de Condorcet – luminaries of the Age of Enlightenment – who envisioned humanity's path as one of inevitable progress towards an ideal society. In 1798, Malthus published *An Essay on the Principle of Population*, in which he expressed his profound scepticism about these prevailing and, to his mind, naive views. He advanced the gloomy thesis that in the long run humanity could never prosper because any gains it made would ultimately be depleted by population growth.

Malthus had considerable influence on his contemporaries. Some of the most prominent political economists of the period, including David Ricardo and John Stuart Mill, were profoundly swayed by his argument. Karl Marx and Friedrich Engels, on the other hand, assailed him for neglecting the role of class-ridden institutions in the prevalence of misery, while the fathers of the theory of evolution, Charles Darwin and Alfred Russel Wallace, credited his treatise with having a decisive influence on the development of their own highly influential thesis.

In retrospect, Malthus's description of the world as it existed in the past was entirely accurate. It was his pessimistic predictions about the future of humanity that turned out to be utterly mistaken.

The Malthusian Thesis

Imagine a village in the pre-industrial age where the inhabitants devise a more efficient method to grow wheat using iron ploughs, considerably increasing their ability to produce bread. At first, the villagers' diets would improve and, trading some of the surplus, their living conditions would rise. The abundance of food might even enable them to reduce their work and enjoy some leisure. But critically, Malthus argued, this surplus would allow them to sustain more surviving children, and accordingly the village's population would grow over time. And since the land available for wheat cultivation within the village is necessarily limited, this population growth would gradually lead to a reduction in each villager's bread ration. Living standards would begin to drop after the initial rise and would only stop falling once the ratio of loaves per villager returned to its original level. Painfully, their technological progress would lead to a larger but not a richer population in the long run.

This trap has had all living beings in its clutches. Consider a pack of wolves on an island. Global cooling causes sea levels to drop and uncovers a land bridge to another island, which is home to a peaceful population of rabbits. The wolves gain new hunting grounds, the availability of additional prey boosts their living standard, and more cubs survive to reach maturity, leading to an explosion of the wolf population. However, as more wolves must share a limited amount of rabbits, the wolves' living standard gradually reverts to the pre-cooling level, while the wolf population stabilises at a larger size. Access to more resources does not make the wolves better off in the long run.

The Malthusian hypothesis is based on two fundamental building blocks. The first is that a rise in resources (agricultural yields, fishing hauls, and hunting and gathering bounties) leads populations to have more surviving offspring, driven by the biological, cultural and religious predisposition to reproduce, and the decline in child mortality that accompanies better nourishment. The second building block is that population growth engenders a decline in living conditions whenever living space is limited. According to Malthus, the size of any population will adapt to the available resources via two mechanisms: *the positive check* – a rise in mortality rates due to the increased frequency of famine, disease and war over resources in societies whose populations have outgrown their food production; and *the preventative check* – a drop in birth rates during periods of scarcity through delayed marriage and the use of contraception.

Did technological advancements in the pre-industrial era lead to larger but not richer populations as implied by the Malthusian thesis? The evidence is clear that technological sophistication and population size were indeed positively associated in this era, but the existence of this relationship does not in itself indicate an impact of technology *on* population. In fact, technological advancements during this period were partly the *result* of larger populations because sizeable societies produced both more potential inventors and greater demand for their inventions. Besides, it may be that other independent factors – cultural, institutional or environmental – contributed to the growth of both technology and population, thus accounting for the positive correlation between the two. In other words, this correlation cannot in itself be taken as evidence of Malthusian forces.

Fortunately, the Neolithic Revolution provides us with an intriguing way to test the validity of the Malthusian thesis. As argued convincingly by Jared Diamond, the evidence strongly suggests that regions that underwent the Neolithic Revolution earlier enjoyed a technological head start over their contemporaries which persisted for thousands of years.[1] We can therefore infer a region's level of technological advancement from our knowledge of when it underwent the Neolithic Revolution (or from the number of domesticable species of plants and animals in the region). Put another way, at any single point in time, regions that had undergone the Neolithic Revolution earlier would be expected to have higher levels of technological sophistication. Thus, all other factors being equal, if a region that underwent the Neolithic Revolution earlier is *also* larger or richer, we can confidently conclude that this has been *caused* by its level of technological advancement.

Using this approach, we can indeed observe the Malthusian mechanism at work prior to the industrial era. In 1500 CE, for instance, higher technological level, as inferred from an earlier onset of the Neolithic Revolution, did indeed lead to greater population density, whereas the impact on per capita income was negligible (Fig. 4).[2]

Separate evidence, meanwhile, shows that fertile soil also contributed to higher population density but *not* to higher living standards. And examining even earlier eras through the same lens reveals an impressively consistent pattern – technological advancements and higher land productivity led primarily to larger but not richer populations, implying that prior to the Industrial Revolution, people across the world enjoyed largely similar standards of living.

The Inevitable Onset of Agriculture

The Malthusian mechanism sheds light on the roots of major events in the course of history that might otherwise appear perplexing. One apparent conundrum is that human remains from early agricultural societies do not attest to improved health or wealth but rather to deteriorating living standards as compared to those of hunter-gatherers living millennia before. Hunter-gatherers evidently lived longer, consumed a richer diet, worked less intensively and suffered fewer infectious diseases.[4] Why, then, did these early farmers and shepherds abandon the relatively bountiful and superior life of hunting and gathering?

As described above, the prehistoric humans who branched out of Africa and settled new ecological niches would have

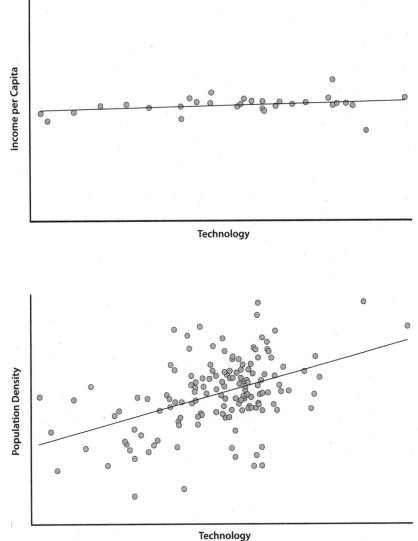

**Figure 4. Effects of Technology Level on Population Density and
Per Capita Income across Countries in the Year 1500 CE**

The chart depicts, based on cross-country variation in the year 1500 CE,
the positive impact of the level of technology (as inferred by the time elapsed
since the Neolithic Revolution) on population density (bottom panel) and
its insignificant effect on per capita income (top panel).

(Each circle represents a region delineated by its modern international borders.)[3]

enjoyed access to plentiful new resources and would have been able to multiply rapidly without reducing their living conditions. Ultimately, however, in accordance with the Malthusian mechanism, this population growth would have balanced out the gains as greater numbers of humans competed for the same stock of wild animals and plants. Living conditions would gradually have reverted to their original subsistence level, despite advances in tools and techniques. In fact, in some societies the decline in living standards, due to excessive population growth, was even worse than a mere reversion and presented the possibility of a societal collapse.

This was particularly severe in regions that *ancient* humans, prior to *Homo sapiens*, had never settled and where the local animals had not adapted to the human threat. In these regions, such as in Oceania and the Americas, the arrival of *Homo sapiens* with their advanced weapons led to such a boom in hunting that it soon brought most large mammals to extinction, forcing the growing number of tribes to compete for resources that were rapidly dwindling.

An extreme and dismal example of rapid population growth and over-extraction leading ultimately to collapse can be seen among the isolated Polynesian tribes, such as those who settled Easter Island in the Pacific Ocean at the beginning of the thirteenth century.[5] For nearly four hundred years, the human population of Easter Island expanded rapidly due to the abundance of vegetation and fishing waters. The Polynesians built a flourishing civilisation on the island and sculpted the famous and impressive moai statues, the largest of which stands ten metres tall. However, population growth eventually placed increasing pressure on the fragile local ecosystem. By the turn of the eighteenth century, Easter Island's bird population had been wiped out and its forests destroyed, making it harder for the inhabitants to build and maintain fishing boats. The tension this engendered sparked frequent internal conflicts and caused the local population to be decimated by nearly 80 per cent.[6] Similar ecological disasters, described by Jared Diamond in his book

Collapse, occurred on the Pitcairn Islands in the Southern Pacific Ocean, among Native Americans who settled territories in present-day south-western United States, in the Maya civilisation in Central America, and among the Nordic tribes who settled Greenland.[7]

Hunter-gatherer societies in the Fertile Crescent experienced comparable pressure nearly 12,000 years ago. Population growth supported by food abundance and technological improvements prompted a gradual decline in per capita food availability from hunting and gathering until their temporarily enhanced living standards reverted towards subsistence. However, the particular biodiversity of the Fertile Crescent with its abundance of domesticable species of plants and animals granted these societies an alternative mode of subsistence that was largely unavailable to the Easter Islanders – adopting agriculture. Climatic conditions contributed, too.[8] With the end of the last ice age, around 11,500 years ago, land became more suitable for agriculture and climatic volatility and seasonality increased. Farming thus became a safer strategy of food production, despite being associated with inferior diet quality, than the richer but less predictable and increasingly scarcer one of hunting and gathering.

The viability of reliance on agriculture in the Fertile Crescent helped avert the ecological crisis that would later destroy the civilisation on Easter Island, allowing the region to support a significantly larger population. Indeed, by some accounts, a single acre of land could feed nearly a hundred times more farmers and shepherds than hunter-gatherers.[9] Ultimately, of course, the population size of agricultural societies stabilised at a new and higher level, but this time, in reverting to subsistence level, their living conditions actually became significantly lower than those of hunter-gatherers who had lived *millennia* before them, when existing ecological niches were not yet densely populated. Compared to the living standards of the hunter-gatherers who were their more immediate ancestors, however, the transition to agriculture was entirely rational, perhaps even inevitable; in fact, it did not reflect a deterioration. Intriguingly, this switch from the bountiful lifestyle of much earlier hunters and gatherers to the impoverished living standards of densely packed farmers may be the origin of the myth of a lost paradise, common to several cultures across the world.

With their larger populations and their technological head start, agricultural societies out-competed the hunter-gatherers who remained until eventually agricultural practices became dominant across vast swathes of the globe. A new epoch had begun and there was no going back.

Population Swings

We can also detect the powerful Malthusian mechanism at work in the population swings that took place in the era after the Neolithic Revolution, triggered by dramatic ecological, epidemiological and institutional upheavals.

One of the most devastating events in human history was the Black Death – a pandemic of bubonic plague that first erupted in China in the fourteenth century and then made its way west with Mongolian troops and merchants as they travelled along the Silk Road to the Crimean Peninsula. From there it continued its journey on merchant ships to the city of Messina in Sicily and Marseilles in France in 1347 and spread like wildfire across the European continent.[10] Between 1347 and 1352 the plague killed 40 per cent of the European population. It was especially lethal in densely populated areas. Within just a few years, many cities – including Paris, Florence, London and Hamburg – lost more than half of their inhabitants.[11]

Though we can envision the lasting psychological trauma of the Black Death, whose survivors lost many of their relatives and friends, the plague did not ravage their wheat fields or flour mills. European farmers were therefore able to resume their work after the terrible devastation and found that demand for their labour had soared. The land desperately needed more working hands, and average labourers soon enjoyed higher

Triumph of Death
Wall painting (1448), Palermo, Italy[12]

wages and better working conditions than they had prior to the Black Death.

In the years 1345–1500, as the population of England collapsed from 5.4 million to just 2.5 million people, real wages more than doubled (Fig. 5). As a result of the improved living standards these wages afforded, birth rates rose and death rates fell, and so the English population slowly started to recover. But in accordance with the Malthusian mechanism, that population growth led eventually to a fall in average wages until, within three centuries, both population and wages had reverted to their pre-plague levels.

Another momentous population swing followed Christopher Columbus's voyages to the Americas in 1492–1504. These continents contained bountiful crops such as cocoa, maize, potatoes,

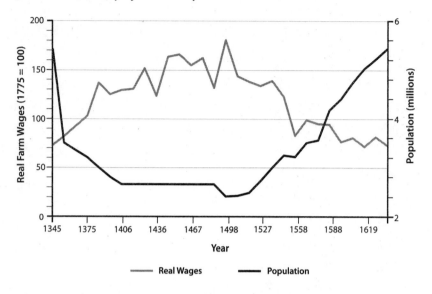

**Figure 5. The Impact of the Black Death on
Wages and Population in England**

The population of England declined sharply after the onset of the Black Death
in 1348, resulting in a temporary rise in real wages, which reverted to their
pre-plague level as population rebounded to its pre-plague level by 1615.[13]

tobacco and tomatoes that were unfamiliar to Europeans, who started shipping them back to Europe. In the opposite direction crops such as bananas, coffee beans, sugar cane, wheat, barley and rice were brought to the Americas for the first time.

The potato reached Europe in approximately 1570 and quickly became a staple of European cuisine. Potatoes had an especially big impact in Ireland, where they became popular among poor subsistence farmers. This crop was particularly well suited to the Irish soil and climate; it boosted farmers' incomes in the short run, and sometimes even allowed them to save enough to buy new livestock.[14] The first peasants to cultivate potatoes enjoyed a significant increase in their calorie consumption and quality of life.

In accordance with the Malthusian theory, however, this improvement was to be short-lived. In the aftermath of the introduction of the potato, the Irish population swelled from about 1.4 million in 1600 to 8.2 million in 1841, keeping living standards close to subsistence.[15] In fact, the situation was to grow even worse than it had been. In the years 1801–45, numerous parliamentary committees debated the situation; most concluded that Ireland's rapid population growth and collapsing living conditions put it on the brink of disaster, since by then much of the Irish population was entirely dependent on potatoes for its subsistence.[16] Worst of all, it was dependent on a single variety of potato.

In 1844, Irish newspapers started reporting that a new fungus – late blight – was ravaging potato crops in the United States. The fungus soon reached European ports aboard American cargo ships. From there, it spread to the fields, destroying crops in Belgium, southern England, France, Ireland and the Netherlands. It is estimated that nearly half of all potato crops in Ireland were blighted in 1845 and three-quarters in 1846. The lack of diversity in Ireland's potato crops meant that farmers had no alternative varieties with which to replace their devastated harvests. In the absence of useful intervention or relief from the British government, whose policies had encouraged dependency on the single crop in the first place, mass famine became inevitable, and during the Great Famine (1845–49) about one million people, mainly in poor rural areas, died from starvation, typhus and diseases that malnourished human bodies were unable to fend off, while more than one million immigrated to Great Britain and North America. Some areas lost more than 30 per cent of their population. Whole villages were emptied of their inhabitants. Thus, over the course of three centuries, the introduction of a superior crop and its subsequent destruction translated into an increase and then a tragic decline in population size, but living conditions in the long run were largely unaffected.

The Europeans were not alone in adopting crops from the New World; the Chinese imported sweet potatoes and maize, which were better suited to their soil than potatoes. Maize reached China in the mid-sixteenth century across three routes: from the north, via the Silk Road, which cut through Central Asia to the province of Gansu; from the south-west, through India and Burma to the province of Yunnan; and from the south-east, aboard Portuguese merchants' ships who traded along the Pacific coast of the Fujian province.[17] Initially, maize spread fairly slowly and its cultivation was limited to these three provinces. It gained popularity in the mid-eighteenth century, and by the turn of the twentieth century it had become a staple across the whole of China. The adoption of maize had such an impact on the country's agricultural output that Chinese researchers later dubbed it their second 'agricultural revolution'.[18]

In many scientific disciplines, controlled experiments enable researchers to determine the impact of a particular factor, such as a novel drug or vaccine, by measuring its effect on an experimental (treatment) group relative to a control group. For historical episodes, however, we cannot wind the clocks back, expose some humans (and not others) to a particular effect, and examine its impact over time. Yet we can draw on *quasi-natural historical experiments* – historical scenarios that reproduce approximate laboratory conditions, and allow us to infer the impact of a particular factor or event by comparing its influence on the exposed population relative to an equivalent control (unexposed) population.[19] The fact that maize arrived at different times in the different provinces of China provides such a quasi-natural historical experiment with which to test the Malthusian thesis within a country rather than across countries.

According to the theory, we should find that in the long run Chinese provinces that adopted maize earlier would end up with greater population densities than those that adopted it later but not with higher income per capita or economic development. However, simply comparing the regions' population densities and living standards is of no use, as provinces that adopted maize earlier may also have had other key differences from the provinces that adopted it later, differences that also affected their population density and living standards. Indeed, China as a whole underwent other major transformations during this period that may have influenced regional levels of population density and living standards, independently of the adoption of maize.

Instead, scholars have compared the long-term *changes* in population density and economic prosperity experienced by the first three Chinese provinces that adopted maize with those *changes* in provinces that did not adopt it until much later. Comparing the 'differences-in-differences' rather than differences in the actual levels permits us to remove these potentially confounding factors.[20] And indeed, consistent with the Malthusian hypothesis, the early introduction of maize in these three Chinese provinces resulted in a 10 per cent larger *increase* in population density than in the other provinces, over the period 1776–1910, and had no apparent impact on wage levels. Overall, the introduction of maize accounts for about a fifth of China's total population growth during this period.

It is apparent, then, that neither surpluses nor shortages prevailed indefinitely during the Malthusian epoch. The introduction of novel crops or technologies magnified the rate of population growth, mitigating their impact on economic prosperity, while the long-term economic devastation of ecological disasters was ultimately averted by their adverse effects on population via famine, disease and wars. An economic ice age was inevitable.

The Economic Ice Age

The Neolithic Revolution, as well as a series of monumental cultural, institutional, scientific and technological advances, had no discernible long-lasting effect on either the economic measure of living standards (per capita income) or the biological one (life expectancy). Like other species, over most of their existence, humans were caught in a trap of hardship and privation, near the subsistence level.

Despite some regional differences, income per capita and

wages for unskilled labourers in different civilisations fluctuated within only a very narrow band for thousands of years. In particular, estimates suggest that wages for a workday were the equivalent of seven kilograms of wheat grains in Babylon and five kilograms in the Assyrian Empire more than three thousand years ago, eleven to fifteen kilograms in Athens more than two thousand years ago, and four kilograms in Egypt under the Roman Empire. In fact, even on the eve of their Industrial Revolution, wages in Western European countries remained in this narrow range: ten kilograms of wheat in Amsterdam, five in Paris, and three to four in Madrid, Naples and assorted cities in Italy and Spain.[21]

Moreover, skeletal remains across various tribes and civilisations over the past 20,000 years indicate that despite some regional and temporary differences, life expectancy (at birth) oscillated within a very narrow band.[22] Remains uncovered in Mesolithic sites in North Africa and the Fertile Crescent suggest that life expectancy was nearly thirty years. During the subsequent Agricultural Revolution it did not change significantly in most regions, though it dropped in some.[23] In particular, skeletons exhumed from burial sites dating from the early stages of the Neolithic Revolution, 4,000 to 10,000 years ago, suggest that life expectancy was about thirty to thirty-five at Çatalhöyük (Turkey) and Nea Nikomedeia (Greece), twenty at Khirokitia (Cyprus), and thirty near the towns of Karataş (Turkey) and Lerna (Greece). Two and a half thousand years ago, life expectancy reached about forty years in Athens and Corinth, but headstones from the Roman Empire indicate yet again an age at death in the range of twenty to thirty.[24] More recent evidence points to fluctuations in life expectancy in the range of thirty to forty years in England from the mid-sixteenth to nineteenth centuries,[25] and comparable values were recorded in pre-industrial France,[26] Sweden[27] and Finland.[28]

For nearly 300,000 years after the emergence of *Homo sapiens*, per capita incomes were scarcely higher than the minimum necessary for survival, plagues and famines were abundant, a quarter of babies did not reach their first birthday, women commonly perished during childbirth, and life expectancy rarely exceeded forty years.

But then, as noted earlier, Western Europe and North America abruptly began to witness a rapid and historically unprecedented rise in living standards across various strata of society, a process that was subsequently experienced in other regions of the world. Remarkably, in the period since the dawn of the nineteenth century, a blink of an eye in relation to the Malthusian epoch, per capita incomes soared by a factor of fourteen in the entire world, while life expectancy more than doubled.[29]

How did humanity, at last, break free from the grip of the Malthusian forces?

3

The Storm Beneath the Surface

A glass kettle is placed on a hot stove. Soon the water within begins to heat up. Looking at the surface of the water, it is hard to detect any change: the water appears peaceful as, at first, the gradual rise in temperature has no visible effects. This calm, however, is deceptive. As the water's molecules absorb heat energy and the intermolecular attractive forces diminish, they are moving ever more rapidly until, past a critical point, the water dramatically changes state – from a liquid to a gas. The water undergoes a sudden *phase transition*. Not all the water molecules in the kettle convert to a gaseous state at once, but the process eventually sweeps them all away, and the properties and appearance of the water molecules that started off in the kettle are soon entirely transformed.

In the past two centuries, humankind experienced a similar phase transition. Like the conversion of the water in the kettle from a liquid to a gas, it was the result of a process that intensified invisibly, beneath the surface, throughout the hundreds of thousands of years of economic stagnation. The transition in state from stagnation to growth appears to have been dramatic and sudden – and indeed it was – but as will become apparent, the fundamental triggers of this transformation were operating from the emergence of the human species, gaining momentum over the entire course of our history. Furthermore, just as some water molecules in the kettle transform to a gaseous state before others, humanity's phase transition occurred at different times across the globe, generating previously inconceivable levels of inequality between the countries that underwent the phase transition relatively early and those that remained trapped for longer.

What brought about this phase transition?

Unified Growth Theory

In recent decades, physicists have attempted to devise a 'Theory of Everything' that would provide a coherent explanation for all the physical aspects of the universe, reconciling quantum mechanics with Einstein's theory of general relativity while integrating the interaction between the four fundamental forces of nature: gravitational, electromagnetic, weak nuclear and strong nuclear. Their efforts have been driven by the conviction that a systematic and more accurate understanding of the physical aspects of the universe must be rooted in a unified framework capable of explaining all known physical phenomena; any theory that is consistent with some but not all known physical phenomena must be partial and therefore, inherently, incomplete.

Nicolaus Copernicus, the Renaissance-era astronomer who maintained that the planets revolve around the sun (and not, as his contemporaries believed, around the Earth), presented an analogous view nearly five hundred years ago. He argued that, in the absence of a unified theory to understand the operation of the universe, 'it is as though an artist were to gather the hands, feet, head and other members for his images from diverse models, each part excellently drawn, but not related to a single body, and since they in no way match each other, the result would be monster rather than a man'.[1]

The development of unified growth theory was fuelled by a similar conviction that an understanding of what drives economic development globally would be fragile and incomplete unless it could reflect the primary driving forces behind the *entire* process of development, rather than merely over isolated periods.[2] Moreover, the advent of the theory was predicated on the realisation that prior analyses, which considered the modern era of economic growth and the Malthusian epoch of stagnation as two distinct and disjointed phenomena, rather than as a unified whole, had led to a limited and even distorted understanding of the growth process itself, neglecting the critical role of historical forces in our understanding of present-day inequality in the wealth of nations.

Unified growth theory captures the journey of humanity over the *entire* course of history, since the emergence of *Homo sapiens* in Africa nearly 300,000 years ago. It identifies and traces the forces that governed the process of development during the Malthusian epoch, eventually triggering the phase transition in which the human species escaped from this poverty trap into an era of sustained economic growth. These insights are essential for understanding the growth process in its entirety, the hurdles faced by poorer economies today in their transition from stagnation to growth, the origins of the great divergence in the wealth of nations in the past centuries, and the fingerprints of the ancient past in the fate of nations.

During the Malthusian epoch, as we have established, deviations from the subsistence level of consumption, due to innovations, conflicts, and institutional and epidemiological changes, generated a powerful counter-reaction of the population, reverting per capita income to its long-run level. What, then, propelled humanity out of the gravitational forces of the Malthusian equilibrium? How did the world wrench itself out of this economic black hole?

In search of the catalyst of the transition from stagnation to growth, one may argue that the Industrial Revolution is the force that gave the world an abrupt external shock that jolted it into the modern phase of growth. However, evidence from the eighteenth and nineteenth centuries when the Industrial Revolution occurred suggests that there was no 'jolt' at any point during this period. While the transition was rapid when compared with the timespan of human history, the productivity gains experienced *during* this period increased *gradually*. Indeed, when the Industrial Revolution first transpired, since technological change was incremental, populations spiked but average incomes increased only very modestly, just as would be predicted by the Malthusian theory. Yet, at a certain point, nearly a century later, the Malthusian equilibrium quite mysteriously *vanished* and tremendous growth ensued.

The conceptual framework I devised in the past few decades to address this conundrum was inspired by insights from the mathematical field of bifurcation theory, which demonstrate how, beyond a certain threshold, minor alterations in a single factor may generate a sudden and dramatic transformation in the behaviour of complex dynamical systems (as is the case when heat crosses a threshold and transforms water from liquid to gas).[3] In particular, this research has focused on identifying the cogs that were whirring invisibly beneath the surface, wheels of change that were turning relentlessly *throughout* the epoch of the Malthusian equilibrium but which ultimately broke its hold and led to the emergence of modern growth – much like the rising temperatures in the kettle.

What are those mysterious wheels of change that operated persistently during the Malthusian epoch and ultimately triggered the dramatic metamorphosis in living standards in the past two centuries?

Wheels of Change

Population Size

One of these wheels of change was population size. At the eve of the Neolithic Revolution, in the year 10,000 BCE, an estimated 2.4 million human beings roamed the Earth. Yet, by the year 1 CE, as the Roman Empire and the Mayan civilisation approached their height, the world's population had multiplied seventy-eight-fold, and soared to 188 million. A millennium later, when the Vikings raided the coasts of Northern Europe and the Chinese first used gunpowder in combat, humanity stood at 295 million individuals. World population had risen to nearly half a billion by the year 1500, at the time when Columbus was in the midst of his expeditions to the Americas, and at the turn of the nineteenth century, in the early phases of industrialisation, the human population nearly crossed the one billion mark (Fig. 6).

The relationship between population size and technological change is a reciprocal one – just as technological advancements during the Malthusian epoch enabled populations to densify and grow 400-fold within a 12,000-year period, so had the size of these human populations contributed to an acceleration in the pace of innovation. As noted above, larger populations were

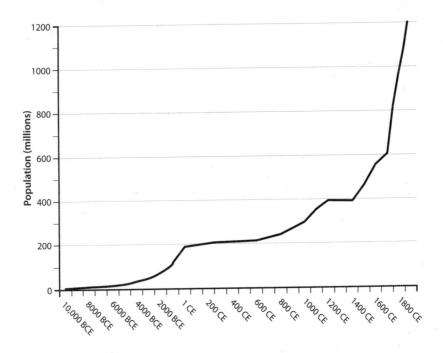

Figure 6. Human Population Growth during the Malthusian Epoch[4]

more likely to generate both a greater demand for new goods, tools and practices, as well as exceptional individuals capable of inventing them. Moreover, sizeable societies benefited from more extensive specialisation and expertise, and greater exchange of ideas through trade, further accelerating the spread and penetration of new technologies.[5] As we have seen, this self-reinforcing, positive feedback loop emerged at the very dawn of the human species and it has been operating ever since.

This impact of population size on the technological level is apparent across cultures and regions throughout the historical record. Regions that experienced an earlier onset of the Neolithic Revolution, such as the Fertile Crescent, gave rise to the largest prehistoric settlements and enjoyed a persistent technological head start. Likewise, territories characterised by more suitable land for agriculture, and therefore higher density of population, possessed more advanced technologies. Intriguingly, even among relatively small Polynesian societies in the Pacific Ocean, larger communities at the time of early European contact, such as the ones in Hawaii and Tonga, employed a wider range of complex and sophisticated marine foraging technologies than smaller societies, such as those on the Vanuatu islands of Malekula, Tikopia and Santa Cruz.[6]

The critical importance of population size to a society's ability to foster technological innovation is exemplified in the printing revolution of the German innovator Johannes Gutenberg. Born in the bustling city of Mainz and having lived part of his adult life in Strasbourg, Gutenberg benefited from the trade networks that passed through these cities, the accessibility of older generations' accumulated knowledge, and the exposure to the diffusion of inventions in the field of print from such far-flung places as Persia, Greece, Byzantium, China and the Mamluk Sultanate. The scale and the prosperity of these towns also enabled him to profit from an apprenticeship as a goldsmith and to have access to funding for the development of his movable-type printing system. If Gutenberg had instead been born in an isolated village, his path to this invention would have been strewn with obstacles. Lacking such rich contact with other civilisations it is far less likely he would have been aware of earlier developments in his field. He would certainly have struggled to secure funding for his invention since the potential market for printing presses in his village would have seemed too small to make the invention profitable. And it is probable he would even have had to devote a major portion of his time to farming because rural populations generally struggled to support a whole class of artists, craftsmen and innovators at this time.

Larger populations were not only more conducive to technological development, they also prevented the kind of technological decline that is a common feature of smaller communities, such as that experienced by the Polar Inuit of north-west Greenland in the 1820s. This society was hit by an epidemic that decimated its adult population, who were the store for the tribe's priceless technological knowledge, such as for kayak construction. In its aftermath, the young survivors could not restore this lost technological know-how, since even the possessions of the old were buried with them, and experienced an extreme technological regression, which drastically eroded their hunting and fishing capabilities. Their population began to dwindle and would surely have continued to wane had they not eventually encountered another Inuit community, who reintroduced them to this lost knowledge a few decades later.[7] Acute technological regression among isolated communities had been experienced by other small communities, such as Aboriginal Tasmanian tribes after the loss of their land bridge with Australia. In contrast, technological regression is much rarer in larger populations which tend to have trading links with other groups, spread their knowledge across society, and enjoy regular infusions of new inventions.

As will become apparent, this reinforcing cycle – technological development sustaining larger populations, while larger populations reinforce technological development – which has operated throughout most of our existence, gradually but continuously intensified until ultimately the rate of innovations reached a critical threshold. This was one of the sparks for the phase transition that hoisted humanity out of the epoch of stagnation.[8]

Population Composition

Population size operated in tandem with another wheel of change – population composition. Like size, population composition was also a product of Malthusian forces.[9] One of the first scholars to realise this was Charles Darwin, who recounted in his autobiography:

> In October 1838, that is, fifteen months after I had begun my systematic enquiry, I happened to read for amusement Malthus on Population, and being well prepared to appreciate the struggle for existence which everywhere goes on from long-continued observation of the habits of animals and plants, it at once struck me that under these circumstances favourable variations would tend to be preserved, and unfavourable ones to be destroyed.[10]

What did Darwin mean by 'favourable variations', and how would their preservation in a Malthusian environment affect the composition of a population?

Very simply, any intergenerationally transmitted trait which makes an organism better adapted to their environment, generating for them more resources, thus affording them greater or more reliable nourishment and protection and thereby fostering for them a larger number of surviving offspring, can be considered 'favourable'. Because of this survival advantage, the prevalence of these 'favourable' characteristics in any population will increase over time. This is the essence of Darwin's natural selection.

One might think that any truly momentous and impactful evolutionary change would take aeons to occur, and so these processes, interesting as they may be, are irrelevant for the understanding of the journey of humanity. But while it took living beings millions of years to develop fully formed eyes out of an early 'proto-eye', the composition of existing traits within a given population can in fact alter quite rapidly. One famous example of rapid adaptation is the change in the dominant colour of common moths in nineteenth-century Britain – from pale to dark. As tree trunks and walls became covered in soot in the industrial parts of the country, the scarcer darker moths suddenly enjoyed better camouflage against predators, and thus a significant survival advantage over their lighter contemporaries, and within a short period came to dominate the overall moth population.[11]

Human beings do not reproduce as rapidly as moths, but even so we have experienced rapid adaptations to diverse environments across the planet. As noted in the previous chapter, this is how we acquired natural immunity to local diseases, boosting our resistance to infection in the aftermath of the Neolithic Revolution. This is how we developed the ability to metabolise the regional food supply – in particular, lactose tolerance in regions where cows, goats and sheep were domesticated[12] – and how we developed the capacity for long-term acclimatisation to high-altitude areas. Regional adaptations also triggered the evolution of a range of skin pigmentation across the globe. In areas of higher UV radiation, populations evolved skin pigmentations as protection from the sun's harmful rays. In contrast, in regions further from the equator that receive less sunlight, a mutation that caused lighter skin tones helped the body generate vitamin D, endowed its bearers with a survival advantage and thus became more prevalent.

Moreover, when the adaptation is cultural rather than biological, these changes can take hold in a population even more rapidly. These processes do not require the passing of genetic mutations from one generation to the next; the principles that lead to their greater prevalence over time are similar but they spread instead through the mechanisms of imitation, education or indoctrination, swiftly giving rise to new cultural traits and their impact on economic and institutional changes.[13] These are the 'favourable variations' that are perhaps most relevant to the journey of humanity.

During the Malthusian epoch, it is reasonable to suppose that cultural traits that were complementary to the techno-logical environment would have generated higher income, and thus a larger number of surviving offspring, leading therefore to a gradual increase in the prevalence of these traits in the popu-lation. And because these traits would in turn reinforce that pace of technological change, they would have contributed to the pace of the development process from stagnation towards growth. As we will see, among the most growth-enhancing of these cultural traits would have been norms, attitudes and cus-toms associated with placing a high value on education, having a 'future-oriented' mindset and embracing what we might call an 'entrepreneurial spirit'.

This process is epitomised by the evolution of the cultural inclination for parental investment in 'human capital' – factors that influence worker productivity, such as education, training and skill, along with health and longevity. Consider a human population caught in the Malthusian equilibrium that consists of two large clans: the Quanty and the Qualy. The Quanty clan adheres to the cultural norm, 'be fruitful and multiply' (Genesis 9:1), bringing as many children as possible into the world and investing its limited resources in raising them. In contrast, the Qualy clan pursues an alternative custom: its members choose to have fewer children but they invest a considerable part of their time and resources in factors that influence their children's productivity and earning capacity. Which of the clans, the Qualy or the Quanty, will have more descendants and thus dominate the overall population in the long run?

Suppose that Quanty households bear on average four chil-dren each, of whom only two reach adulthood and find a reproductive partner. Meanwhile, Qualy households bear on average only two children each, because their budget does not allow them to invest in the education and health of additional offspring, and yet, thanks to the investment that they do make, both children not only reach adulthood and find a reproductive partner but they also find jobs in commercial and skill-intensive occupations, such as blacksmiths, traders and carpenters. At this stage, neither the fraction of Quanty nor Qualy is expanding over time and the composition of the population remains stable. But now suppose the society in which they live is one where technological development boosts the demand for the services of blacksmiths, carpenters and other trades who can manufacture tools and more efficient machines. This increase in earning capacity would place the Qualy clan at a distinct evolutionary advantage. Within a generation or two, its families are likely to enjoy higher incomes and amass greater resources. Their offspring will then be able to afford to bear on average, say, three children, educate all three of them, raise them to adulthood, and marry them off. In contrast, the uneducated offspring of the Quanty clan will not be affected by this technological development, their incomes will remain unchanged, and thus, on average, still only two children from each Quanty household will be likely to reach adulthood.

This mechanism suggests that in societies where technological innovation offers economic opportunity and thus where reproductive success is enhanced by the investment in human capital that allows one to seize it, a positive feedback loop will lead the Qualy clan to dominate the population in the long run: the increasing dominance of Qualy families will foster technological progress, while technological progress will increase the share of Qualy families in the population.

It is worth mentioning that this basic trade-off between a larger number of offspring or greater parental nurturing is common to all living organisms:[14] bacteria, insects and small mammals, such as rodents, evolved to follow the 'quantity strategy' of reproduction, whereas larger mammals such as humans, elephants and whales, as well as parrots and eagles, evolved to follow the 'nurturing strategy'.[15]

The extensive genealogical records of nearly half a million

progeny of European settlers in Quebec between the sixteenth and eighteenth centuries provide a unique opportunity to test the validity of this theory. Tracing the number of offspring of the founder populations in Quebec over four generations, it is apparent that the largest dynasties originated with moderately fertile settlers who had only a moderate number of children (and invested proportionately more in their children's human capital), while the more fertile founders, who formed large families (and invested proportionately less in each of them), had fewer descendants over time. In other words, the evidence suggests that, perhaps paradoxically, a moderate rather than a large number of children per family was conducive to a larger number of descendants after several generations. This reflects the beneficial effects of a smaller number of children on each individual child's likelihood to survive, marry, acquire literacy and reproduce.[16] Evidence from England in the period 1541–1851 reveals a similar pattern: families who tended to invest in their children's human capital had the largest number of children who survived into adulthood.[17]

The conditions the founder populations of Quebec faced during this period of high fertility would have resembled those that humans encountered during their dispersal across the planet in at least one sense: having settled new territories, both populations would have found themselves in an environment with a carrying capacity that was an order of magnitude greater than the size of the founder population. Extrapolating from this evidence, then, it is not unlikely that during periods of high fertility within the Malthusian epoch – periods in which the pace of adaptation could have had a significant impact on the composition of the population – the prevalence of individuals with a stronger inclination towards investment in the survivability of fewer offspring gradually increased.

These, then, were the wheels of change that have been whirring beneath the surface for the entire course of human existence: technological innovations sustained larger populations and triggered the adaptation of the human population to their ecological and technological environments; larger and more adapted populations fostered in turn the ability of humankind to design new technologies and gain increasing control of their environment. Taken together, it was these wheels of change that led ultimately to a spectacular explosion of innovations on a scale never seen before in human history – the Industrial Revolution.

4

Full Steam

The classic images of the Industrial Revolution are gloomy and sombre: a cluster of textile factories with thick black fumes rising from their chimneys, set in stark contrast to the once-idyllic English countryside, along with small children engaged in gruelling manual labour in polluted and precarious urban environments.[1] Such representations have been engraved into our collective imagination by authors such as William Blake and Charles Dickens, but they distort the essence of this unique period.

After all, if the factories that polluted the air and rivers were the core of the Industrial Revolution, why was it there and then that life expectancy surged and infant mortality plummeted? If the effect of the Industrial Revolution was to transform cheerful farmers into miserable day labourers, then why have farmers around the world been migrating into major industrialised towns ever since? And if the Industrial Revolution, at its core, was about child exploitation, why did legislation banning child labour and establishing primary schools appear during this era, of all times, and in the most industrialised regions and nations, of all places?

The fact is that industrialisation lent this revolutionary period its name since it was its most novel and glaring characteristic, but to fully grasp the implications of the Industrial Revolution it is important to realise that industrialisation itself was secondary. In the words of the economic historian Deirdre McCloskey:

'The Industrial Revolution was neither the age of steam, nor the age of cotton, nor the age of iron. It was the age of progress.'[2]

Acceleration of Technological Development

The progress of this era took various forms, of which one is most obviously connected to the phenomenon of industrialisation: a stunning *acceleration* of technological development, the likes of which had never been seen in recorded history. Each of the inventions that emerged in this period deserves a place of honour in the technological annals of humankind. The nearly unfathomable surge in the pace of technological advancement had been gathering pace since the Age of Enlightenment, and over the course of the next few hundred years the number of significant inventions that emerged in Europe and North America exceeded all of those developed previously by human civilisation over thousands of years. The technological landscape in these regions was utterly transformed.

The appearance of this veritable tsunami of ideas in such a short time and in such a limited geographic region is even more remarkable. But once again it is impossible to identify a 'jolt' or single invention that catalysed the wave. From the eve of the Industrial Revolution throughout its various phases, Britain's economic productivity improved gradually and continuously.[3] From a distance, it may appear to have happened overnight. In fact, it took significantly longer than the lifespan of any individual.

This accelerated development was not exclusive to industrial technology. Science also advanced at great speed across the European continent, while art, literature and music similarly benefited from an unprecedented flourishing of talent and new genres. This was a process that in fact began during the seventeenth century, when the leading philosophers in Western culture started to depart from the ancient traditions of Greece and the

Church to pen engrossing treatises on the nature of humankind and the world.

Nonetheless, one of the most important inventions of the period was indeed an industrialising one. The steam engine, designed by the British ironmonger Thomas Newcomen, entered commercial use in 1712. It had a fairly simple and banal purpose: to pump water out of coal mines – a complex task that demanded a significant workforce back in the eighteenth century. This novel technology was further advanced in the years 1763–75 by the Scottish engineer James Watt, who adapted the engines for the operation of factory machinery, proliferating its commercial use.

The repetitive operation of the steam engine might seem as uninspiring as the content of the first written documents in human history – Sumerian tablets recording ordinary business deals and tax rates, around 3400 BCE. Those writings, however, fired the starting gun of a process that within a few thousand years would lead to the *Epic of Gilgamesh*, the *Mahabharata*, the *Arabian Nights*, Virgil's *Aeneid*, Shikibu's *The Tale of Genji*, Dante's *Divine Comedy*, Shakespeare's *Hamlet*, Cervantes's *Don Quixote*, Goethe's *Faust*, Hugo's *Les Misérables* and Dostoevsky's *Crime and Punishment*. Meanwhile, the Newcomen steam engine set in motion the technological leap that, in just 250 years, would allow the Soviets to launch sputnik into space and the Americans to land humans aboard *Apollo 11* on the moon.

The textile industry was the cutting edge of the Industrial Revolution, the high-tech sector of its day. A pantheon of British inventors – most notably John Kay, Richard Arkwright, James Hargreaves, Edmund Cartwright and Samuel Crompton – designed sophisticated machines that automated much of the textile manufacturing process. Automation slashed the hours of labour needed to produce each roll of fabric, reducing the price of finished garments and enabling poor families in Europe and its colonies to purchase clothes of a superior quality. Initially, the new machines were operated with water wheels in factories built next to rivers and waterfalls. Yet the advent of the steam engine liberated the industry from its dependence on running water and enabled the development of industrial towns across Europe and North America, although proximity to coal mines remained necessary.[4]

But technological development also revolutionised the construction of large-scale structures more generally, as well as transportation by land, sea and air. This began in the early eighteenth century, when the ironmonger Abraham Darby invented a new and cheaper method of smelting iron ore, encouraging the widespread use of this metal and ultimately the construction of bridges and skyscrapers. In the middle of the nineteenth century, the inventor and industrialist Sir Henry Bessemer developed a cheap and rapid method for production of strong and supple steel. Improvements in the iron and steel industries led to the development of new and transformative cutting and processing tools, which had a significant impact on a variety of industries, and contributed to the rise of steam locomotives, which in turn dramatically reduced travelling times across long distances. At the beginning of the nineteenth century, the journey from New York to what would soon be Chicago lasted nearly six weeks, but by 1857, the railway had shortened the trip to just two days. The steamboat likewise reduced travel distances and time across the seas, liberating maritime trade from its reliance on the winds, and vastly accelerating the pace of globalisation.[5]

This period saw other breakthroughs in the field of communication. The American inventor Samuel Morse built the first commercial electromagnetic telegraph in 1844; within only three decades, the world's main arteries were lined with telegraph wires, and messages could be transmitted across seas and oceans in a matter of minutes. In 1877, another American inventor, Thomas Edison, unveiled the phonograph, the first audio recording device in history, and two years later he invented the incandescent light bulb – or perhaps more accurately, he improved the bulb invented by his predecessors. While switching on his light bulb, Edison proclaimed, 'We will make electric light so cheap that only the rich will burn candles,' underlining the broad impact of this innovation.[6] Edison then founded the world's first commercial power station in New York in 1882, following which electrical power was quickly adopted across an array of fields and gradually replaced the steam engine in factories. The late nineteenth century also witnessed the invention of the internal combustion engine, which soon allowed automobiles to supersede the horse-drawn carriage as an ordinary method of local transportation.

This partial list of innovations does not do justice to the plethora of advances in the practices of chemistry, agriculture, woodwork, mining, canal-digging and in the production of materials such as concrete, glass and paper; nor to the long list of other groundbreaking inventions such as the bicycle, the hot-air balloon, the industrial production line and the elevator (which made the construction of skyscrapers practical); nor does it begin to touch on the host of novel financial instruments that evolved to fund these ventures. Virtually every field of human endeavour was radically transformed during this age of innovation.

The transformation in technological power of European nations and the US swung the balance of power across the globe. The change was so rapid that it caught even technologically developed societies elsewhere off guard; lacking the resources to resist European military power, their native populations were subjected to oppression and exploitation. In particular, the rulers of the Qing Dynasty, who decided in 1839 to ban trade with British merchants who had flooded China with opium, quickly discovered that China's creaking imperial navy was no match for a small fleet of British gunboats, driven by steam engines and shielded with steel armour. Britain's victory in the First Opium War (1839–42) was especially ironic given that both the gunpowder and steel plating that reinforced its battlefield advantage were produced with technology that had originated in China centuries earlier.

A decade later, technological advantage allowed the US Navy under Commodore Matthew C. Perry to coerce Japan into signing an agreement that ended more than two hundred years of isolationism. This outcome triggered a series of power struggles within Japan's ruling elite, between those who supported the ancient order and those who recognised the technological power of Europeans and Americans and the need for dramatic reforms. This internal conflict ultimately ended with victory for the forces championing technological, social and industrial progress. They promoted the Meiji Restoration – the termination of Japan's feudal system of government and the restoration of the imperial power – which transformed Japan into an economic and military powerhouse.

Dramatic innovation and rapid change became hallmarks of the way in which Europeans and their North American descendants thought, operated, dined, dressed, spent their leisure time, viewed works of art and culture, and of course butchered each other on blood-soaked battlefields of the Napoleonic wars and the American Civil War. Meanwhile, the ideas propounded by European philosophers, writers and scientists during this era radically revised collective conceptions of human nature, society and the cosmos. Among some social circles, it became a mark of status to be educated, up to date on the latest ideas and debates, and able to express enlightened views about, say, *The Communist Manifesto*, Victor Hugo's latest novel, or Charles Darwin's sensational theory about the origin of species.

But the fundamental characteristic of this era – namely, the acceleration in the rate of innovation – had a more profound impact on education than merely turning it into a cultural commodity among the middle classes and the elites. It placed it centre stage in the process of economic development. Arguably, in fact, this transformation of education was more significant and lasting than the mechanisation of manufacturing, for it transformed education's very purpose – and brought it for the first time to the masses.

Education in the Pre-Industrial Era

For most of human history, formal education was available only to a small, privileged section of society. As early as in the Mesopotamian and the Egyptian civilisations, children of elites learned to read, write and perform basic arithmetic tasks in order to prepare themselves for occupations such as scribes, priests and for a range of administrative positions. They were also frequently introduced to astrology, philosophy and theology, for the sake of spiritual and cultural enrichment and as an entry pass into the intellectual strata.

When education was provided to wider sections of society, it served primarily cultural, religious, social, spiritual and military purposes. Education in ancient Persia, Greece and Rome, for example, was aimed largely at cultivating obedience and discipline with intellectual and physical training geared towards cultural, religious, and military ends. In contrast, Confucian and Buddhist education was devised to inculcate the virtues of morality, respect for elders and good character, as these were seen to be the foundation of social harmony. The education systems advanced by monotheistic religions, meanwhile, were designed to cultivate faith, morality, adherence to and fulfilment of the religious laws and the transmission of these values across generations. In particular, one of the earliest mass education systems, the Jewish *cheder* – formed more than 2,000 years ago – was designed to educate boys as young as four years old, so as to enable them to fulfil their religious obligation of reading the Torah and to enhance their faith, morality and ethnic identity. Similar religious institutions subsequently emerged in the Muslim world, as well as the Christian, especially in regions influenced by the Protestant Reformation. Nevertheless, in none of these systems was the development of skills that would be useful for adult professional occupations a primary consideration.

Literacy rates over most of human existence were insignificant. Estimates from the Middle Ages, which are primarily based on the proportion of people who could sign their name on various documents, point to rates below 10 per cent in countries such as China, France, Germany, Belgium and the Netherlands, and even lower levels elsewhere in Europe and across the globe.[7]

But in the centuries leading up to industrialisation, as Europe started to make strides in technology and trade, the importance of education began to intensify. As early as the Renaissance, European civilisations were markedly more technologically sophisticated than other contemporary societies. Among their major inventions in the pre-industrial era were the printing press, the pendulum clock, the eyeglasses, the telescope, the microscope, and countless improvements in agriculture and seamanship. By this time, for reasons explored in the second part of the book, other civilisations that had previously out-paced Europe in technological development, including the Chinese and the Ottoman, had started to lag behind, and in the few centuries after the year 1500, the world's most advanced technology became virtually indistinguishable from European technology.[8] This technological divergence was reflected in a widening literacy gap between Europe and the rest of the world.

The extent to which Gutenberg's printing press affected literacy rates – or indeed economic growth in Europe – remains debat-able;[9] what is undisputable is that growing literacy at this time contributed to the growth and the proliferation of the printing industry, and that mass printing of books significantly increased the desire to read and write among those Europeans who were equipped to do so. In the second half of the fifteenth century, Europe printed nearly 13 million copies of books; in the sixteenth century, over 200 million; in the seventeenth century over half a billion copies; and in the eighteenth century that number soared to approximately one billion copies of books – a growth rate far exceeding that of the population on the continent.[10]

What is also apparent is that the rapid growth of the European book industry spurred further technological and cultural change, which in turn contributed to the enhancement of human capital formation. The late fifteenth century saw the mass printing of 'commercial mathematics', textbooks, written to teach trainee merchants how to price their stocks, convert currencies, and calculate profit margins and interest payments. Others disseminated the essential discipline of double-entry bookkeeping, an innovation that allowed merchants to manage their accounts rationally and professional textbooks proliferated across the European continent and became an indispensable source of knowledge for doctors, lawyers and teachers. Not surprisingly, therefore, cities that embraced the printing press in the late fifteenth century experienced greater population growth, predominantly due to inward migration, and became major hubs of intellectual thought and literature, further promoting literacy as a noble pursuit for respectable citizens and as a virtue in its own right.[11]

During this period, Europe became the most literate and technological place in history. By 1800, literacy rates were 68 per cent in the Netherlands, 50 per cent in Britain and Belgium, and around 20 per cent in other Western European nations. In non-European societies, however, literacy rates started to rise only in the twentieth century. For humanity as a whole, the adult literacy rate stood at a mere 12 per cent in 1820, only crossed the 50 per cent mark around the mid-twentieth century, and currently stands at about 86 per cent (Fig. 7).

Yet education in pre-industrial Europe was still not geared towards the provision of skills to a mass workforce. One of the pioneers of modern education, the seventeenth-century Czech philosopher John Amos Comenius, promoted innovative pedagogical methods such as learning in vernacular languages (instead of Latin), introducing pupils to a range of subjects with gradually increasing degrees of complexity, and enhancing logical thinking over dull memorisation. However, even Comenius's most revolutionary inclusive teaching enterprise, integrating women and the poorer segments of society into the education system, was designed to instil moral and cultural values, not to impart expertise vital for work. Few children, including those fortunate enough to gain a rudimentary education, acquired skills and knowledge

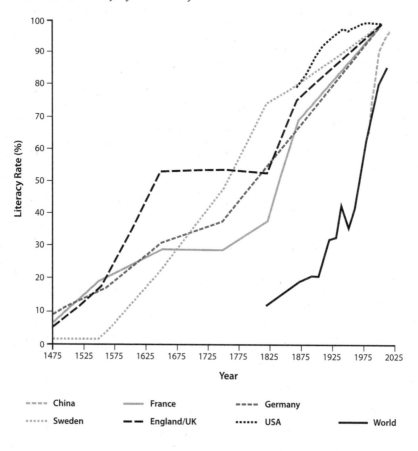

Figure 7. Rising Literacy Rates around the World, 1475–2010[12]

at school that were relevant to their adult working lives; those skills were learned predominantly on the job – tilling the fields, performing housework, or serving as apprentices.

Starting in the mid-seventeenth century, Western Europe became home to philosophers who championed a notion of progress based on cumulative scientific knowledge, a rationalist rejection of mysticism and religious dogma, and sometime progressive values such as equality of opportunity, freedom of expression and individual liberties, as well as curiosity and scepticism. During this Age of Enlightenment, education – and its corollary, enhanced human capital – became increasingly important, both culturally and economically. Even so, the meta-morphosis in the nature of education – geared towards industrial and commercial purposes – had yet to come.

Industrialisation and Human Capital

In the earliest phase of the Industrial Revolution, literacy and numeracy played a limited role in the production process, and thus the enhancement of these aspects of human capital would have had a limited effect on workers' productivity. Although some workers, supervisory and office personnel in particular, were required to be able to read and perform elementary arithmetical operations, a large portion of the tasks in industry was successfully performed by people who were illiterate.

During the subsequent phases of the Industrial Revolution, the demand for skilled labour in the growing industrial sector markedly increased. From here on, and for the first time in history, human capital formation – factors that influence worker productivity, such as education, training, skills and health – was designed and undertaken with the primary purpose of satisfying the increasing requirements of industrialisation for literacy and numeracy as well as mechanical skills among the workforce. This was the case across a wide range of industrial nations but was particularly apparent among the first countries that experienced industrialisation – England, France, Germany and the United States.

In England, the first phase of the Industrial Revolution was associated with the intensification of the mechanisation of the production process, but without a corresponding increase in the employment of skilled workers. In 1841, for instance, only 5 per cent of male workers and only 2 per cent of female workers were employed in occupations in which literacy was required.[13] Workers developed skills primarily through on-the-job training, and child labour was highly valuable. During the latter stages of the Industrial Revolution, however, the scale of education in

England dramatically changed. The proportion of children aged five to fourteen in primary schools rose from 11 per cent in 1855 to 25 per cent in 1870, and in the period 1870–1902, as the government assumed responsibility for providing a free education system for the public, that proportion rose to nearly 74 per cent.[14] Thus, literacy rates among English men, which were at around 67 per cent in the 1840s, increased significantly, reaching 97 per cent by the end of the century.[15]

In France, the development of the education system occurred well before the Industrial Revolution, but the process was deepened and transformed to satisfy industrial needs during the early phases of industrialisation. The provision of elementary and secondary education in the seventeenth and eighteenth centuries was dominated by the Church and religious orders, although some state interventions in technical and vocational training were designed to reinforce development in commerce, manufacturing and military efficiency. After the French Revolution, the state established primary schools and selective secondary and higher education, with the objective of producing effective elites to operate the military and governmental apparatus.[16] In view of the growing industrial demand for human capital, the provisions of primary and higher education was then extended, and the number of communities without schools fell by 50 per cent between 1837 and 1850. By 1881–82, a universal, free, compulsory and secular primary school system had been established, emphasising technical and scientific education, and the proportion of children aged five to fourteen in primary schools increased from 52 per cent in 1850 to 86 per cent in 1901.[17]

In Prussia, as in France, the initial steps towards compulsory education took place at the beginning of the eighteenth century, well before the Industrial Revolution, and education was viewed primarily as a way to unify the state. In the second part of the eighteenth century, education was made compulsory for all children aged five to thirteen, though these regulations were not strictly enforced partly due to the lack of funding. At the beginning of the nineteenth century, motivated by the need for national cohesion, military efficiency and trained bureaucrats, the education system was further reformed. Schooling became compulsory and secular for a three-year period, and the gymnasium was reconstituted as a state institution that provided nine years of education for the elite.[18] As in England and France, industrialisation in Prussia coincided with the implementation of universal primary schooling. Secondary schools started to serve industrial needs as well; the *Realschulen*, which emphasised the teaching of mathematics and science, were gradually adopted, and vocational and trade schools were founded. Overall, total enrolment in secondary school increased six-fold from 1870 to 1911.

Industrialisation in the United States also increased the importance of human capital in the production process and in the economy as a whole.[19] The rise of the industrial, business and commerce sectors in the late nineteenth and early twentieth centuries increased the demand for managers, clerical workers and educated sales personnel who were trained in accounting, typing, shorthand, algebra and commerce. By the late 1910s, technologically advanced industries demanded blue-collar craft workers who were trained in geometry, algebra, chemistry, mechanical drawing and related skills. The structure of education was transformed to meet these needs, and total enrolment in public secondary schools increased seventy-fold from 1870 to 1950.[20]

This historical evidence clearly suggests that technological advancements in the course of industrialisation have been associated with human capital formation. But is there substantial evidence that this association is indicative of industrialisation being the cause and skill formation the effect? After all, it could be that this association reflects the impact of human capital formation on the evolution of the industrial sector, or else that some other cultural or institutional factors gave rise to both industrialisation and education. In order to establish a line of causality between technological acceleration and

industrialisation on the one hand and human capital formation on the other, we can refer to a *quasi-natural historical
experiment*.

In France, the steam engine – one of the most important
inventions in the early stages of the Industrial Revolution – was
first introduced in a mine in Fresnes-sur-Escaut, a sleepy village
near the French–Belgian border. Evidence suggests that, due to
the regional diffusion of this novel technology, over the course
of the mid-nineteenth century the closer a local region or *département* (an administrative unit created in 1790) was to this
village, the more rapidly it adopted the steam engine for itself.
Geographical distance from Fresnes-sur-Escaut could therefore
predict the relative presence of steam engines in each region.
In other words, while the *actual* number of steam engines in
any place may have been affected by the pre-existing level of
education in that *département* and other potential confounders, *distance* from Fresnes-sur-Escaut can be used to assess the
potential causal impact of technology on education because it
(a) directly predicts the presence of steam engines, (b) cannot
be affected by pre-existing levels of education or indeed by
other confounders and (c) has no direct effect on the level of
education, only an indirect one through its impact on the number of steam engines. (After all, Fresnes-sur-Escaut was not,
we may be sure, the first place to adopt *education* in France,
and was therefore not the origin for its spread throughout the
country.)

Using this method, we can establish that technological
acceleration in the form of industrialisation, as reflected by the
number of steam engines in each French *département*, and as
inferred by distance from Fresnes-sur-Escaut, had a *positive*
impact on several measures of human capital formation in the
1840s, including the share of primary school students in the population and literacy rates among army conscripts. The more steam
engines in each *département*, the greater the investment in human
capital.[21] Similarly, separate evidence shows that the use of

steam engines in early-nineteenth-century Britain increased the skill intensity of the nearby workforce, especially in mechanical occupations.[22]

The impact of technological advancement on human capital formation is also observed in the United States.[23] Evidence based on the expansion of railroads into new American towns during the period 1850–1910 suggests that counties that were fortunate enough to be plugged into the national train network were characterised by higher literacy rates and more skilled workers, such as engineers, technicians, doctors and lawyers, and had a lower share of the population employed in the agricultural sector.[24]

This wide range of findings suggest that technological and commercial development during the Industrial Revolution *stimulated* various forms of investment in human capital. In some societies, human capital took the form of literacy and formal education, while in others it was associated with the development of professional crafts.

Given the argument of the previous chapter – that technological development and human capital created a mutually reinforcing cycle – it will come as no surprise that there is also evidence that this enhanced human capital facilitated *further* technological advancement.[25] Indeed, one of the reasons why some argue that the Industrial Revolution broke out in Britain rather than elsewhere in Europe was Britain's comparative advantage in human capital, which proved to be particularly beneficial in the early stages of industrialisation. After all, Britain was undoubtedly rich in coal, which was an essential fuel for the first steam engines, but so were many other countries. However, Britain also had a more unusual raw material – human capital. Historians describe the presence at that time of a broad class of professional carpenters, metalworkers, glassblowers and others who were able to support the work of the finest inventors and build or even improve their innovating designs.[26] These craftsmen passed on their skills to their apprentices, whose numbers soared in the early stages of the Industrial Revolution and were instrumental in the adoption, advancement and proliferation of industrial technologies.[27]

Indeed, engineers who emigrated from Britain became the industrial pioneers of many other countries, including Belgium, France, Switzerland and the United States. The first textile factory in North America, for instance, was built in the town of Pawtucket in Rhode Island in 1793 – just a few miles from Brown University, where this book was written. Funded by the American industrialist Moses Brown, the factory was the initiative of the British-American industrialist Samuel Slater, who arrived in the United States at the age of twenty-one. Slater had worked in a textile factory in Britain since the age of ten, where he developed a first-hand understanding of the technicalities of Richard Arkwright's spinning frames. Hoping to protect its technological advantage, the British government banned the export of the machine, and even the blueprints required for its construction. Nevertheless, Slater found a simple, yet fiendishly difficult, way to get around the prohibition – by memorising the designs. The influence of Slater, who is known as the 'Father of the American Industrial Revolution', was so significant that some Britons in his city of birth smeared him as 'Slater the Traitor'.

The contribution of an educated workforce to technological development is further corroborated by historical evidence from some of the other countries that first experienced industrialisation.[28] In nineteenth-century Prussia, for instance, literacy had a positive impact on innovation, as reflected by patent registration.[29] Moreover, remarkably, a study suggests that subscriptions to the *Encyclopedie* in eighteenth-century French towns (reflecting the size of their educated elite) were positively correlated with technological innovations by French firms in the same towns a full century later.[30] Similarly, cross-country analysis establishes that the number of engineers in various countries had a persistent effect on per capita income,[31] and in today's world, human capital formation encourages entrepreneurship, the adoption of new technologies and working methods, and, more broadly, economic growth.[32]

So how in practice did this rise in public mass education come about?

The Advent of Universal Public Education

In 1848, one of the most influential books in human history was released in London: Karl Marx and Friedrich Engels's *The Communist Manifesto*. Marx and Engels believed, quite rightly, that the social and political upheavals the world was then experiencing were directly related to the rapid technological change in production methods at the time. They argued that the rise of the capitalist class had played a major role in uprooting the feudal order and generating economic progress, but further maintained that ever-intensifying competition among capitalists could only result in a reduction in their profits, inducing them to deepen the exploitation of workers. Class struggle would therefore be inevitable since society would necessarily reach the point where the 'proletarians have nothing to lose but their chains'.

The central pillar of the Marxist thesis was the unavoidable power struggle between capitalists and workers that would lead ultimately to a revolution and the shattering of the class-based society. It is indeed the case that industrialised nations experienced fierce and often violent conflicts between capitalists and organised labour in the late nineteenth and early twentieth centuries. However, the communist revolution Marx and Engels foresaw happened in 1917 in Russia of all places, where at the time the share of employment in the agricultural sector exceeded 80 per cent. In fact, the most heavily industrialised capitalist nations have never experienced a successful class revolution, neither during Marx and Engels's lifetimes nor ever since.

How was the 'inevitable class struggle' and the communist revolution their *Manifesto* prophesised averted in most societies? One explanation is that the threat of revolution prompted industrialised nations to adopt policies designed to alleviate inter-class tensions and mitigate inequality – primarily, the expansion of voting rights and thus the power to redistribute wealth, as well as the rise of the welfare state.[33]

But an alternative hypothesis is centred around the critical role that human capital began to play in the production process during the era of industrialisation. According to this view, investing in the education and the skills of the workforce became increasingly *more* important to the capitalist class, not less so, as they came to realise that of all the capital at their disposal, it was human capital that held the key to preventing a decline in their profit margins.[34] In particular, the importance of specific craft skills that were instrumental in the country's first steps towards industrialisation soon diminished and were replaced not by an absence of skill, as some might suppose, but by a need for a general-purpose, adaptable sets of skills that would allow the workforce to navigate the challenges associated with *rapidly changing* technological and institutional environments. In such conditions, workers benefited from having a broad and flexible education, rather than exclusive, vocational skills that comple-mented a particular task or occupation.[35]

By this account, contrary to Marx's conjecture that the Indus-trial Revolution would erode the importance of human capital, allowing the owners of the means of production to exploit their workers more viciously, ongoing technological transformation of the production process in fact made human capital an increas-ingly critical element in the boosting of industrial productivity. Instead of a communist revolution, therefore, industrialisation triggered a revolution in mass education. Capitalists' profit margins stopped shrinking and workers' wages started rising, and ultimately the threat of class conflict – the beating heart of Marxism – began to fade. Put simply, industrial societies around the world, even those who resisted other aspects of Western modernity, supported the provision of public education pre-dominantly because they realised the importance of general mass education in a dynamic technological environment, both for business owners and for the workers themselves.

Nevertheless, industrialists were reluctant to fund the education of their potential workforce, as there was no guarantee that these workers would not take their newly acquired skills and find employment elsewhere. Indeed, in 1867, the British iron magnate James Kitson testified to an official commission that individual manufacturers were holding back on funding schools because they feared that their competitors would reap the rewards.[36] In the Netherlands and Britain, a handful of industrialists did fund their own private schools, but they had limited success. The few capitalists who did open and maintain schools in this period, such as the Welsh textile manufacturer Robert Owen, were predominantly motivated by philanthropic, rather than commercial, reasons.

As it became increasingly apparent that skills were necessary for the creation of an industrial society, previous concerns that the acquisition of literacy would make the working classes receptive to radical and subversive ideas were jettisoned and capitalists began lobbying governments for the public provision of the education. Industrialists in Belgium, Britain, France, Germany, the Netherlands and the United States became actively engaged in influencing the structure of their countries' public education systems and encouraged their leaders to amplify investment in mass education. Ultimately, national governments caved to pressure from the industrialists, and increased their expenditure on elementary-level education.

In 1867–68, the British government established the parliamentary Select Committee on Scientific Instruction. So began nearly twenty years of various parliamentary investigations into the relationship between the sciences, industry and education, designed to address the capitalists' demands. A sequence of reports based on these investigations underlined the inadequacy of the training that supervisors, managers, proprietors and workers generally had been receiving. They argued that most managers and proprietors did not understand the manufacturing process and thus failed to promote efficiency, investigate innovative techniques, or value the skills of their workers.[37] The reports made several recommendations, including the need to redefine primary schools, revise the curriculum throughout the entire school system (particularly with respect to industry and manufacturing), and improve teachers' training. Moreover, they recommended the introduction of technical and scientific education in secondary schools.

The government gradually yielded to the capitalists and increased contributions to primary as well as higher education. In 1870, it assumed responsibility for ensuring universal primary education, and in 1880, prior to the significant extension of the electoral franchise in 1884, education was made compulsory throughout Britain.

There was resistance from some quarters to the provision of public education in Britain. What is telling is that it came from the landed rather than industrial elite. In 1902, when Parliament legislated the Education Act that established the provision of a free education system for the public, there was growing demand in the manufacturing and services industries for technicians, engineers, clerks, lawyers and workers able to read blueprints, instruction manuals and warehouse inventories. Industrialists stood to gain from an investment in human capital that would enhance their workers' productivity. But from the point of view of a wealthy landowning family, the output of an educated farmer was scarcely higher than that of their uneducated peers, so there was no incentive to support public education. On the contrary, were you lucky enough to be one, you might very well have vigorously lobbied to *stop* your tenant farmers from investing in their children's education so as to reduce their incentive to leave your land in pursuit of the new opportunities being created for educated workers. Indeed, Members of Parliament from constituencies with relatively high proportions of workers in industrial professions voted predominantly in favour of the Education Act, while the constituencies that most opposed the establishment of comprehensive education were the agricultural-intensive ones, where the landed gentry held most sway.[38]

Another major factor in the opposition to public education was concentration of land ownership. In agricultural areas where land was relatively equally distributed, landowners had little incentive to impede education reforms, since their earnings from agriculture were relatively limited in comparison to the impact education would have on their own children's well-being. In places where land was concentrated in the hands of a few, however, landowners who relied heavily on agriculture for their wealth and who wished to staunch the exodus of their workers to nearby towns were particularly hostile to the establishment of comprehensive public education.[39]

In such a manner, historical inequality in land ownership may have had a powerful effect on the pace of the transition from agriculture to industry, and the emergence of the modern growth regime. This is borne out by the varying pace of educational reforms across the United States in the early twentieth century, where unequal land distribution had an adverse effect on education spending.[40] In fact, the relatively egalitarian distribution of land in Canada and the US as compared to Latin America might provide a partial explanation for the educational gap between the two regions. Furthermore, within South America, educational standards are higher in countries such as Argentina, Chile and Uruguay, where distribution of land ownership was (relatively) more even. And in other areas of the world such as Japan, Korea, Taiwan and Russia, the enactment of agrarian reforms that partially equalised land ownership predicated further reforms that improved the education of the general populace.

Ultimately, in the second phase of industrialisation, the allied interests of children, parents and industrialists trumped the interests of landowners, and education spread to all layers of society among the first industrialised nations. Though at the turn of the nineteenth century relatively few adults in Western countries had received basic schooling, by the turn of the twentieth century, education had been completely overhauled, and nearly 100 per cent of adults in Britain, the United States and other industrial nations had completed an elementary education – a truly seismic shift that occurred in the developing world in the mid-twentieth century, once the pace of technological advancement induced this transformation.

This, surely, was progress and it led in turn to other indisputable improvements in workers' lives. Fifty years after Marx prophesied the spectre of class struggle, workers' wages were rising, class boundaries began blurring, and mass education enabled the democratisation of further opportunities as well as the phasing out of a particularly insidious but widespread practice: child labour.

Child Labour No More

In 1910, the American photographer Lewis Hine snapped a portrait of a barefoot twelve-year-old girl dressed in rags, leaning against a large machine in a textile factory. Her name was Addie Card and her serious expression was haunting. Hine and other photographers immortalised many similar images of child labour in the United States and Britain, and their pictures soon became some of the most iconic symbols of the Industrial Revolution. These photographs aroused fierce public protest and led to legislation banning the employment of children. But contrary to popular belief, child labour was neither an innovation of the Industrial Revolution nor a significant factor in the industrialisation process. Nor, in fact, was child labour eradicated as a result of the legislation against it.

Child labour has been an intrinsic element of human societies throughout history as the challenges of a subsistence existence demanded that young children perform a plethora of back-breaking tasks, both domestic and agricultural. But when the Industrial Revolution broke out, the prevalence of the phenomenon had reached an unprecedented magnitude. Families'

Addie Card, 12 Years. Spinner in North Pownal Cotton Mill.
Vermont, 1910[41]

earnings in urban areas were barely above subsistence, and children as young as four were sent for employment in the industrial and the mining sectors. Child labour was particularly prevalent in textile factories where delicate hands were advantageous for unclogging the machines. The dismal, abusive and hazardous working conditions that children experienced over this period, along with educational deprivation, reinforced the cycle of poverty.[42]

But rapid technological change in the course of industrialisation and its impact on the demand for educated labour gradually reduced the profitability of child labour for parents as well as industrialists in two ways. First, the new machines reduced the relative productivity of children by automating the simpler tasks that children were capable of, thus magnifying the difference between the earning capacity of parents and children and reducing parental benefit from child labour. Second, the rise in the importance of human capital in the production process induced parents to invest their children's time and energy in education rather than work, and led industrialists, keen for their workforce to be better equipped with the relevant skills, to support laws which limited and ultimately prohibited child labour.[43]

The first effective legislation to limit child labour was passed initially in Britain in 1833. This Factory Act banned the employment in factories of children under the age of nine, limited the working hours of children aged nine to thirteen to nine hours per day, and prohibited night shift for children below the age of eighteen. In 1844, Parliament passed a new act, limiting children aged nine to thirteen to six and a half hours of work, so that they could devote three hours a day to schooling, restricted the working hours of children aged fourteen to eighteen to twelve hours per day, and imposed safety requirements in the operation and the cleaning of the machines by children. In subsequent years, Britain passed additional measures that consistently raised the minimum age of employment and compelled factory owners to pay for the education of their younger workers.

Since the assorted regulations amounted to a tax on employing children, many have argued that the legislation played a critical role in eradicating child labour in Britain. But while that may well have been a contributing factor, child labour was in fact on a downward slide in Britain well before this state intervention.[44] In the British cotton industry, the proportion of workers younger than thirteen dropped from nearly 13 per cent in 1816 to 2 per cent in 1835, before any significant enforcement of the new labour code. A similar trend occurred in the linen industry. Technological advancements played an important role in phasing out child labour long before legislation did, partly because machines, like Richard Roberts's self-acting spinning mule, had already reduced the need for child labour in many sectors. And while the silk industry was exempted from the restrictive child labour legislation, due to its struggle to compete with foreign producers who had access to cheaper raw material, the proportion of child workers in silk factories still fell, from nearly 30 per cent in 1835 to 13 per cent by 1860. If this trend is representative, it is not inconceivable that, even without legislation, child labour would have diminished significantly in other sectors.

In fact, in the latter half of the nineteenth century, public funding for education relieved employers of the full burden of financing their employees' schooling, effectively decreasing the 'tax' on child labour. Yet the number of children employed in factories never returned to its turn-of-the-century level. In the period 1851–1911, the proportion of boys aged ten to fourteen employed in factories fell from approximately 36 per cent to less than 20 per cent; for girls the proportion declined from nearly 20 per cent to nearly 10 per cent.[45] Similar trends were recorded in most developed countries. Legislation appears to have played only a subsidiary role in these processes while the main factors that reduced the employment and the exploitation of children were the widening parental-children income gap and changing attitudes towards education.

Given that these changes in attitudes were in large part due to rising demand for human capital, it is unsurprising that the scourge of child labour first disappeared in the most industrialised nations and, within them, in the most industrialised areas.[46] In the United States, laws limiting child labour were first passed in 1842 in Massachusetts, a major industrialised state. The governors of industrialised states were not necessarily more enlightened; rather, the rapid pace of technological progress exacerbated their demand for human capital, reduced their reliance on child labour, and diminished their opposition to legislation restricting it. Soon enough, similar laws were passed in all states that had been transformed by the Industrial Revolution, and only later did they spread to the more agricultural states of the country. As the pace of technological progress gained momentum in the US, and the importance of education became increasingly more apparent, child labour was slowly phased out. Between the years 1870 and 1940, the proportion of American boys aged fourteen to fifteen who were in work dropped from 42 to 10 per cent. Similar patterns were recorded among girls and younger children.

A fascinating illustration of the perception of the impact of technology on child labour at the time is reflected in a tractor

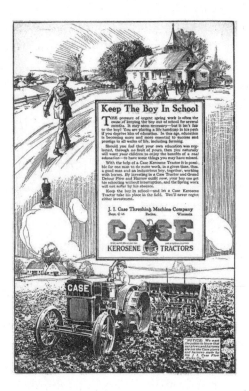

Tractor Advertisement, 1921
Keep The Boy In School

THE pressure of urgent spring work is often the cause of keeping the boy out of school for several months. It may seem necessary – but it isn't fair to the boy! You are placing a life handicap in his path if you deprive him of education. In this age, education is becoming more and more essential for success and prestige in all walks of life, including farming.

With the help of a Case Kerosene Tractor it is possible for one man to do more work in a given time, than a good man and an industrious boy, together, working with horses. By investing in a Case Tractor and Grand Detour Plow and Harrow outfit now, your boy can get his schooling without interruption, and the Spring work will not suffer by his absence.

Keep the boy in school – and let a Case Kerosene Tractor take his place in the field. You'll never regret either investment.[47]

advertisement from 1921. In order to persuade farmers to purchase a tractor, marketers emphasised the growing importance of human capital. Their campaign stressed that the main benefit of the new technology was the workforce it saved, allowing farmers to send their children to school even during the spring – the busiest season of the agricultural year. Interestingly, the advertisers emphasised the importance of human capital 'in all walks of life, including farming'. Perhaps they were trying to allay American farmers' concerns that their educated children would choose to work in the booming industrial sector instead of staying on the family farm.

A stunning increase in the rate of technological innovation, the arrival of mass education, the end of child labour: in these three key ways, the Industrial Revolution was indeed the age of progress. Nevertheless, it was the impact of these factors on women, families and childbirth that brought about the phase transition and the escape from the Malthusian trap.

5

Metamorphosis

During the early phases of the Industrial Revolution, amid rapid technological progress and rising incomes, the populations of most industrialising nations expanded rapidly. Yet, in the second half of the nineteenth century, that trend reversed: population growth and birth rates in developed countries fell sharply – a pattern that was repeated in the rest of the world at a faster pace during the twentieth century.[1] Between 1870 and 1920, fertility rates declined by 30 to 50 per cent in most Western European nations (Fig. 8), and in the United States they plummeted even more precipitously.[2] This dramatic collapse in fertility rates along with the fall in mortality rates, which often preceded it, have become known as the Demographic Transition.

The Demographic Transition shattered one of the cornerstones of the Malthusian mechanism. Suddenly, higher incomes were no longer channelled towards sustaining an expanded population; 'bread surpluses' no longer had to be shared among a larger number of children. Instead, for the first time in human history, technological progress led to an elevation in living standards in the long run, sounding the death knell for the epoch of stagnation. It was this decline in fertility that prised open the jaws of the Malthusian trap, and heralded the birth of the modern era of sustained growth.[3]

Why did the Demographic Transition occur? From our contemporary vantage point, one might suppose contraception

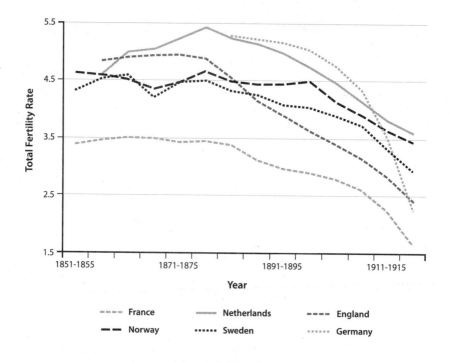

**Figure 8. Children per Woman
in Western European Nations, 1850–1920**[4]

was a major factor. In the absence of modern forms of birth
control, the most common ways of avoiding pregnancy at this
time were the age-old strategies of delayed marriage, abstinence and of course the withdrawal method. In Western Europe,
during periods of scarcity, the average age of marriage rose, as
did the prevalence of celibacy – both of which resulted in a
drop in birth rates. Indeed, as William Cobbett, the English MP
and leading campaigner against the changes brought by the
Industrial Revolution, observed, this was a '[s]ociety in which
men, who are able and willing to work, cannot support their
families, and ought, with great part of the women, to be compelled to lead a life of celibacy, for fear of having children to be
starved'.[5] By contrast, in times of prosperity, the average marriage age dropped and birth rates rose accordingly. This is
known as the 'European Marriage Pattern', which prevailed

between the seventeenth century and the early part of the twentieth century (Fig. 9).[6]

Elsewhere, customs such as dowry payments in Eurasian and North African societies, and 'bride price' in sub-Saharan Africa, Asia, the Middle East and Oceania, further solidified the link between living standards, marriage age and birth rates. During periods of prosperity, a larger number of families could afford these payments, and therefore marry off their children at younger ages – causing the marriage age to drop and birth rates to rise, whereas in times of scarcity fewer families could afford these transfers, delaying the age of marriage and lowering fertility rates.

Induced abortion was also practised in a wide range of preindustrial societies, at least as early as ancient Egypt.[7] Intense physical activity such as back-breaking labour, climbing, weightlifting or diving could be deliberately undertaken to induce

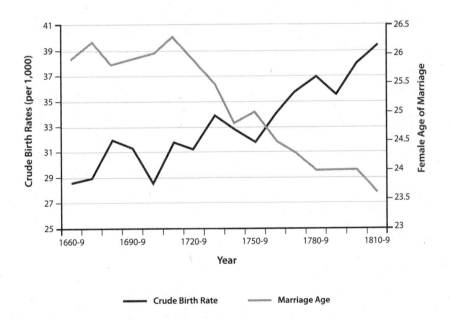

Figure 9. Fertility Rates and Women's Age of Marriage in England, 1660–1820

miscarriage, for example. Other techniques included fasting, pouring hot water onto the abdomen, lying down on heated coconut shells, or consuming medicinal herbs such as silphium (which was driven to extinction before the fall of the Roman Empire, arguably due to excessive use). And some evidence suggests that spermicides and primitive condoms were used in the ancient civilisations of Egypt, Greece and Rome.[8]

But since all these methods of managing fertility had been present throughout history and had not changed on the eve of the Demographic Transition, the catalysts for such a major, sudden and widespread decline in fertility must have been more profound.

Triggers of the Demographic Transition

The Rise in the Return on Human Capital

As seen in the previous chapter, the growing importance of education in response to a rapidly changing technological environment contributed to human capital formation. A large number of occupations in manufacturing, trade and services now required the abilities to read and write, perform basic arithmetic operations, and conduct a range of mechanical skills, so parents were induced to invest in their children's literacy, numeracy, skills and even health. As a result, the balance in the timeworn *quantity–quality trade-off* that parents had been forced to wrestle with throughout human history shifted – and thus precipitated the dramatic decline in fertility of the Demographic Transition.[9]

Similar patterns can be observed in earlier periods of human history. In the first century BCE, for example, when Jewish sages decreed that all parents should acquire education for their sons, Jewish farmers who struggled to meet the cost of education faced a stark choice: either they disobeyed or even abandoned their religion, as many did, or they settled for fewer children.[10] In time, this mandate gradually elevated the proportion of individuals within the Jewish community who were favourably inclined towards the investment in the education of their children.

Technological progress during the Industrial Revolution affected the quantity–quality trade-off anew in several key respects. First, it boosted parental income, meaning that parents could afford to invest more in their children should they wish to. This *income effect* acted to increase the resources being invested in the raising of children overall. Second, the growth in earning capacity also amplified the *opportunity cost* of raising children – the income a parent would have to forgo in order to raise a child instead of working. This *substitution effect* acted to reduce the number of births.

It is conceivable that historically the income effect dominated the substitution effect, leading to an increase in birth rates. Indeed, empirical studies show that rises in household income in the Malthusian epoch and in early phases of industrialisation had precisely this outcome. However, at the time of the Demographic Transition there were additional forces at play.[11] The new opportunities available specifically to those with an education led parents to invest a higher proportion of their earnings educating their children, further suppressing the degree to which the income effect might have increased birth rates. Ultimately, then, it was the increase in the *return* on parental investment in their children that overpowered the income effect, forcing birth rates down.

At the same time, this mechanism was reinforced by several important changes that were triggered by the advances in technology. The surge in life expectancy and the decline in child mortality amplified the likely *duration* of the return on education, further enhancing the incentive to invest in human capital and reduce fertility. Technological development and the rise in industrial demand for education also had the knock-on effect of reducing the relative productivity and thus profitability of child labour, which presented a disincentive to bear children as a source of labour. Finally, migration from the countryside into towns and cities, where the cost of living was higher, increased the cost of child rearing, further contributing to the fertility decline.

The geographical diffusion of the Protestant Reformation in Prussia provides a quasi-natural experiment that reveals the effect on fertility rates of greater investment in education. On 31 October 1517, Martin Luther nailed his *Ninety-Five Theses*, protesting the Church's sale of indulgences, to the door of All Saints' Church in Wittenberg, sparking the Protestant Reformation. Luther argued that the Church had no role mediating between man and God, and encouraged independent Bible reading – a radical belief that incentivised his followers to strive for literate children. Prior to 1517, the evidence suggests that proximity to Wittenberg had no effect on a region's economic or educational development. After 1517, however, as waves of Protestantism rippled out of Wittenberg, parents in nearer regions experienced a greater exposure to these revolutionary ideas, increasing their inclination to invest in their children's literacy. The effect of the Reformation on human capital formation was so persistent that three and a half centuries later Prussian counties closer to Wittenberg were characterised by higher levels of education and, in line with the quantity–quality trade-off, experienced a larger reduction in birth rates than counties further away.[12]

Another quasi-natural experiment that sheds light on the relationship between education on fertility rates occurred in the United States. In 1910, the Rockefeller Sanitary Commission launched an initiative to eradicate hookworm in the American South. This intestinal parasite was known to cause infected children to be less attentive at school, and its eradication would therefore boost their ability to learn and complete their studies. In other words, if the initiative was successful – which it was – there would be an increase in the return on investment in the children's human capital. Comparing the *changes* in parental birth rates in areas that benefited from this intervention with those in similar regions that were unaffected by the programme suggests that the greater returns on children's education did indeed trigger a reduction in parental birth rates.[13]

The role of the quantity–quality trade-off in the decline in fertility rates has also been observed in other countries, such as

China, France, England, Ireland, and Korea, as well as in cross-country analyses of developing societies in the past decades.[14] In particular, data from England in the period 1580–1871 suggests that the birth of an additional child within a family reduced the probability that other siblings would be able to read and write and acquire skilled trades.[15] Similarly, evidence from China, between the thirteenth and twentieth centuries, indicates that children born into smaller families were more likely to apply for the rigorous entry exams for China's public service positions.[16]

The impact of human capital on labour productivity was clearly not the only reason for parents choosing to invest in the education of fewer children. As noted in the previous chapter, societies have invested in education for thousands of years, reflecting religious, cultural and national aspirations – factors that have surely affected rates of fertility and technological innovation too. Nevertheless, it is not a coincidence that the investment in human capital and the provision of public education became especially widespread in industrialised nations towards the end of the nineteenth century. Nor is it any coincidence that this took place in parallel with the onset of the Demographic Transition.

However, there was an additional important factor at play: the narrowing of the gender wage gap and the rise in women's paid employment.

The Decline in the Gender Wage Gap

Today, over half a century after pay discrimination became illegal in the United States and the United Kingdom, and despite the fact that women achieve higher education levels than men, women in both countries and throughout the world receive on average lower pay than men do. This gender wage gap is the result of various factors: greater employment of men in senior positions and higher-paying sectors; the adverse effect of parental leave on career advancement and paid working hours; straightforward forms of discrimination.

Not long ago, however, the gender wage gap was far greater than it is today, having declined significantly across the globe since the second phase of industrialisation began. In 1820, the average working woman in the US earned only 30 per cent of a man's salary. In 1890, the total wages of women stood at 46 per cent of the wages of men, and by the Second World War, it had risen to around 60 per cent.[17] Perhaps not surprisingly, the narrowing of the gap between men's and women's wages coincided with greater access to education for women. In 1840, literacy rates for British men stood at 67 per cent compared to 50 per cent for women, while by the end of the century, that gap had dramatically shrunk and more than 90 per cent of men and women were literate.[18] A similar pattern was observed in Western European nations in the course of their industrialisation, and across the developing world in the twentieth century.[19]

Various economic, cultural, institutional, legal and social factors contributed to the narrowing of the gender wage gap.[20] In particular, the mechanisation of the production process diminished the importance of low-skilled heavy manual labour, traditionally considered to be 'men's work', while fostering the significance of mentally intensive work, both of which served to reduce gender disparities in earning and education. In addition, widespread access to education, as well as legislation designed to secure property rights in the economy as a whole, planted the seeds for women's electoral enfranchisement and ultimately for the legal prohibition of gender discrimination and its condemnation as morally unacceptable.

In the early nineteenth century, when automation in the textile industry reduced the demand for handspun fabrics made by women in home-based workshops, the gender wage gap in England widened and birth rates rose.[21] But over the course of the century, the gender wage gap narrowed dramatically across sectors, partly due to the rapid mechanisation of the production process and the increasing importance of mental skills.[22] Indeed, for almost a century, between the years 1890–1980, sectors in the US that experienced more rapid technological progress witnessed women's employment rates rise relative to men's.[23]

The surge in women's wages had conflicting effects on fertility rates. On the one hand, rising women's wages eased household budget constraints and permitted a larger number of children – an income effect. But, on the other, women's higher wages increased the household's opportunity cost of having more children, as well as of marrying daughters earlier, inducing delayed marriage and suppressing birth rates – a substitution effect. Since historically in most cultures the burden of raising children fell mainly on women, the substitution effect dominated the income effect, and fertility declined.[24]

The decline in gender wage gaps reinforced the drop in birth rates that had been triggered by the rise in the return on human capital. Data from the 1911 census in England and Wales suggests that as job opportunities for women increased and the gender wage gap declined, birth rates also fell.[25] Comparable patterns emerge from an examination of textile factories in Germany in the time period 1880–1910,[26] the United States in the period 1881–1900,[27] and Sweden in 1860–1955.[28]

This rich historical evidence suggests then that technological advances during the Industrial Revolution led to higher returns on investments in human capital, the narrowing of the gender wage gap, a decline in child labour, an expansion in life expectancy and an increase in migration from rural to urban regions, and that these factors contributed to the decline in fertility in the course of the Demographic Transition.

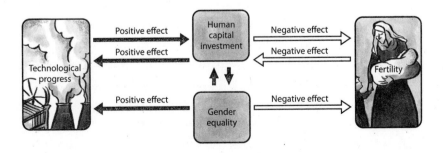

But how did these grand transformations affect the daily lives of ordinary families?

Family Tales

Consider three fictional families, each representing the typical experience of birth rates, education levels and living standards in a different historical period. The first family lives in the Malthusian epoch, during which the economic well-being of the population remained unchanged in the long run and food surplus was predominantly channelled into raising a larger number of children. The second family lives at the dawn of the Industrial Revolution, a period in which increased income led to even larger families and sporadic training of children. Finally, the third family lives in the post–Demographic Transition era, marked by a reduction in the number of children per family, increased investment in their education, and significant improvements in living conditions.

The first family, the Kellys, owns a modest plot of land in sixteenth-century rural Ireland. They have three children – two girls and a boy – and are still grieving the death of their youngest daughter, who passed away from pneumonia a few months ago. The family's small farm yields a meagre income, which scarcely keeps them at a subsistence level. They live in a tiny, dilapidated shack whose roof leaks when it rains and their children suffer from cold, hunger and the diseases of malnutrition.

It is hard for Mrs Kelly not to envy her sister, Anne, who married a wealthy landowning man from the neighbouring village and has thus far borne five healthy children, who help with the farm and household duties. During a family gathering, Anne's husband regales the adults with tales of a promising wonder crop from the Americas: the potato. Mr Kelly appears somewhat sceptical but his wife convinces him to take the risk and replace their wheat with the newfangled potato. They soon discover that, by growing potatoes, they can squeeze more calories out of their small allotment. Their children gradually gain strength and start helping the parents sell their surplus yield in a nearby market town.

Flush with some cash at last, the Kelly family can afford to repair the house and the leaky roof, and to buy warm clothes before the arrival of the harsh winter months. Soon, Mrs Kelly becomes pregnant again. The couple is delighted that their family is about to expand with an additional child and their lives are on the mend. Since Mrs Kelly is healthier this time around, the baby is stronger, and she is able to breastfeed and look after her infant while her older children take over the housework. The newborn will reach adulthood, as will two of their three older children and one of the next two children that will soon join the family.

Mr and Mrs Kelly do not consider investing in their children's education. They are both illiterate, as is everyone else they know, apart from the local mayor and the priest from the nearest town. The vast majority of their neighbours are illiterate farmers, and the skills of the local blacksmiths, carpenters, fishermen and assorted tradesmen generate only slightly higher income than they have. Basic literacy is not required for any of these professions, which instead depend on skills acquired on the job. Professions that demand education – such as medicine and law – are scarce and are typically reserved for the children of the aristocracy and bourgeoisie, who study in distant, elite institutions. The Kellys, therefore, have no motive to spend their modest income procuring an education for their children, especially since it implies losing valuable pairs of hands both on the farm and at home.

Since the Kellys have few reasons to invest in their children's education, they spend their additional income that the potato yield permits to improve their household's living space and diet, and on raising more children. Caught in the Malthusian trap, the Kelly family's wealth soon proves to be short-lived. Their children have more children of their own whenever their incomes rise above subsistence level, and since the family only owns a small plot of land, their living standards gradually drop. Within a few generations, their descendants are suffering the same harsh conditions as their ancestors: the family stops growing, and their income is near subsistence, and when the potato blight eventually ravages Ireland, some of them tragically die of starvation and others migrate to America.

The Joneses, the second family, live' in early-nineteenth-century England. Like the Kellys, they own a run-down house and farm a small plot of land. They, too, have three children – two boys and a girl – and they too are mourning the recent death of their youngest, a son who succumbed to smallpox. However, turn-of-the-century Britain is experiencing a whirlwind of change due to the mechanisation of the textile, coal and metals industries, as well as the growing transatlantic trade.

Mrs Jones's sister, Ellen, has recently married and moved to the neighbouring city of Liverpool, where her husband is the manager of a textile factory. At a family gathering, he invites Mr Jones and his two sons to work at the factory. Mr Jones is initially hesitant, but Mrs Jones persuades him to take up the offer. So the couple leaves their village and relocates to Liverpool. The work in town is not easy, but the wages of three factory hands far exceed their previous income from farming. A few months later, the Joneses can afford to buy their children new clothes and move into a more spacious flat.

It is not long before Mrs Jones is pregnant again, and she soon gives birth to a healthy baby girl. While his wife nurses the baby at home, Mr Jones takes his elder son, William, to meet the chief technician at the textile factory and offers to pay for his training as an apprentice, learning the tricks of the trade. The teenager is not excited by the thought of being a technician's apprentice and the gruelling work it involves, but his mother persuades him and explains that, with this expertise, he will earn a much higher wage and the daughter of the family next door may be willing to marry him. His younger brother is frustrated. He is fully aware that his parents lack the funds to provide him with similar training; he will have to endure the drudgery of being a humble factory hand for the rest of his life. While investing in their elder son's skills, the Joneses have two additional healthy babies who are destined to life in poverty.

During the Joneses' lifetime, birth rates soar despite the fact that many parents also start investing in their children's education and skills, but the growing number of mouths to feed only partially offsets the positive effects of technological progress on living conditions. In contrast to the Kellys, the Joneses have begun a journey that leads ultimately out of the Malthusian trap; they, their children and particularly the grandchildren born to William will enjoy increasing prosperity over time.

The third family are the Olssons, who have a modest home in early-twentieth-century Stockholm. They have two sons and a daughter. However, unlike the Kellys and the Joneses, they have not been forced to mourn the loss of any of their children. During their lifetime, technology has developed at a dazzling pace across the Western world. The new buildings that surround them are plugged into the electricity grid, and fewer of their neighbours than ever before are employed in agriculture. Steam locomotives coupled with steamboats connect Sweden to the rest of Europe, and the first automobiles have begun rolling through the streets of Stockholm.

Like almost everyone they know, Mr and Mrs Olsson can read and write. They married at a later age than the Joneses and Kellys because they wanted to accumulate sufficient wealth before settling down. Mr Olsson owns a small fishing vessel and Mrs Olsson, who was employed in a textile factory before the wedding, now works part-time for a local newspaper and devotes her free time to advancing the feminist cause. The Olssons' daughter will soon start school; the two older boys have concluded their education and are currently employed, one as a newspaper delivery boy, the other at a warehouse at the docks.

Mrs Olsson's sister, Ingrid, has married a wealthy banker, bought a spacious house in the suburbs, and sends her children to an expensive private secondary school. At a Christmas lunch, Ingrid's husband turns to Mr Olsson and suggests that he should borrow from his bank to invest in a new steam-powered trawler. The Olssons hesitate but decide to pursue the opportunity. The new boat vastly increases Mr Olsson's fishing hauls, and with their new-found wealth, the couple decides to send their two sons to secondary school and live without the children's extra income during the school term, in the hope that their education will lead to a respectable and fruitful trade.

The Olssons are living through a time when the importance of human capital is turning education into a powerful status symbol, indicating one's place in the social hierarchy and affecting one's ability to find a suitable spouse, forge meaningful social and commercial ties, and more. Since the children's education is costly, and Mrs Olsson's time is valuable, the parents prefer not to have any additional children. The fertility rate in Stockholm is still higher than the mortality rate, but the moderate growth in population only partially offsets the rise in living standards, which are soaring at breakneck speed.

Hundreds of thousands of years after *Homo sapiens* emerged on this planet, Mr and Mrs Olsson are born into one of the first generations to have escaped the Malthusian trap, and their family is one of millions in Western Europe and North America who escape poverty during this period. The improvements in the Olsson family's quality of life – a direct product of technological progress – do not recede over the next few generations but only intensify. The descendants of the Jones family will have lived through the Demographic Transition and been liberated from the Malthusian trap a little earlier than the Olssons, towards the end of the nineteenth century, while those of the Kelly family will have broken free of it soon after them in the early part of the twentieth century.

At last, thanks to the Demographic Transition, humanity has undergone its phase transition.

Phase Transition

From the dawn of humankind, technological progress helped generate a gradual increase in population size as well as the proliferation of traits that were conducive to further technological progress. However, as discussed in earlier chapters, for hundreds of thousands of years, the gravitational forces of the Malthusian trap thwarted any meaningful sustainable increase in living standards. Nonetheless, beneath the surface the great cogs of human history – the interplay between technological progress and the size and composition of the population – were turning from the start, gathering pace at first imperceptibly but accelerating faster and faster until eventually, in the late eighteenth century, they unleashed the technological explosion of the Industrial Revolution. One hundred years later, the acceleration of technological innovation and its impact on the growing appetite for educated workers who could navigate the changing technological environment, along with the rise in life expectancy, the decline in child labour, and the reduction of the gender wage gap set off the Demographic Transition, liberating economic growth from the counterbalancing effects of population growth. At last, societies escaped from the long arms of the Malthusian octopus, allowing living conditions to soar.

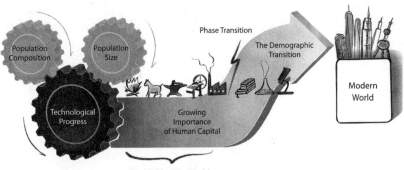

The Cogs of Change

The trajectory of the journey of humanity – the progression out of the Malthusian trap and into the modern era of growth – might now appear inevitable. But its timing and pace were influenced by other monumentally important factors. To return to our earlier kettle analogy, the precise moment of water's phase transition from a liquid to a gas depends on temperature, yes, but other variables too, such as humidity and atmospheric pressure. Under the influence of these additional conditions, evaporation may occur below or above the threshold of 100 degrees Celsius. Similarly, while the phase transition in the journey of humanity was brought about by the deepest tectonic shifts, which propelled technological progress in every era and corner of the globe and lifted most societies out of the Malthusian trap, aspects of local geography, culture and the institutions that shaped and defined societies accelerated this transition in some places and hindered it in others. Uncovering these forces and understanding their effects will be the goal of the second part of our journey.

But first, what if the rise in living standards we have been experiencing ever since this phase transition turns out to be only a temporary anomaly? What if our current era of growth were to end abruptly, as some believe it must? Have we indeed reached the promised land? Is industrialisation conducive for prosperity in the long run? Is the journey of humanity sustainable?

6

The Promised Land

In the late nineteenth century, the vast majority of people across the planet lived in homes that had no electricity, running water, toilets, sewerage or central heating. Their diet was meagre and monotonous, and they had no access to refrigerators, not to mention washing machines or dishwashers. Few could even have envisioned the use of cars – let alone planes – for daily transportation. Radio had just been invented, television and computers did not exist, communication over the telephone was very limited and the mere concept of the mobile phone, or the internet, would have appeared to most as witchcraft.

Yet these living conditions transformed in a heartbeat. The proportion of households in the US with running water spiked from 24 per cent in 1890 to 70 per cent by 1940, while the percentage with an indoor toilet rose from 12 to 60 per cent. Only an insignificant fraction of American homes had electric-powered lighting in 1900, but by 1940, millions of households had been connected to the power grid, and electricity lit 80 per cent of them. Central heating, which was first introduced in the early twentieth century, rapidly spread throughout the US and by 1940 was keeping 42 per cent of households warm. And while most American families could hardly imagine owning an automobile, a refrigerator or a washing machine a few decades earlier, by 1940, nearly 60 per cent of them owned a car, 45 per cent possessed a refrigerator and 40 per cent had a washing machine.[1]

Similar trends occurred during the same period in other Western countries, and have taken place in other world regions since the second half of the century. Behind these figures lay an improvement in the average person's quality of life of such a magnitude that those of us today who have never lived without running water, electricity or an indoor toilet may scarcely comprehend.

Health is self-evidently one of the most important factors in the quality of life, and there too the world experienced a massive leap forward. Long before the advent of modern medicine in the latter half of the twentieth century, the contribution of the French scientist Louis Pasteur to the recognition of the germ theory of disease and the subsequent installation of sewerage and water networks in major towns at the turn of the twentieth century led to a sharp decrease in deaths from infectious diseases. Moreover, the introduction and diffusion over the next few decades of vaccinations against diseases, including smallpox, diphtheria and whooping cough, generated a further drop in death rates.

This unprecedented rise in living standards contributed to an extraordinary increase in life expectancy. For millennia, as income per capita was near subsistence, life expectancy had oscillated in a narrow range, between thirty and forty years. Changes in resources, as well as wars, famines and epidemics, triggered temporary swings in fertility and mortality rates, but life expectancy remained relatively stable because the Malthusian mechanism prevented sustained improvement or deterioration in living conditions. However, in the middle of the nineteenth century, as income per capita began its unprecedented ascent, life expectancy started to soar (Fig. 10). Again, these trends began in industrialised nations from the middle of the nineteenth century onwards, during their escape from Malthusian forces, and proceeded in developing countries towards the second half of the twentieth century, predominantly affecting the poorest sections of society, who were most vulnerable to cold, hunger and disease.

These improvements to public health reinforced the virtuous

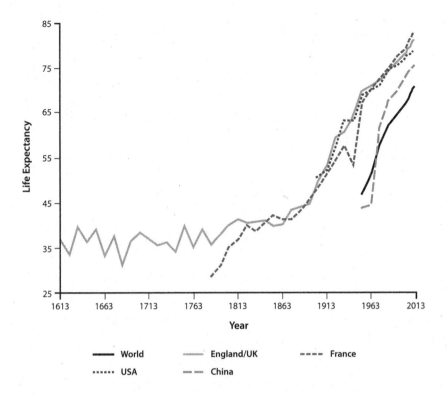

**Figure 10. Evolution of Life Expectancy (at birth)
across the Globe, 1613–2013[2]**

circle between technological progress and human capital formation. Technological advancements contributed to a decline in morbidity rates and a rise in life expectancy, which in turn boosted the incentive to invest in education and fostered further technological innovations. In particular, the eradication of malaria at the start of the twentieth century in the American South, as well as in countries such as Brazil, Colombia, Mexico, Paraguay and Sri Lanka towards the middle and the end of the century, has improved not only children's health but also their education, skills and earning capacity decades into the future.[3]

Naturally, one's standard of living is not just a matter of health, material goods and physical comfort but is influenced by the social, cultural and spiritual dimensions of our existence too.

In these respects, technological advancements during this period provided far greater access to information, cultural exchange and social contact irrespective of physical distance. The first consequential development in this regard was the rapid proliferation of Gutenberg's printing technology, which facilitated the diffusion of information and culture via books and newspapers. Subsequently, the reforms championed by Sir Rowland Hill in the nineteenth-century British postal service allowed ordinary citizens to exchange letters, while the advent of the telegraph – a quantum leap in information transmission technology – made near-instantaneous communication possible between remote regions such as the different sides of the Atlantic.

In an age of such rapid transformations, however, even the extraordinary invention of the telegraph was soon eclipsed. In 1876, Alexander Graham Bell – a Scottish-born inventor who had emigrated to Canada and then to the United States – conducted the first call on his newly invented telephone. By the turn of the century, about 600,000 telephones were ringing across America, and by 1910, the number had risen ten-fold to 5.8 million;[4] phone use per capita was equally impressive over this period in Denmark, Sweden, Norway and Switzerland.[5] It is hard to comprehend the leap in the quality of life experienced by people across the globe in the early twentieth century, who could suddenly communicate with relatives, friends and collegues in distant places rather than waiting weeks (or longer) to correspond via letters or spend a fortune on short telegrams.

The advancements of the period also included a unique cultural dimension. When Edison conceived of the phonograph in 1877, he hoped it would be used to record important political speeches and teach elocution. Yet, by the 1890s, phonographs played music in cafes and restaurants, and in the early twentieth century they spread to private homes. The phonograph was a genuine sensation, although the biggest improvement in terms of public access to culture and entertainment was still yet to come with the development of the radio by the Italian inventor Guglielmo Marconi in 1895.

Wireless transmission technology had appeared in the late nineteenth century and was promptly embraced by the world of shipping. In 1912, the *Titanic* sent wireless distress signals when it hit an iceberg, though tragically the transponders on the ship that could have made a difference were switched off and the signals were not received. World War I briefly postponed the arrival of radio technology on the open market, and the first commercial radio broadcast was not aired until November 1920 in the US. But during the 1920s, a large number of stations sprang up like mushrooms across Europe, North America, Asia, Latin America and Oceania, including the BBC, Radio Paris and Funk-Stunde AG Berlin. Radio appears to have had a more dramatic impact on lifestyles and culture than any other invention preceding it. For many families in remote and isolated areas, the radio was their only exposure to the outside world, replete with political intrigue in the nation's capital, modern music and news from across the ocean. As depicted in the film *Radio Days*, America in the 1930s and '40s was a nation addicted to radio shows, panicking when H. G. Wells's novel *The War of the Worlds* was dramatised in 1938, and gripped by a live broadcast of the rescue effort of an eight-year-old girl who had fallen down a well.

Following the first film screening by the Lumière brothers in Paris in 1895, the proliferation of cinemas in the early part of the twentieth century turned actors such as Charlie Chaplin, Mary Pickford and others into international stars. Black-and-white silent movies soon gave way to Technicolor 'talkies', and in 1939, tens of millions of cinephiles worldwide were astonished to behold the burst of colour in *The Wizard of Oz*: 'Toto, I've a feeling we're not in Kansas anymore . . .' Dorothy (played by Judy Garland) tells her dog. 'We must be over the rainbow!' Indeed, after more than a century of dizzying technological progress, parts of humanity itself finally appeared to be over the rainbow.

Or was it? Alongside this breathtaking technological progress and the vast improvement in living standards, the human species also experienced several catastrophes in the first half of the twentieth century. Tens of millions of people died in the trenches of World War I and in the Spanish flu pandemic that convulsed the world in 1918–20. The Great Depression, which began in 1929, pushed many countries into not only poverty and unemployment but also devastating political extremism, and the first shot of atrocity-ridden World War II was fired ten years later.

Meanwhile, within some of the most advanced societies, prosperity over this period of ascent in living conditions was not equally shared across the various layers of society. Unequal opportunities, discrimination and social injustice had contributed to massive social and economic inequality, reflecting racial prejudice, and gender biases, as well as the legacy of the dark age of slavery. In fact, disparities in health and education were augmented, civil liberties remained the privilege of some but not others, and social injustice became in certain respects more prevalent.

And yet, ultimately, even these dreadful events of the last hundred years have not diverted humanity from its new phase of sustained economic growth and the grand arc of the advancement of humanity. Living standards of humanity as a whole, seen through a broader lens, have swiftly recovered from each of these catastrophes.

This progress is captured crudely by the unprecedented growth of income per capita that has taken place across the globe since the onset of the Demographic Transition. Between 1870 and 2018, worldwide average income per capita surged by a previously inconceivable factor of 10.2 to $15,212 a year. Income per capita in the US, Canada, Australia and New Zealand rose by a factor of 11.6 to $53,756 a year; in Western Europe it rose by a factor of 12.1 to $39,790 a year; in Latin America, by a factor of 10.7 to $14,076 a year; in East Asia, by a factor of 16.5 to $16,327 a year; in Africa, while this improvement had been significantly smaller, income per capita still rose by a factor of 4.4 to $3,532 a year.[6]

Perceived from a distance, then, the main trend of the past two centuries has been the transition from a world in which most people were illiterate and indigent farmers who toiled incessantly, ate like paupers, and bore large numbers of children only to watch nearly half of them die before reaching adulthood, to one in which most of the world's population bears children they can expect will outlive them; enjoys varied diets, entertainment and culture; works in a relatively less perilous and strenuous environment; and benefits from significantly higher incomes and longer lives. To date, the forces that exploited technological progress to amass power, destroy and oppress have had a secondary impact compared to the forces that leveraged it to create, promote equality of opportunity, reduce human misery and build a better world.

As we consider the sustainability of this growth, however, one major and intriguing shift in recent decades demands a deeper reflection: the continued rise in living conditions towards the end of the twentieth century has taken place not because of industrial manufacturing, but perhaps despite it. What does this signify?

The Twilight of Industry

In the latter half of the nineteenth century, one of the Western world's fastest-growing industrial towns rose over the banks of the Great Lakes of North America: Detroit, Michigan. Nicknamed the 'Paris of the West' thanks to its spectacular architecture and wide boulevards lined with electric lamps, the city was located at the heart of an extensive commercial network, connecting Chicago to New York and the rest of the East Coast. In the early twentieth century, Henry Ford founded his immensely successful Ford Motor Company in the town, which soon attracted an influx of entrepreneurs, turning it into the world capital of the automobile industry. Detroit reached its zenith in the 1950s, when it became home to 1.85 million people, making it the fifth-largest city in the United States. Automobile workers enjoyed higher wages than their peers in other industries, and car manufacturers employed a large class of managers and engineers, whose superior income enabled them to build luxurious houses in the suburbs, dine at exclusive restaurants, and enjoy plays at Detroit's lavish theatres.

In the 1960s, however, Detroit's fortunes began to turn. Competition in the auto industry intensified, and some manufacturers moved parts of their operations to Mexico, Canada and the Southern states to save on labour costs. This caused an exodus from the city; whole neighbourhoods became ghost towns. In 1967, as Detroit's economy continued to slump, a five-day riot broke out and claimed the lives of forty-three residents. The city was mired in corruption, crime and unemployment, an image that made its way into popular culture with films such as *Robo-Cop*. In 2013, the municipality filed for bankruptcy after sinking further in debt than any other American city had before. Currently, Detroit's population is less than one-third of its size in the 1950s, with numerous streets lined with deserted and neglected buildings – in sad contrast to its glorious past.

The case of Detroit is not unique. Many other cities in the industrial heartlands of the American North-East and Midwest such as Buffalo, Cleveland and Pittsburgh experienced a significant decline in the latter half of the twentieth century – a pattern that gave the region the unflattering name 'Rust Belt'. Britain, France, Germany and other developed countries also saw industrial regions that had boomed in the early twentieth century fall far behind their neighbours. In fact, in the period immediately after 1980 the developed world as a whole witnessed an overall decline in manufacturing jobs. In advanced economies, the share of employment in the manufacturing sector declined sharply from nearly 25 per cent in the period 1970–79 to about 13 per cent in the period 2010–15;[7] UK manufacturing went from employing 21.8 to 7.6 per cent of the workforce in the period 1981–2019;[8] and in the United States it dropped from 21 to 8 per cent.[9] In contrast, in emerging markets and developing economies, employment in the manufacturing sector declined only slightly from 13 per cent in the period 1970–79 to 12 per cent in 1981–2019, whereas

China experienced a sharp increase from 10 per cent to 21 per cent over this period.[10]

As we saw in the previous chapters, rising living standards in the West during the Industrial Revolution were predominantly the result of human capital formation and rapid technological advancement, each reinforcing the other. This technological advancement took the form of industrialisation but the rise in living standards was not contingent on the process of industrialisation itself. True, in the earlier phases of industrialisation, the two processes went hand in hand: the growth in income per capita rose in parallel to the growth of industry. But in the twentieth century, as the pace of technological change in low-skilled industries slowed down, the impact of industrialisation on the standard of living was transformed. Instead of encouraging the cultivation of human capital and economic growth, low-skilled industry stifled it – just as agriculture had in the past.

Consider France as an example. Regions that experienced rapid industrialisation and economic growth in the mid-nineteenth century remained relatively wealthy until the 1930s, but by the turn of the twenty-first century, they had fallen behind other, less industrial areas. In the short run, the industrial heartlands' specialisation in manufacturing had enriched local residents. Over time, however, the reliance of the industrial sector on workers with only basic education reduced the incentive to invest in higher education in these heavily industrial areas, further limiting the educational aspirations of their populations. The disparities in human capital formation between low-skilled industrial regions and regions characterised by higher-skill industries and services deepened over time. This, in turn, impeded the adoption in the former industrial heartlands of technologies that demanded high levels of education, further reinforcing their tendency to focus on low-skilled sectors and reducing their prosperity.[11]

The repercussions of the relative decline in the importance of manufacturing are illustrated by some of the most high-profile political events of recent years. Donald Trump based his 2016 election campaign on a promise to make American industry 'great again'. Indeed, much of Trump's pivotal support came from states in the Rust Belt, such as Indiana, Michigan, Ohio and Pennsylvania, and from other districts that were hollowed out and ravaged by the unemployment generated by industrial decline.

The United Kingdom's recent departure from the European Union may also be associated with the decline of manufacturing. Britons working in manufacturing or living in areas that were dependent on industrial production, such as north-east England, were more likely to vote in favour of Brexit.[12] And in France, Germany and other developed nations as well as Britain, politicians frequently assist domestic industries through subsidies, tariffs, quotas and various benefits in the hope of discouraging corporations from shifting their operations to developing countries where wages are significantly lower, though to no great avail.

Industries that relied on a limited set of basic skills sent the torch of the dual engines of economic growth – technological progress and human capital investment – in search of new sectors to illuminate, including services, finance and digital technology. The decline of industrial towns and regions has been deeply distressing for the communities founded in them, with some older workers losing their livelihoods indefinitely and with a significant number of younger residents being forced to uproot themselves and migrate to find jobs elsewhere. Investment in general human capital, though, in the form of a rounded basic education and transferable skills, has enabled an increasing fraction of these workers in dying industries to switch to booming sectors of the economy and reap the fruits of continuously rising living standards.

A key lesson from the twilight of low-skilled industries in Western societies is that developing countries may benefit from the allocation of resources towards human capital formation and skill-intensive sectors rather than towards the development of traditional low-skilled intensive industrial sectors.[13]

The Age of Growth

In the latter half of the twentieth century the great wheels of change continued to spin at an ever-intensifying pace. It was during this period that the age of growth finally reached economies worldwide, boosting the living conditions of billions of people on the planet, although often very unevenly. Once again, this transformation brings into view the pivotal role that human capital has played in improving the quality of life in our modern world, a trend that led the American economic historian Claudia Goldin to name the twentieth century 'the century of human capital'.

Among the major technological breakthroughs of the twentieth century were the harnessing of nuclear energy, the introduction of personal computers, the development of antibiotics, and the advancement of automobiles and aeroplanes, as well as the radio, the television and, of course, the internet. Alongside these entirely new inventions, however, technological change also upgraded our most enduring and essential agricultural commodities. The development of exceptionally high-yield and disease-resistant varieties of wheat, corn and rice improved agricultural productivity nearly overnight. Described as the 'Green Revolution', the adoption of these new bumper crops increased harvests tremendously and reduced hunger across the world. Thanks to them, Mexico became self-sufficient in grain in the 1960s, while India and Pakistan almost doubled their wheat harvests over the years 1965–70 and became self-sufficient in cereal production in 1974.

In many other cases, innovation was primarily organisational rather than technological or scientific. In 1968, the International Organization for Standardization recommended American entrepreneur Malcolm McLean's design for the modern intermodal shipping container as the standard template worldwide. The adoption of this uniform design across all modes of transportation made loading and unloading at ports significantly more efficient, dramatically reducing the costs of freight transport and contributing to a boom in international trade.

As ever, this diffusion of technologies intensified both the demand for and the value of human capital formation, bringing the Demographic Transition to every corner of Planet Earth. Between 1976 and 2016, worldwide growth in human capital investment led to a rise in literacy among the world's adult population: from 61 to 83 per cent among women, and from 77 to 90 per cent among men. Meanwhile, the proportion of primary-school-age girls *not* in school fell from 35 per cent in 1970 to 10 per cent in 2016, and among boys it dropped from 20 to 8 per cent. Yet more remarkably, in nations defined by the World Bank as 'low income', the proportion of school-age girls not enrolled in school dropped from 72 per cent in 1970 to 23 per cent in 2016, and that of school-age boys fell from 56 per cent to 18 per cent.

And just as you would expect by now, wherever human capital formation was growing, the birth rate was falling (Fig. 11).

In the latter half of the twentieth century, many developing countries finally broke out of the Malthusian trap. Across Africa, Asia and Latin America, families started having fewer children and investing more in the ones they had. In the period 1970–2016, fertility rates dropped from a worldwide average of 5 children per mother to 2.4 children. To varying degrees, this decline occurred across every region of the planet. In high-income countries, fertility rates dropped from 3 children per woman to 1.7; in low-income countries, they decreased from 6.5 children to 4.7; in sub-Saharan Africa, from 6.6 to 4.8; in the Arab world from 6.9 to 3.3; and in the most populated countries in the world, they dropped sharply: from 5.7 to 1.6 in China, largely due to its one-child policy enacted in 1979, and from 5.9 to 2.3 in India. In fact, barring migration, the populations of some of the most developed countries – including Germany, Italy and Japan – are expected to shrink in the coming decades, as current fertility rates have fallen below the rate of replenishment.

Combined with rapid economic growth, these declining birth rates led to a dramatic improvement in living standards all

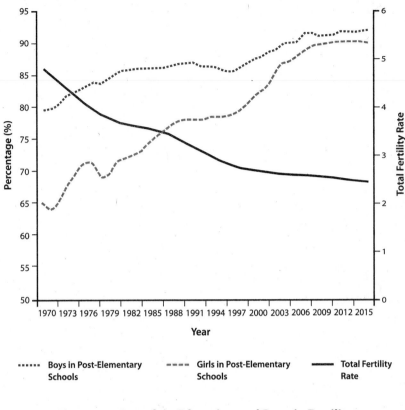

Figure 11. Growth in Education and Drop in Fertility across the World, 1970–2016[14]

around the globe. In the 1970s and '80s, nearly 40 per cent of the world's population lived below the poverty line – a threshold defined by the World Bank as an income of $1.90 a day (Fig. 12). In particular, 61 per cent of people lived below this poverty line in sub-Saharan Africa in 1994, and among the world's most populous nations, 66 per cent of Chinese people lived below the poverty line in 1990, and 63 per cent of Indians in 1972. This proportion has dropped sharply in recent decades, except for in sub-Saharan Africa. Today, about 10 per cent of the world still lives below the poverty line – including 40 per cent of sub-Saharan Africans, but less than 5 per cent in Latin America and the Caribbean, and in the largest nations in the world, this

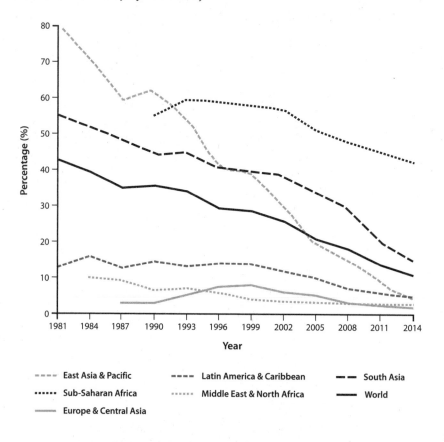

**Figure 12. The Fall in the Proportion of People
on Sub-Poverty Income Levels across the World, 1981–2014**[15]

proportion dropped to 22 per cent of Indians in 2011, and most impressively to less than 1 per cent of Chinese in 2016.

The contribution of economic growth to living standards is evident from myriad health indicators. Between 1953 and 2015, global average life expectancy rose from forty-seven to seventy-one years, and infant mortality rates declined as impressively. This remarkable progress signifies billions of children studying in schools, billions of women giving birth in hospitals that practise basic hygiene, and hundreds of millions of elderly people enjoying financial support in their old age. In large parts of the globe, it implies that children born in the twilight of the twentieth century are among the first generations who are able to look beyond the grind of daily existence and not just dream of a better future but have cause to expect one – a future of sustained improvement in their quality of life.

Of course, the pace of economic growth in any one place and time has been also affected by a wide range of temporary factors. In the aftermath of World War II, many countries experienced an intense and rapid economic growth spurt, due partly to the post-war reconstruction effort. In the 1970s and '80s, by contrast, the global pace of growth slowed as a result of the 1973 oil crisis and demographic trends. In the 1990s, growth picked up again thanks to the revolution in information technology, globalisation, outsourcing, and the astounding expansion of China and other developing countries. Most recently, the financial crisis in 2008 and the Covid-19 pandemic have had adverse temporary effects of the global growth trajectory. But despite these short-run fluctuations due to major crises, economic growth in Western Europe and North America over the past 150 years – that is, since the onset of the Demographic Transition – has maintained an average pace of about 2 per cent a year.

In one of his most famous aphorisms, the British economist John Maynard Keynes said that 'in the long run, we are all dead'. This was meant as a criticism of economists who focused on long-term developments rather than the immediate effects of short-term crises on millions of people's lives.[16] But Keynes's maxim is quite misleading. In fact, to a large extent, we are all the product of, and all contend with, the repercussions of events and behaviours that began decades, centuries and even millennia before we were born. As we will see in the second part of the book, contemporary economic prosperity at the societal level is, to a large extent, a product of deep historical, geographical, institutional and cultural features, rather than, say, the grave consequences of the atrocities and destruction of World War II or the devastating impact of the Great Depression. Human suffering during and in the aftermath of these events has been horrendous. And yet, considering the gravity of the human losses and traumas that occurred over these periods and beyond, the effects of these events on *societal* (rather than individual) measures of living conditions have been remarkably short-lived, typically fading within years or decades, while the fundamental forces explored in this book have an impact that lasts hundreds, thousands or even tens of thousands of years.

In recent decades, while large segments of the developing world have joined this age of growth and billions of people have been liberated from the vulnerability to hunger, disease and volatility, a new, looming peril has appeared over the horizon: global warming. Will this phenomenon also turn out to be short-lived, even while it may be devastating for the generations who live through it, or will it be the single historical event that derails humanity from its journey thus far, bringing the most catastrophic long-lasting consequences of all?

Growth and Environmental Degradation

The Industrial Revolution set the stage for humanity's alarming impact on the environment.[17] Since its early phases, pollution has increased dramatically in major industrialised cities, contributing to the climate crisis we currently face. In particular, the burning of fossil fuels has elevated the level of heat-trapping greenhouse gases in the Earth's atmosphere and fostered global warming. The anticipated climb in temperatures across the planet in the coming decades is predicted to engender major environmental changes, leading to the extinction of a large variety of plants and animals, and disrupting the complex balance of life on Earth. Furthermore, the forecast rise in sea levels is expected to displace tens of millions of people, affecting the world food supply and generating significant economic losses and human suffering. The gradual adoption of environmental regulations and environmentally sustainable technologies, such as harnessing solar and wind energy, recycling and waste management, and wastewater treatment have partly mitigated this trend, but our pollution of the planet remains alarming.

Earlier predictions of mass starvation due to the inability of Planet Earth to support our exploding population were largely proven false by the remarkable surge in food supply over the course of the Green Revolution, along with a gradual decline in population growth. Nevertheless, the seven-fold surge in world population and the fourteen-fold rise in income per capita in the past two hundred years, dramatically increasing worldwide consumption, have been major driving forces of environmental degradation. Some are concerned that the journey of humanity as we know it may no longer be viable. The insufficient pace of the transition towards sustainable energy sources and the ongoing production of eco-unfriendly goods contribute to the growing view that avoiding an environmental disaster will necessitate slowing the pace of economic growth.[18]

Is economic growth indeed incompatible with the preservation of Earth's natural environment? Must we choose between the two? Not necessarily.[19] Cross-country analysis suggests that an increase in the size of a population leads to an increase in carbon emissions that is an order of magnitude larger than would result from a comparable increase in the material well-being of that population. In other words, a region with 50 million people and an income of $10,000 per capita emits significantly more carbon than a region with 10 million people and an income of $50,000 per capita, despite the fact that the two regions have precisely the same aggregate income. This implies that economic growth fuelled by a decline in fertility rates – growth arising due to an increase in the relative size of the working-age population (known in the economic discipline as a 'demographic dividend') – would permit significant reductions in the projected level of carbon emissions.

In fact, the decline in fertility rates since the onset of the Demographic Transition has been reducing the burden of exponential population growth on the environment. So while the Industrial Revolution triggered our current period of global warming, the concurrent onset of the Demographic Transition may well serve to mitigate its effects, diminishing the potential trade-off between economic growth and environmental preservation. Essentially, sustaining economic growth while mitigating further environmental degradation and reducing the likelihood of 'collapse' will rely on some of the same key factors that have brought us to our current predicament: technological innovation to facilitate the transition away from reliance on fossil fuels and towards environmentally friendly technologies, and a decline in fertility to reduce the population burden on the environment and to engender further economic growth. As the American technologist, business leader and philanthropist Bill Gates puts it: 'We should spend the next decade focusing on the technologies, policies, and market structures that will put us on the path to eliminating greenhouse gases by 2050.'[20]

Among these policies and structures should be ones that foster worldwide gender equality, access to education and the availability of contraceptives, and thus contribute to fertility reduction across the globe. By mitigating the current trend in global warming, they will buy us valuable time for the development of the game-changing technologies that will be required in this battle. The formal endorsement of demographic measures such as these may garner greater political support among most developing countries than conventional climate policy recommendations: adopting clean energy technologies and environmental regulations are costly to administer and enforce, whereas policies associated with fertility reduction provide the benefits of economic growth along with environmental preservation.

If we can avoid complacency and commit the proper resources, the incredible power of human innovation that was so spectacularly unleashed during the age of progress, twinned with fertility decline – both fuelled by human capital formation – should permit the timely advancement of the revolutionary technologies that will be needed, turning this climate crisis into a fading memory in the centuries to come.

Coda: Resolving the Mystery of Growth

The development of humankind has been extraordinary – breathtaking in its path and radically different from the evolution of any other living species on Planet Earth. Early humans roamed the savannahs of East Africa using fire for light, warmth and cooking, and chiselling stones to make blades, axes and other tools. Several million years later, one of their descendants writes this book on a portable device capable of performing complex, split-second mathematical calculations using nanotechnology-based processors with 100,000 times more processing power than the computers used only fifty years earlier to land a man on the moon.

The first spark that set humanity on its distinctive journey was the development of the human brain, whose growing capabilities were born from adaptation to evolutionary pressures that were unique to our species. Equipped with their powerful brains, humans developed progressively better technologies, improving their hunting and gathering efficiency. Such advances enabled the population to swell, while attributes that made humans better able to use those technologies bestowed a survival advantage. Thus emerged *Homo technologicus*: human beings whose fingers adapted to sculpt raw materials into useful hunting and cooking objects, whose arms developed to hurl spears, and whose brains evolved to store, analyse and transmit information, to reason and communicate using languages, and to facilitate cooperation and complex trade relations.

Over hundreds of thousands of years, these processes unceasingly enhanced the adaptation of humankind to its ever-changing environment, allowing the species to thrive and grow and permeate new ecological niches as it ventured out of Africa. It learned to protect itself from precarious weather conditions and refine its hunting and gathering skills in a wide range of habitats until, about 12,000 years ago, it experienced its first major transformation: some humans adopted sedentary lifestyles and began farming their food, generating evolutionary pressure on the species as a whole to follow suit.

The Neolithic Revolution had an enduring effect on humanity. In a matter of only a few thousand years, the majority of humans abandoned their nomadic lifestyle and began cultivating the land, raising cattle, sheep and goats, and adapting to their new surroundings. Agricultural societies benefited from significant technological advantages, which persisted for thousands of years. Technological innovation in the form of irrigation and cultivation methods generated higher agricultural yields and led to greater population density, fostering specialisation, and the emergence of a non-food-producing class, dedicated to knowledge creation. They spurred further technological progress, as well as advancements in art, science and writing, leading to the onset of civilisation. The human habitat had been gradually transformed: farms grew into villages, and villages expanded into towns and walled cities. These cities sprouted magnificent palaces, temples and fortresses, the bastions of elites who created formidable armies and slaughtered their enemies in battles for land, prestige and power.

For most of the history of our species, the interplay between technological progress and the human population was a persistent reinforcing cycle. Technological progress enabled the population to grow, and encouraged the adaptation of societal traits to these innovations, while the growth and the adaptation of the population widened the pool of inventors and expanded the demand for innovations, further stimulating the creation and adoption of new technologies. For aeons, these great cogs of human history whirred beneath the surface, propelling humanity on its journey. Technologies improved, populations grew, societal traits that suited new technologies spread – and these changes triggered further technological progress in every civilisation, on every continent and in every era.

Nevertheless, one central aspect of the human condition remained largely unaffected: living standards. Technological progress over most of human history failed to engender any meaningful long-term betterment in the material well-being of the population, since – like all other species on Earth – humanity was caught in a poverty trap. Technological progress, and the associated expansion of resources it allowed, invariably contributed to population growth, dictating that the fruits of progress had to be divided among a growing number of mouths. Innovations led to a rise in economic prosperity for a few generations, but ultimately population growth brought it back down towards subsistence levels. When populations enjoyed fertile land and political stability, technology made significant strides. This occurred variously in ancient Egypt, Persia and Greece, in the Mayan civilisation and the Roman Empire, in the Islamic caliphates, and in medieval China. Bursts of technological progress spread new tools and production methods across the surface of the globe and temporarily elevated living standards. Yet these improvements were short-lived.

Eventually, however, the inevitable acceleration of technological advancement over the course of human history reached a tipping point. The innovations of the Industrial Revolution that began in a small pocket of northern Europe in the eighteenth and nineteenth centuries was sufficiently rapid to foster demand for a very particular resource: the skills and knowledge that would enable workers to navigate a technological environment that was not just new but continuously changing. In order to equip them for such a world, parents increased their investment in the upbringing and education of their children, and thus were forced to bear fewer of them. The surge in life expectancy and the decline in child mortality augmented the duration of the return on education, further enhancing the incentive to invest in human capital and reduce fertility. Meanwhile, the decline in the gender wage gap increased the cost of child rearing and contributed further to the attraction of smaller families. These joint forces triggered the Demographic Transition, severing the persistent positive association between economic growth and birth rates.

This dramatic drop in fertility liberated the development process from the counterbalancing effects of population growth, and allowed technological improvements to raise prosperity permanently instead of in fleeting spurts. Thanks to a better-quality workforce, and heightened investment in human capital, technological progress accelerated further, boosting living conditions and catalysing sustained growth in income per capita. Humanity was undergoing a phase transition. Just as the Neolithic Revolution spread from a few hubs such as the Fertile Crescent and Yangtze River to other regions, so the Industrial Revolution and the Demographic Transition began in Western Europe and over the course of the twentieth century rippled out across most of the globe, raising prosperity levels wherever they reached.

The past two hundred years, therefore, have been revolutionary: living standards have taken an unprecedented leap forward by every conceivable measure. Average per capita incomes across the world have risen by a factor of fourteen and life expectancy has more than doubled. The cruel world in which child mortality was mounting gave way to a prosperous one, in which the death of a single child is an extraordinary tragedy. Yet improvements in living conditions have meant more than just better health and higher incomes. Technological progress also led to a decline in the use of child labour, a shift to less perilous and strenuous occupations, the ability to communicate and engage in commerce across vast distances, and the proliferation of mass entertainment and culture on a scale that our ancestors could never have imagined.

Although this spectacular technological advancement and the

immense improvement in living standards have been shared unevenly across the planet, and sometimes grotesquely so within societies themselves, and though natural disasters, pandemics, wars, atrocities and political and economic upheavals have occasionally rained destruction on countless individuals, these tragedies and injustices – dramatic and horrific as they have been – have not diverted the journey of humanity from its long-term path. Viewed via a wider prism, the living standards of humanity as a whole have recovered from each of these calamities with remarkable haste and have kept hurtling forward – propelled by the great cogs of technological progress and demographic change.

Yet the industrialisation process also triggered a warming of the planet that now threatens the livelihoods – and the lives – of people all across the world, causing some to question the ethics of our lavish consumption and the sustainability of our journey. Fortuitously, the sources of these high living standards could also be their preservation: the power of innovation accompanied by fertility decline may carry the inherent potential to reduce the trade-off between economic growth and environmental preservation. The development of and transition to eco-friendly technologies, and the reduction in the environmental burden due to further decline in population growth that will be brought about by increasing returns to education and gender equality, may permit economic growth to sustain its current pace while mitigating the current trend of global warming, providing valuable time for the development of the revolutionary technologies that will be essential if we're to reverse the current course of global warming.

The journey of humanity is abundant with captivating episodes. It is easy to become adrift on the ocean of detail, pounded by the waves and oblivious to the mighty currents underneath. The first part of this book has focused on these undercurrents: the interplay between technological progress and the size and the composition of the human population. It is virtually impossible to understand the history of humankind without grasping the contributions of these forces to the progression of the human species – the evolution of the human brain, the two monumental revolutions (the Neolithic and the Industrial), the growth of human capital investment and the Demographic Transition, the major trends that made us the dominant species on Planet Earth. These undercurrents provide a unifying conceptual framework, a clear axis from which to understand this journey. In their absence, the history of human development would be merely a chronological list of facts – an incomprehensible wilderness of rising and falling civilisations.

And yet the pace of progress in living standards has been neither universal nor inevitable. Indeed, modern humanity is exceptional in that the standard of living of humans across the planet largely depends on their place of birth. What are the root causes of this vast wealth disparity across nations and regions? Are human societies inevitably trapped by the history and geography of the places in which they sprouted? Was the emergence of these inequalities predominantly deterministic or random? What is the role of deeply rooted institutional, cultural and societal characteristics in the divergence in the wealth of nations?

Having followed the journey of humanity from the past to the present, our exploration of the Mystery of Inequality will involve gradually winding the clock back in search of its deepest origins, reverting ultimately to the roots of our journey – the exodus of *Homo sapiens* from Africa tens of thousands of years ago.

II

The Origins of Wealth
and Inequality

7

Splendour and Misery

In the past decade, scores of boats overloaded with migrants from Africa have sunk just off the coast of Libya and thousands of passengers have lost their lives. The survivors of these traumatic incidents have often expressed disappointment at having failed to reach their intended destination, Italy, but have rarely regretted their decision to embark on the perilous voyage to Europe.

In 2015 alone, more than a million people crossed the Mediterranean in similar crafts, and over the course of this ongoing humanitarian crisis many thousands more from Africa, the Middle East and Latin America have died attempting to reach European and US borders. This desperate mass exodus, in which people not only endanger their lives but leave behind their families and homeland, and pay considerable sums they can scarcely afford to human traffickers, is primarily a result of the immense inequality in living standards across world regions – manifesting as gaps in human rights, civil liberties, socio-political stability, quality of education, life expectancy and earning capacity, as well as, most urgently in recent years, the prevalence of violent conflict.

This disparity in living conditions is so vast that the reality of life at one end of the spectrum is difficult to conceive for someone at the other. In 2017, in most developed nations, life expectancy exceeded eighty years, infant mortality was lower

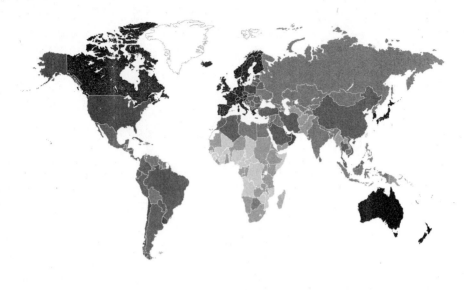

| | 52 - 61 | | 62 - 68 | | 69 - 74 | | 75 - 77 | | 78 - 80 | | 81 - 85 |

Figure 13a. Life Expectancy at Birth across the World, 2017

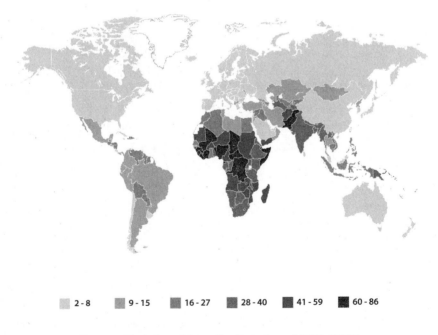

| | 2 - 8 | | 9 - 15 | | 16 - 27 | | 28 - 40 | | 41 - 59 | | 60 - 86 |

Figure 13b. Infant Mortality Rate (per 1000), 2017

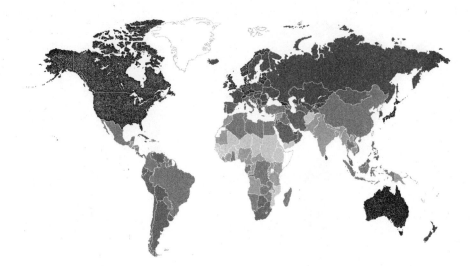

| | 1.5 - 4.3 | | 4.4 - 6.7 | | 6.8 - 8.7 | | 8.8 - 10.8 | | 10.9 - 12.6 | | 12.7 - 14.1 |

Figure 13c. Average Years of Schooling, 2017

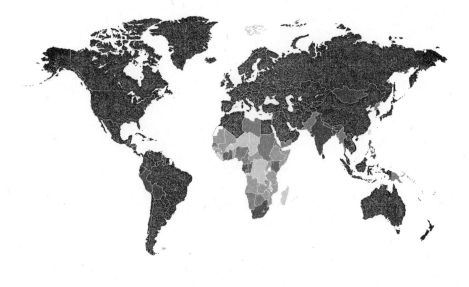

| | 9 - 26 | | 27 - 46 | | 47 - 63 | | 64 - 80 | | 81 - 96 | | 97 - 100 |

**Figure 13d. Percentage of the Population
with Access to Electricity, 2017**

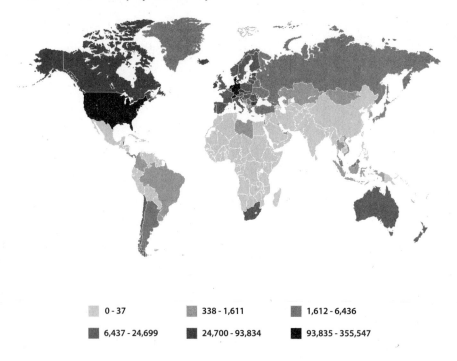

0 - 37	338 - 1,611	1,612 - 6,436
6,437 - 24,699	24,700 - 93,834	93,835 - 355,547

Figure 13e. Secure Internet Services (per million people), 2017

than five deaths per 1,000 live births, nearly all the population had access to electricity, a significant fraction had internet connection, and the prevalence of undernourishment was about 2.5 per cent. In the least developed nations, by contrast, life expectancy was lower than sixty-two years, infant mortality rates surpassed sixty deaths per 1,000 births, less than 47 per cent of the population had access to electricity, less than a tenth of 1 per cent had internet connection, and 19.4 per cent suffered from undernourishment (Figs 13a–13e).[1]

Equally disconcerting is the gap in living standards across social, ethnic and racial lines within societies, manifesting as disparities in education, income and health. In 2019, prior to the impact of Covid-19, in the world's richest country, the United States, life expectancy of African Americans was 74.7, whereas that of white Americans was 78.8; infant mortality rates per 1,000 were 10.8 for African Americans and 4.6 for white Americans; and 26.1 per cent of African Americans had a college degree by the age of twenty-five, in contrast to 41.1 per cent of white Americans.[2]

Even so, the gulf in living standards between the richest and the poorest countries is so much larger that millions of women and men risk their lives in the attempt to reach the developed world.

Disparate Factors

At the surface of this global inequality is the fact that income per capita in developed nations is significantly higher than that in developing countries (Fig. 14), resulting in a much higher expenditure on education, health care, nutrition and housing.

But why do the citizens of some countries earn significantly more than the residents of others? This earning gap partly reflects differences in 'labour productivity': each hour of work in some world regions produces goods or services of greater value than an equivalent hour of work elsewhere. Agricultural labour productivity, for instance, varies enormously across countries. In the United States agricultural productivity per worker in 2018 is nearly 147 times higher than in Ethiopia, 90 times higher than in Uganda, 77 times higher than in Kenya, 46 times higher than in India, 48 times higher than in Bolivia, 22 times higher than in China and 6 times higher than in Brazil.[4] But again, why do American farmers reap a far bigger harvest than the farmers of sub-Saharan Africa, South East Asia and most of South America?

The answer should come as no surprise: these differences are primarily a reflection of the technologies for cultivation and harvesting that are used in each country, as well as the skills, education and training of farmers. American farmers use tractors, trucks and combine harvesters, for example, while farmers

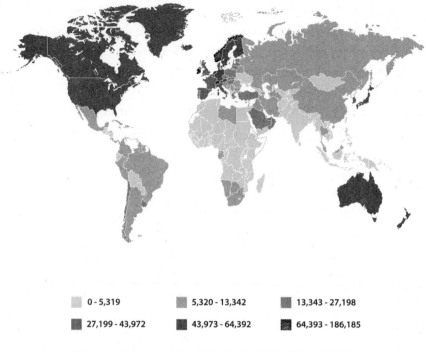

Figure 14. Income Per Capita in US Dollars, 2017[3]

in sub-Saharan Africa are more likely to rely on wooden ploughs often pulled by oxen. Moreover, American farmers are better trained and can use genetically modified seeds, advanced fertilisers and refrigerated transportation, which may not be feasible or profitable in the developing world.

Nonetheless, this chain of proximate causes does not shed light on the *roots* of the disparity. It simply directs us to a more fundamental question: Why does the production process in certain countries benefit from more skilled workers and more sophisticated technologies?

Rusty Tools

Previous attempts to understand economic growth, like that of Nobel Prize-winning economist Robert Solow, focused on the importance of the accumulation of physical capital – straw baskets, rakes, tractors and other machines – to economic growth.

Suppose that a couple harvests enough wheat to bake a few dozen loaves of bread a week. They use some of these loaves to feed their family and sell the remainder at the village market. Once they have saved enough, they purchase a plough, increasing their stock of physical capital, their harvests and ultimately the number of loaves of bread they can bake per week. As long as the couple does not have additional children, this accumulation of capital (the addition of a plough) will help them increase their per capita income. The impact of this physical capital accumulation, however, is constrained by the *law of diminishing marginal productivity*: as the amount of land and time available to them is limited, then if that first plough boosts the couple's output by five loaves of bread a week, a second plough might only contribute three more loaves, while the fifth plough may hardly boost productivity at all.

The important corollary of this analysis is that only perpetual improvements in the efficiency of the plough will deliver long-term income growth for these villagers. Furthermore, the acquisition of a new plough would spur faster growth on a poor farm than it would on a more advanced farm of equal size, because this would likely be the first on the poor farm, whereas it might be the third or the fourth on the rich one. Thus, a relatively poor farm should grow more quickly than a more advanced one, and over time the income gap between the poor and the rich farms should narrow.

Solow's growth model suggests therefore that economic growth cannot be sustained indefinitely in the absence of technological and scientific progress.[5] Moreover, it predicts that, with time, income disparities between countries that differ only in their *initial* levels of per capita income and capital stocks should diminish.

Imagine a marathon race in which the further runners get from the starting point the harder each additional step

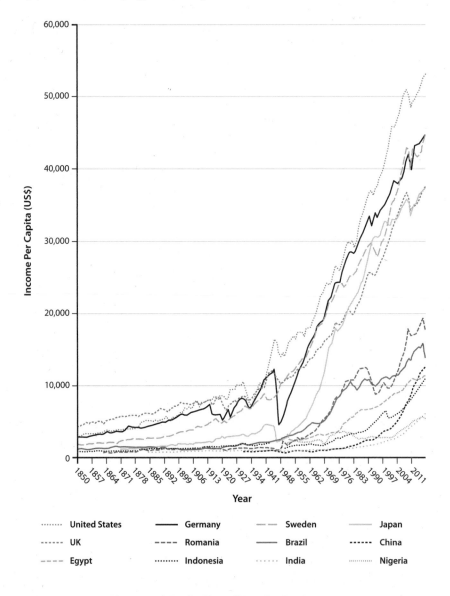

**Figure 15. Evolution of Per Capita Income
across Countries, 1850-2016**[6]

becomes. If one group of runners starts the race a few minutes earlier than a second, equally talented group of runners, the first group will keep ahead of the latecomers, but the gap between the two will be narrowing with every stride they take.

Analogously, in the context of countries that differ only in their initial levels of per capita income and capital stock, those poorer economies that started the race later should gradually converge with those richer economies that started the race earlier, and thus the income gaps across these nations should eventually decline.

Yet, as Figure 15 shows, the economies of the developed and developing nations have not converged. Quite the contrary, in fact: the gaps in living standards between regions have largely expanded over the past two centuries.

What prompted this great divergence between some countries? And what are the forces that have prevented some poorer nations from catching up with richer ones? In the second half of the twentieth century, policymakers advanced programmes with the aim of raising the living standards of developing countries based on the insight that technological progress and the accumulation of physical and human capital stimulate economic growth. However, inequality across nations persists to such an extent as to suggest that these policies have had a limited impact.[7] Too narrow a focus on observable factors on the surface – the manifested disparities – rather than on the underlying causes that created them has prevented the design of policies that would help poorer nations overcome the less visible, but more persistent, obstacles they face. These forces could have created a barrier that inhibited investments, education and the adoption of new technologies, contributing to uneven development across the globe. It is these underlying causes and obstacles that we will need to identify if we wish to decipher the Mystery of Inequality and foster global prosperity.

Trade, Colonialism and Uneven Development

During the nineteenth century, international trade rose significantly. It was triggered by the rapid industrialisation of north-western Europe, enabled and fuelled by colonialism and encouraged by the reduction of trade barriers and transportation costs. Of the entire world's output in 1800 only 2 per cent was traded internationally. By 1870 that share had risen five-fold to 10 per cent; by 1900 it was 17 per cent and by 1913, on the eve of World War I, it stood at 21 per cent.[8] While a major portion of this commerce was taking place between the industrialised societies, developing economies were an important and growing market for their exports. The patterns that emerged over this period were unambiguous: north-western European countries were net exporters of manufactured goods, whereas the exports of Asian, Latin American and African economies were overwhelmingly composed of agricultural-based products as well as raw materials.[9]

While technological advances during this era could have spawned the Industrial Revolution without the contribution of the expansion of international trade, the pace of industrialisation and the rate of growth in Western European nations was intensified by this commerce, as well as by the exploitation of colonies, their natural resources, their native populations and enslaved Africans and their descendants. Likewise, the Atlantic triangular trade, which was at its height in the preceding centuries, and the growing trade with Asia and Africa had a major impact on Western European economies. Not only was the trade in goods itself highly profitable, it provided raw materials such as timber, rubber and raw cotton for the process of industrialisation, all cheaply produced through slave and forced labour. Meanwhile, the production in the European colonies of agricultural products such as wheat, rice, sugar and tea enabled European nations to enhance their specialisation in the production of industrial goods, and benefit from the expanding markets for their products in the colonies.[10]

In the UK especially, the share of national income derived from international trade grew: from 10 per cent in the 1780s to 26 per cent in the period 1837–45, and to 51 per cent in 1909–13. Exports were critical for the viability of some sectors, especially the cotton industry, in which 70 per cent of UK output was exported in the 1870s.[11] Other European economies experienced a similar pattern. The proportion of national income resulting from foreign trade on the eve of World War I was 54 per cent in France, 40 per cent in Sweden, 38 per cent in Germany and 34 per cent in Italy.[12]

This expansion of international trade in the early phases of industrialisation had a significant – and asymmetrical – effect on the development of industrial and non-industrial economies. In industrial economies, it encouraged and enhanced specialisation in the production of industrial goods that required a relatively highly skilled workforce. The associated rise in demand for skilled labour in these nations intensified their investment in human capital and expedited their demographic transition, further stimulating technological progress and enhancing their comparative advantage in the production of such goods. In non-industrial economies, by contrast, international trade incentivised specialisation in the production of relatively low-skilled, agricultural goods and raw materials. The absence of significant demand for educated workers in these sectors limited the incentive for investment in human capital and thus delayed their demographic transition, further increasing their relative abundance of low-skilled labour, and enhancing their comparative disadvantage in the production of 'skill-intensive' goods.

Accordingly, globalisation and colonisation contributed to the divergence in the wealth of nations in the past two centuries. While in industrial nations the gains from trade were directed primarily towards investment in education and led to growth in income per capita, a greater portion of the gains from trade in non-industrial nations were channelled towards increased fertility and population growth. These forces persistently affected the distribution of population, skills and technologies worldwide, widening the technological and education gaps between industrial and non-industrial economies and so enhancing rather than diminishing the initial patterns of comparative advantage.[13] The premise of this argument – that international trade generated opposing effects on fertility rates

and education levels in developed and less developed economies –
is supported by regional and cross-country analysis based on
contemporary as well as historical data.[14]

This asymmetric impact of globalisation and colonisation is
also strikingly evident from the rate at which industrialisation
itself took place in developed and developing countries. The
level of industrialisation per capita in the United Kingdom rose
50 per cent between 1750 and 1800, quadrupled between 1800
and 1860, and nearly doubled between 1860 and 1913. In the
United States, it increased four-fold between 1750 and 1860,
and six-fold between 1860 and 1913. A comparable pattern was
experienced by Germany, France, Sweden, Switzerland, Belgium
and Canada. In contrast, developing economies experienced a
decline in per capita industrialisation during the nineteenth century, and it took nearly two centuries for them to revert to their
initial levels, before finally taking off in the second half of the
twentieth century (Fig. 16).[15]

The trading relationship between the UK and its colony India
exemplifies this pattern. Between 1813 and 1850, as India experienced a rapid expansion in its volume of exports and imports, the
country gradually transformed from being an exporter of manufactured products – largely textiles – into a supplier of agricultural
goods and raw materials.[16] Trade with the UK was fundamental
in this process. The UK supplied over two-thirds of India's
imports (primarily manufactured goods) for most of the nineteenth century and was the market for over a third of its exports.[17]

The effect this had in the UK will by now be familiar. By fostering the process of industrialisation, trade helped contribute
to the significant increase in demand for skilled labour in the
second phase of the Industrial Revolution. The average years of
schooling of the male labour force of England, which did not
change significantly until the 1830s, had tripled by the beginning of the twentieth century. School enrolment at the age of ten
increased from 40 per cent in 1870 to nearly 100 per cent in
1902.[18] In the 1870s, the overall fertility rate in the UK started
to drop, and in the subsequent fifty years, it declined from about

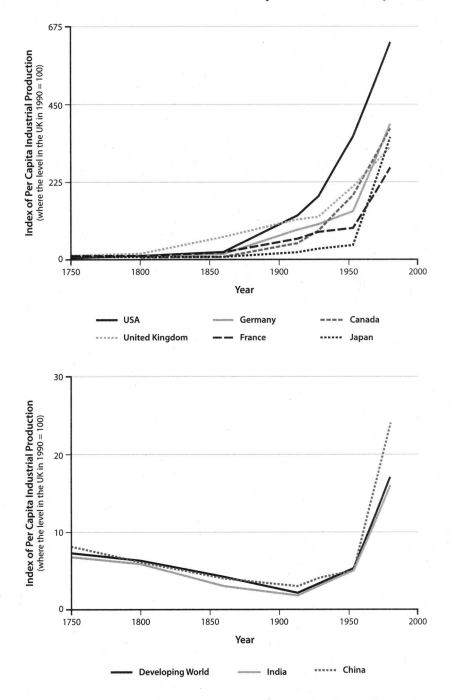

**Figure 16. The Impact of Globalisation:
Industrialisation and Deindustrialisation across the Globe**

five children per woman to nearly 2.5. Over this same period, the economy transitioned into a state of sustained growth in income per capita at a rate of nearly 2 per cent per year.

In contrast, India experienced a decline in its per capita level of industrialisation. The entrenchment of the agricultural sector in India, for which education was not essential, contributed to the persistence of widespread illiteracy well into the twentieth century. Attempts to enlarge primary education in the twentieth century were hampered by low attendance and high dropout rates.[19] Despite the gradual spread of education, 72 per cent of Indians beyond the age of fifteen had no schooling in 1960. In the absence of significant human capital formation, the demographic transition in India was delayed well into the second half of the twentieth century.

Thus, while the gains from trade in the UK expedited its fertility decline and led to significant growth in income per capita, in India they were channelled predominantly towards higher fertility rates. Since 1820, the size of the Indian population relative to that in the UK has doubled while income per capita in the UK relative to that in India has also doubled.

And yet, domination, exploitation and asymmetric trade patterns during the colonial age enhanced pre-existing patterns of comparative advantage rather than generating them in the first place. What accounts for the uneven development that took place *prior* to the colonial period? What allowed some countries to become industrialising colonisers and forced others to become the non-industrialised colonised?[20]

To decipher the Mystery of Inequality we will need to unveil factors that are more deeply rooted than the ones identified thus far.

Deep-Rooted Factors

Imagine that one bright morning you pull yourself out of bed, brew a cup of coffee and, while stepping outside to greet the day, discover to your surprise that the grass is greener outside your neighbours' house.

Why is their lawn so lush? A technical reply might be that your neighbours' grass reflects light at wavelengths in the green range of the spectrum, while yours reflects light closer to the yellow range. This explanation, while perfectly accurate, is not particularly helpful – it gets us no closer to understanding the root of the matter. A more thorough, less pedantic response would focus on the differences in the timing, intensity and methods that you and your neighbours have used in taking care of your lawns: irrigating, mowing, fertilising and applying pesticides.

Nevertheless, these reasons, important as they may be, still might not uncover the root causes for your neighbours' grass being greener. They represent *proximate causes* for the visible differences in the quality of the two lawns, behind which are the *underlying reasons* that explain why your neighbours irrigate their lawn more regularly, or why they are more successful at pest control. If you fail to understand the roles of these deep-rooted factors, your attempts to emulate your neighbours' gardening methods, persistent as they may be, might not yield the dazzling green hue that you desperately crave.

Geographical factors might lie behind the visible differences between the two lawns – variations in soil quality and exposure to sunlight might frustrate your efforts to mimic your neighbours' success. Alternatively, the differences might reflect underlying *cultural factors* that reflect the environment in which they and you were raised and the nature of the education you received – cultural traits, such as an especially future-oriented mindset, that drive them to lavish great care and attention on their lawn, watering and mowing it at the optimal times.

It might be that the two properties are under the jurisdiction of different municipal authorities. Your local council has imposed a watering ban to conserve water, while your neighbours are free to water their lawn to their heart's content. So it could be an *institutional factor* that prevents you from imitating your neighbours' gardening techniques and closing the gap between the two lawns. Or it could be a deeper reason, still in your respective municipalities, that leads to these institutional differences, something associated with the very make-up of your neighbours' community. More homogeneous communities are better positioned to implement regulations and collective decisions about public investment in irrigation infrastructure and the eradication of pests, while more heterogeneous communities might benefit from the cross-fertilisation of diverse innovative gardening techniques. In this sense, it could be that *population diversity* is the underlying cause of the gap between the two lawns.

Like the differences between the two lawns, the immense disparities in the wealth of nations are rooted in a chain of causal factors: at the surface are *proximate factors*, such as the technological and educational differences between countries; at the core are the deeper and *ultimate factors* – institutions, culture, geography and population diversity – that lie at the root of it all. Although it may be challenging to disentangle the impact of proximate and ultimate factors, the distinction is critical if we are to understand how these deep-rooted factors have affected the speed at which the great cogs of human history have turned and thus governed the pace of economic development in different places.

8

The Fingerprints of Institutions

This satellite image is surely one of the most haunting photographs ever taken from space.

The Korean Peninsula
Satellite imagery of night-time light, 2012[1]

In the bottom portion of the picture is the prosperous country of South Korea, late in the evening: a glittering galaxy of stars radiating the light of prosperity. South Koreans drive back from work on illuminated roads, spend their evenings in restaurants, malls and cultural centres flooded with light, or else with their families in their well-lit homes. In contrast, the top segment of the picture contains one of the poorest countries on Earth – North Korea, engulfed in darkness. Most North Koreans prepare for an early bedtime in the gloom of intermittent power outages. Their country does not produce sufficient energy to keep its electricity grid permanently switched on even in the capital city, Pyongyang.

The disparities between North and South Korea are neither the result of geographical or cultural differences, nor a reflection of North Koreans' lack of knowledge about how to build and maintain a functioning electricity grid. For most of the past millennium, the Korean Peninsula largely formed a single social entity, whose inhabitants shared a common language and culture. However, the partition of Korea after World War II into Soviet and American spheres of influence brought about divergent political and economic institutions. North Korea's poverty and technological underdevelopment – like that of East Germany prior to the fall of the Berlin Wall – originates in political and economic institutions that restricted personal and economic freedoms. Insufficient constraints on government power, limited rule of law, insecure property rights, along with inherently inefficient central planning, have hindered entrepreneurship and innovation, while encouraging corruption and fostering stagnation and poverty. Not surprisingly, South Koreans enjoyed per capita income levels twenty-four times higher than that of their northern neighbours in 2018, and a life expectancy eleven years longer in 2020; differences based on other measures of quality of life are no less drastic.[2]

More than two hundred years ago, the British political economists Adam Smith and David Ricardo highlighted the importance of specialisation and trade for economic prosperity. Yet, as argued by the Nobel Prize–winning American economic historian Douglass North, a critical precondition for the existence of trade is the presence of political and economic institutions, such as binding and enforceable contracts, that enable and encourage it. Put simply, if the governing institutions fail to prevent the violation of agreements – or indeed racketeering, theft, intimidation, nepotism or discrimination – trade is likely to be significantly harder and the typical gains it conveys less available.[3]

In the distant past, societies relied on kinship ties, tribal and ethnic networks, and informal institutions to facilitate and foster trade. Medieval Maghribi traders, for example, imposed collective sanctions on those who violated agreements, and built on the special ties between far-flung communities to develop a flourishing transnational trade across North Africa and beyond.[4] However, as human societies grew larger and more complex, it became necessary to formalise these norms. Societies that ultimately developed institutions conducive to trade – shared currencies, property rights protections, and a set of laws that was uniformly enforced – would have been better able to foster economic growth, reinforcing the virtuous cycle between the size and composition of the population and technological progress. Societies that were late to develop pro-trade institutions would have lagged behind.

Over the course of human history, the concentration of political and economic power in the hands of a narrow elite, empowering them to protect their privileges and preserve existing disparities, has typically held back the tide of progress. It has stifled free enterprise, prevented significant investment in education, and suppressed economic growth and development. Scholars refer to institutions that enable elites to monopolise power and perpetuate inequality as *extractive institutions*. In contrast, institutions that decentralise political power, protect property rights, and encourage private enterprise and social mobility are considered *inclusive institutions*.[5] In their book *Why Nations Fail*, the economists Daron Acemoglu and James A. Robinson have demonstrated that differences in political institutions of this sort have contributed to the gaps between nations. Extractive institutions have typically hindered human capital accumulation, entrepreneurship and technological progress, thereby delaying the transition from stagnation to long-term economic growth, whereas inclusive institutions have reinforced these processes.

Yet history suggests that extractive political institutions need not be detrimental at every stage of economic development. In fact, dictators have occasionally orchestrated major reforms in response to external threats to their regimes, as happened in Prussia in the aftermath of its defeat by Napoleon in 1806 and in Japan in the late nineteenth century during the Meiji Restoration. Moreover, for decades after the partition of the Korean Peninsula, South Korea was a dictatorship – it did not begin its transition towards democracy until 1987 – and yet over these three decades it enjoyed impressive growth while North Korea remained undeveloped. Both Koreas were ruled initially by autocracies; their fundamental difference lay in their economic doctrines. The dictators in Seoul adopted private property protections, as well as far-reaching agrarian reforms that decentralised political and economic power, while their rivals in Pyongyang opted for a massive nationalisation of private property and land and centralised decision-making. These early differences provided South Korea with an immense economic head start over North Korea, long before it became a democracy. Similarly, the non-democratic regimes that used to rule Chile, Singapore and Taiwan – and the ones that still govern China and Vietnam – successfully spurred long-term economic growth by promoting investment in infrastructure and human capital, the adoption of advanced technologies, and the promotion of a market economy.

Nevertheless, while non-inclusive political institutions can coexist with viable inclusive economic institutions, this has been largely the exception rather than the rule – and at critical junctures in human history, the rule appears to have been a pivotal one. The existence of inclusive institutions might partly explain why the Industrial Revolution first began in Britain of all places, whereas the presence of extractive institutions may shed light on why some previously colonised parts of the world continue to lag behind, decades after their official liberation from colonial rule.

Institutional Origins of the British Ascent

Britain's unprecedented leap forward during the Industrial Revolution allowed the country to seize control of vast swathes of the planet and build one of the most powerful empires in history. And yet for most of human history, the inhabitants of the British Isles lagged behind their neighbours in France, the Netherlands and northern Italy in terms of wealth and education; Britain was a mere backwater on the edges of Western Europe. British society was agricultural and feudal; political and economic power was held by a narrow elite; and in the early seventeenth century many sectors of the economy were aristocratic monopolies by royal decree.[6] Given the dearth of competition and free enterprise in England, these monopolised industries were spectacularly unproductive in developing new technologies.

Like many other rulers, English monarchs were hostile to technological change and thwarted their kingdom's technological progress. One famous and ironic example is associated with the delayed inception of the British textile industry. In 1589, Queen Elizabeth I refused to grant the clergyman and inventor William Lee a patent for his novel knitting machine. She feared that his invention would harm the local guilds of hand knitters, fostering unemployment and, therefore, unrest. Rejected by the English queen, Lee relocated to France, where King Henry IV gladly awarded him the desired patent. Only several decades later did William Lee's brother sail back to Britain to market this cutting-edge technology, which became the cornerstone of the British textile industry.

In the late seventeenth century, however, Britain's governing institutions were radically overhauled. King James II's efforts to entrench an absolutist monarchy along with his conversion to Roman Catholicism provoked stiff opposition. The king's rivals found a saviour: William of Orange, stadtholder of various Protestant counties of the Dutch Republic (and husband of Princess Mary, the king's eldest daughter). They urged him to seize power in Britain. William heeded their call, deposed his father-in-law, and was crowned King William III of England, Ireland and Scotland. This coup, known as the Glorious Revolution because it was considered, somewhat mistakenly, to be associated with relatively little bloodshed, transformed the balance of political forces in Britain: as a foreign king without a domestic base of support in England, William III depended heavily on Parliament in a way that his predecessor had not.

In 1689, the king gave royal consent to the Bill of Rights, which abolished the monarch's powers to suspend parliamentary legislation and to raise taxes and mobilise armies without Parliament's consent. England became a constitutional monarchy. Parliament began to represent a relatively wide range of interests, including those of the rising mercantile class, and Britain established inclusive institutions that protected private property rights, encouraged private enterprise, and promoted equality of opportunity and economic growth.

In the aftermath of the Glorious Revolution, Britain intensified its attempts to abolish monopolies. The Royal African Company, to which King Charles II had awarded a monopoly over the African slave trade, was just one of many companies to lose power. Parliament also passed new legislation to promote competition in the growing industrial sector, undermining the economic interests of the aristocracy. In particular, it reduced taxes on industrial furnaces while raising duties on land, which was largely owned by the nobility.

These reforms, which were unique to Britain at the time, created incentives that did not exist elsewhere in Europe. In Spain, for example, the Crown zealously guarded its control on profits from its transatlantic trade, often funnelling them into funding wars and the consumption of luxury goods. In Britain, by contrast, the gains from the transatlantic trade in raw material, goods and enslaved Africans were shared by a broad class of merchants and were therefore largely invested into capital accumulation and economic development. These investments laid the foundations for the unprecedented technological innovations of the Industrial Revolution.

Britain's financial system also underwent a dramatic metamorphosis at the time, further enhancing economic development. King William III adopted the advanced financial institutions of his native Holland, including a stock exchange, government bonds and a central bank. Some of these reforms expanded access to credit for non-aristocratic entrepreneurs and encouraged the English government to be more disciplined in its balancing of government expenditure and tax revenue. Parliament gained stronger powers of oversight over the issuance of public debt, and bondholders – those who had lent money to the Crown – won representation in the decision-making process concerning fiscal and monetary policies. Britain thus came to enjoy greater credibility in the international credit market, reducing its borrowing costs in comparison to other European kingdoms.

In fact, the early onset of the Industrial Revolution in England may have been contributed to by even earlier institutional reforms.[7] As described in Chapter 2, in the fourteenth century the Black Death killed nearly 40 per cent of the inhabitants of the British Isles. The resulting scarcity of agricultural workers increased the serfs' bargaining power and forced the landed aristocracy to raise their tenant farmers' wages in order to prevent their migration from rural areas to the cities. In hindsight, the plague had delivered a fatal blow to the feudal system, and England's political institutions became more inclusive and less extractive. They decentralised political and economic power, encouraged social mobility, and allowed a larger segment of society to innovate and participate in wealth creation. In Eastern Europe, by contrast, the existence of a harsher feudal order as well as lower rates of urbanisation, along with a growing demand for agricultural output from the West, strengthened the landed aristocracy and its extractive institutions in the aftermath of the Black Death. In other words, what might have been insignificant institutional variations between Western and Eastern Europe before the Black Death led to a major divergence after its outbreak, placing Western Europe on a radically different growth trajectory from Eastern Europe.[8]

The relative weakness of the guilds in Britain also contributed to some of the institutional changes that preceded Britain's Industrial Revolution. The guilds, which operated across Europe as a whole, were institutions that defended the interests of their members – skilled craftsmen engaged in a particular trade. They often used their monopolistic powers to stifle entrepreneurship and technological progress. For example, the Scribes Guild in late-fifteenth-century Paris managed to bar the entry of the city's first printing press for nearly twenty years.[9] In 1561, the Red-Metal Turners Guild of Nuremberg pressured the city council to deter a local coppersmith by the name of Hans Spaichi, who had invented a superior slide rest lathe, from spreading his invention, ultimately threatening to jail anyone who dared to adopt his new production techniques.[10] In 1579, the Danzig city council ordered the inventor of a new ribbon loom, which threatened traditional ribbon weavers, to be drowned in secret.[11] And in the early nineteenth century, an angry mob of the Weavers Guild in France protested against Joseph-Marie Jacquard (1752–1834), the inventor of an innovative loom operated using a series of punched cards – technology that would later inspire the programming of the first computers. In contrast, the British guilds were less powerful than their European counterparts, which may have been partly a consequence of the rapid and largely unregulated rebuilding of the City of London in the aftermath of the Great Fire of 1666, as well as rapid market expansion elsewhere, leading to a greater demand for craftsmen than the guilds could supply. Their weakness made it easier for Parliament to protect and enable inventors, allowing British industrialists to adopt new technology more quickly and efficiently.

It was thanks to these institutional reforms that Britain in the late eighteenth century was influenced by the assorted interests of merchants and entrepreneurs rather than predominantly by those of a landed elite determined to avert technological progress and perpetuate their power. In this respect, Britain had become the world's first modern economy, and the rest of Western Europe was quick to follow suit. Thus, while deep-rooted forces were bringing humanity as a whole to the end of the Malthusian age and to the brink of the age of growth, these institutional developments, in conjunction with other factors that will be explored shortly, made Britain an exceptionally fertile ground for rapid technological development at precisely the time when humanity was ripe for its phase transition.

Both the early onset of the Industrial Revolution in Britain and the divergence of the economies in the Korean Peninsula show the profound impact that institutions can have on development and prosperity. But might these especially dramatic examples be the exception rather than the rule? When in the course of history institutions have evolved more gradually, did institutional reforms affect economic prosperity or was it in fact economic prosperity that led to institutional changes? Or might some other factors be responsible for the apparent relationship between the two?

Institutions and Long-Run Development

Over the past two centuries, richer countries have tended to be more democratic.[12] Some have argued that democracy equips the public with the power to overcome special interest groups in society, thus improving equality of opportunities and the allocation of talents across occupations, which in turn boosts productivity and encourages economic prosperity. Put another way, because democracy is politically inclusive it is also economically inclusive.

Yet, although democracies have experienced faster economic growth that does not necessarily mean that democracy *causes* growth.[13] In fact, it might be that economic growth has fostered the emergence of a middle class with the power to challenge the political status quo and push for democratic reform; inclusive institutions might be the result, not the cause, of growth. Indeed, some studies have argued in favour of the 'Modernisation

Hypothesis' whereby economic growth is conducive to democratisation.[14] Alternatively, this positive correlation might reflect the impact of other factors that promote both democracy and prosperity. It might be, for example, that growth happened to take place in a democracy – for reasons that are specific to that locale – but that geographical and cultural proximity to that location encouraged other countries to adopt both its technologies and its democratic institutions, thus generating a positive association between democracy and growth.

One promising method for resolving this conundrum is to examine the impact of historical events, caused by forces unrelated to local economic development, which led to sudden institutional transformation in some regions but not in others. Comparing the changes in economic prosperity over the long term in the affected and unaffected regions would enable us to disentangle the impact of institutions from that of other, confounding factors. Episodes of conquest and colonialism provide quasi-natural experiments of this sort.

The Spanish conquistadors' *mita* system of forced labour offers an insightful example of the persistent and adverse effect of extractive institutions on economic development. The *mita* system compelled indigenous villages in certain areas, but not others, to surrender one-seventh of their male workforce to labour in the Spanish silver mines. Although this system was abolished in 1812, Peruvian regions that were subjected to it remain poorer and have higher child malnutrition rates compared to nearby areas that were not exposed to the system. These findings appear to reflect the long-term effects of the migration of the most productive men out of *mita* areas (to escape their conscription to the silver mines), as well as the emergence of large rural communities outside the *mita* areas, which supported the development of public infrastructure in their villages and contributed to their inhabitants' long-term well-being.[15]

Another episode is provided by the Napoleonic conquest of parts of Prussia shortly after the French Revolution. In areas under their occupation, the French established inclusive institutions that encouraged economic growth, such as legal systems based on equality before the law, the abolition of the monopolies of professional guilds, and a reduction in the privileges of Prussian aristocracy. Although invasions are typically associated with disarray and exploitation in the occupied territories, decades after the French retreated, the formerly occupied parts of Prussia were indeed more economically developed, as reflected by their higher rates of urbanisation, relative to neighbouring areas that had not been occupied.[16]

These particular historical events would suggest that institutions can indeed have a long-term influence on the process of development. But does the broader history of colonialism and conquest corroborate this?

The Legacy of Colonialism

The colonial era witnessed the immense enrichment of colonial powers and the immiseration of generations of indigenous peoples and enslaved Africans. As seen in the previous chapter, in the midst of the Industrial Revolution, colonial trade further exacerbated this stark divergence in their fortunes. While the colonisers often had devastating and horrific ramifications on native populations across the vast colonised world, it is plausible that over the longer term the sweeping political and economic institutions that colonisers – predominantly Britain, France, Portugal and Spain – imposed and left behind had the more persistent effects on their former colonies' standard of living.

Large regions of North America, Australia and New Zealand, which had been relatively sparsely populated and less advanced technologically, enjoyed rapid economic growth after they were colonised, though of course the growth was experienced not by the native populations of these lands, but rather by a rapidly expanding immigrant population from Europe. Conversely, the densely populated regions of Meso and South America that had given rise to the most advanced pre-Columbian civilisations – home to the flourishing Aztec, Inca and Maya cultures – encountered slower development in the modern era and were overtaken by the European colonies in North America.[17]

This was largely an unanticipated reversal of fortunes. The French philosopher Voltaire spoke for many when he belittled the British and French skirmishes over their colonies in North America as fighting 'over a few acres of snow'. The Seven Years War in the period 1756–63 ended with a British victory. During the subsequent territorial negotiations, many argued that Britain should demand France's Caribbean possessions, where the economy of plantations, farmed with slave labour, were producing immense profits, instead of its holdings in North America, which had just been ravaged by colonial wars.[18] And yet, in later years, these 'few acres of snow' became one of the wealthiest regions on Earth. The causes of this apparent reversal of fortunes has provoked a stormy academic debate over the past few decades. How did the legacy of colonialism affect long-term development? Why did some colonies grow into prosperous nations while others came to be mired in poverty?

One hypothesis focuses on the fact that most former colonies inherited the legal systems of their colonisers. Former British colonies and protectorates, including Australia, Canada, Hong Kong, India, New Zealand and Singapore, adopted English-style common law systems, whereas former Spanish and Portuguese colonies, such as Angola, Argentina, Bolivia, Brazil, Chile, Colombia, Indonesia and Mexico, embraced civil law systems in various forms. Common law systems provide stronger protections for investors and property rights, and empirical studies point to a positive correlation between the adoption of the common law legal system and economic prosperity; former British colonies enjoyed greater long-term prosperity, as measured by income per capita, than the former colonies of other world powers.[19] Yet we cannot disregard the possibility that the British happened to colonise regions that had greater economic potential, or that the

British colonisers themselves brought to bear particular skills, attitudes and approaches to running an economy.

Different climatic conditions might also have contributed to the long-term effects of colonisation on local institutions. The climate and soil in Central America and the Caribbean were best suited for growing coffee, cotton, sugar cane and tobacco – crops for which efficient cultivation requires large plantations. The agricultural sector that emerged in these regions during the colonial era was therefore characterised by centralised land ownership, which led to unequal wealth distribution, coerced labour and even slavery – the most extractive of all institutions – entrenching inequality and inhibiting growth. In fact, even in later periods the severe concentration of land ownership in Central and South America, the Caribbean and the US South stifled economic development. As seen in Chapter 4, landowners who relied heavily or exclusively on rural labour for their income, as tended to be the case where landownership was highly concentrated, had a strong incentive to thwart investments in public education in order to prevent the migration of their workers to urban areas where educated labour was in higher demand. These forces directly impeded human capital accumulation, industrialisation and economic growth.[20]

In contrast, climatic conditions in the colonies of North America (except for the US South), which were better suited to mixed farming of grains and livestock, encouraged the growth of a network of small family farms, a more equal distribution of wealth, and the adoption of inclusive political institutions, such as democracy, equality before the law and security of property rights, which were conducive to long-term prosperity.[21] Ironically, these institutions were themselves highly discriminatory: the denial of civil liberties and the exploitation of African Americans and Native Americans were integral to this 'inclusivity'.

A related hypothesis maintains that the reason why Meso and South America, once technologically more advanced than their northern neighbour, ended up becoming the poorer part of the Americas, was an indirect and macabre consequence of variations in *population density* in the pre-Columbian era. During this Malthusian period, as technological development and population density went hand in hand, densely populated areas were naturally the ones where civilisations were most advanced. In these prosperous regions, therefore, colonial regimes had a greater incentive to form institutions that would extract the wealth of the vast indigenous population. When these colonies gained independence, the powerful local elites who succeeded the European colonisers maintained these extractive, growth-retarding institutions, so as to sustain and gain from the persistence of economic and political disparities, condemning these regions to underdevelopment.[22] By contrast, in less advanced areas with lower population density, colonial regimes tended to settle and develop these regions for themselves, commonly after they had destroyed, displaced or subjugated the native population. They therefore formed inclusive, growth-enhancing institutions for their own benefit and for that of their descendants. While highly discriminatory towards African American and Native American populations, these institutions contributed to the overall economic development of these regions, fostering the reversal of fortunes.

Yet, the colonial era gave rise to all sorts of transformations in the colonised world apart from the institutional ones, and the growth potential of these colonies was hardly uniform given their vast differences in agroclimatic characteristics. How might we disentangle these various forces and isolate the persistent impact of institutions alone?

Europeans tended not to immigrate in significant numbers to colonies that had relatively higher mortality rates from such diseases as malaria and yellow fever. Most Europeans who relocated to these regions were not settlers, as they were in North America, but rather members of the ruling elite – officials and military servicemen – who arrived for temporary duty and established institutions that exploited and enslaved local populations. In contrast, European immigrants settled en masse in areas with relatively lower prevalence of these fatal diseases, such as North America, where they supported the establishment of more inclusive institutions, conducive to further European immigration and long-term economic growth. At the end of the colonial era, the independent nations that emerged in North America, Australia and New Zealand maintained these semi-inclusive institutions, while many of the local elites in Africa, Latin America and the Caribbean inherited and perpetuated their extractive institutions.

The mortality rate of different settler populations might therefore serve as a predictor of the nature of modern institutions that arose in their wake. And provided that settler mortality rates (and the underlying disease environment) have no direct effect on present-day economic prosperity, these rates can be used as a variable with which to assess the causal influence of these institutions on economic prosperity. Studies using this method suggest that historical governing institutions have indeed had a major impact on the wealth of nations in the modern era.[23]

But this argument is not without its critics, who argue that since the same diseases may have also been lethal for native populations, their prevalence might have diminished native productivity and thus undermined prosperity independently of any indirect effect via political institutions.[24] Indeed, mortality rates today continue to be higher in regions where settler mortality rates were high in the past. Perhaps, then, it was not only the nature of the colonial institutions established in disease-ravaged regions, but also the perilious disease environment itself that condemned these regions to centuries of economic underdevelopment.

It is equally challenging to disentangle the effects of colonial institutions from the impact of the skills of European settlers. When Europeans migrated to colonies, displacing vast native populations, they brought with them certain knowledge and skills as well as commercial ties to their European homelands. Indeed, evidence suggests that colonies consisting of large concentrations of European populations in the nineteenth century were significantly more likely to enjoy economic growth than colonies comprised predominantly of indigenous populations.[25] What appears to be a major impact of institutions might partly reflect the direct effect of European immigrants themselves, with their imported human capital, on economic development. Some have even argued that past levels of human capital are a stronger predictor of modern-day per capita income than the nature and quality of political institutions.[26]

From this perspective, the relatively rapid economic development of North America compared with that of Meso and South America is not the reversal of fortunes it first appears to be. It clearly does not reflect changes in the well-being of the descendants of the native pre-colonial populations, who in North America were either exterminated or displaced. Rather, it indicates a *persistence* of fortune, as the wealthy regions of North America today are predominantly home to people whose ancestors emigrated from the richer regions of the world.[27]

It is also worth noting that the power of colonial institutions to shape economic development may in some regions have been outweighed by that of other, pre-existing institutions. Consider the African continent. Many of Africa's ethnic groups were arbitrarily divided by artificial borders imposed by European imperial powers during the era known as the Scramble for Africa (1884–1914). These borders divided regions that shared the same ethnicity, tribal organisation and language between different nations, subjecting them to distinct central governing institutions. Intriguingly, the evidence suggests that present-day economic development in Africa has been primarily influenced by the pre-existing local social structures and ethnic institutions rather than by the national central institutions that persisted from the colonial era.[28]

To recapitulate, then: during the colonial era extractive institutions were formed and persisted in some colonies, while more inclusive ones prevailed in others, reflecting geographical characteristics, the disease environment and population density. The current body of evidence suggests that these institutions had a significant lasting effect on the economic development of former colonies, although important confounding factors – notably the disease environment and the human capital of the colonisers – may preclude firm quantitative conclusions. But what about societies that were not colonised? What was the origin of their institutions, and why did institutions conducive to technological progress and economic prosperity first arise in Europe rather than in, say, the sizeable and advanced civilisations of Asia? And within Europe, why first in Britain rather than France or Germany?

Origins of Institutions

Institutional reforms at critical junctures in the course of history, triggered by war; disease; capricious, charismatic or brutal leaders; or the quirk of fate, have occasionally been the direct cause of a divergence in development trajectories across the globe.[29] If medieval Europe had been spared the Black Death, or if James II had repelled William of Orange on the battlefield, then feudalism and absolute monarchy might have lasted longer in England, and ultimately the Industrial Revolution might have occurred somewhere else or in a different time period. Indeed, in some cases, as on the Korean Peninsula, a relatively arbitrary political decision – the division of the country along the 38th parallel – condemns two segments of the same people to an entirely different economic fate, despite the stability of their basic geographical and cultural environments. In other words, it may be that some institutional shifts at critical junctures end up being the fork in the road at which the growth path bifurcates and disparities between nations are born. And unlike geographical and cultural factors, which are inherently persistent over time, institutions can alter very rapidly and may for that reason have particularly dramatic effects.

Yet, 'random' institutional transformations are rather uncommon. Institutions typically survive for centuries and adapt very slowly, even when technological and commercial developments call for urgent reform. The main impact of institutions might in fact lie in their *continuity* and thus in their persistent effect on development, as has been the impact of extractive institutions in Latin America and growth-enhancing institutions in North America.

For the most part, institutions have evolved gradually in response to long-term pressures and trends: as the complexity of societies intensified; as shifts in the environment opened up new opportunities for trade and led to demand for public infrastructure; as climatic conditions required cooperation in the formation of irrigation systems; as the increasing scale and diversity of populations enhanced the importance of social cohesiveness.[30] It is these other factors – cultural, geographical and societal – that will need to be examined if we are to shed light on the origins of the prevailing institutions in non-former colonies across the globe.

Moreover, we may reach the limits of the power of political institutions to account for differences in economic prosperity when we begin to examine the great variation among Western European democracies whose income per capita in 2020 ranged from $17,676 in Greece to $51,126 in Sweden, to $86,602 in Switzerland to $115,874 in Luxembourg.[31] Similarly, additional factors will surely be required to explain the centuries-long endurance of significant disparities *within* countries, such as the gulf between northern and southern Italy, which have in principle shared the same central governing institutions since the country was politically unified in the second half of the nineteenth century.

We have seen how growth-enhancing political and economic institutions have intensified the virtuous circle between technological progress and the size and composition of populations, hastening the transition to the era of modern growth. We have also explored how growth-retarding institutions, in contrast, have put a spoke in this wheel, impeded development and contributed to long-term economic stagnation. But as will become apparent, a broad range of cultural, geographical and societal factors have affected and interacted with institutions, in some places curtailing innovation and human capital formation, in others fostering technological progress, investment in education, and the Demographic Transition.

To properly understand the role of these factors, we must journey further back in time – exploring initially the origins of the cultural traits that have affected the growth process.

9

The Cultural Factor

'It is easier for a camel to go through the eye of a needle,' contended Jesus, 'than for a rich man to enter into the kingdom of God.' This was a common theme of the Church's earliest founders, and for many centuries Christian theologians argued against the pursuit of personal wealth, considering it an obstacle to spiritual development and salvation. Paul the Apostle supposedly went so far as to argue that 'the love of money was the root of all evil'. Later theologians shared similar sentiments, and Thomas Aquinas declared in the thirteenth century that 'covetousness' was a sin. Moreover, Christianity maintains that on Judgement Day the social order will be overthrown and the meek 'shall inherit the earth'.[1]

In 1517, Christendom was shaken to the core when the German monk and theologian Martin Luther nailed his *Ninety-Five Theses* to the door of a Wittenberg church, decrying the Catholic Church's sale of indulgences. Luther's intention was to reform the Church, not to break away from it, but the ferocious debate that ensued between Luther and supporters of the papacy caused an irreparable rift. In 1520, Pope Leo X formally threatened to excommunicate Luther, who responded by publicly burning the papal bull – *Exsurge Domine* – along with volumes of canon law. In the bonfire, he also burned his final bridges with the Catholic Church, shaping Lutheranism as a distinct movement in the Christian world, and sparking the Protestant Reformation in Western Europe.

Protestantism unleashed a wave of new religious norms and beliefs on a range of issues, including thrift, entrepreneurship and wealth. As noted in Chapter 5, Luther (1483–1546) argued that the Church had no role mediating between man and God, encouraging independent Bible reading – a radical practice that incentivised his followers to acquire literacy skills. The French theologian Jean Calvin (1509–1564), founder of the Calvinist branch of Protestantism, asserted that all faithful Christians were duty-bound to serve God through diligent work, frugal living, and abstinence from waste and licentiousness; economic success, in his view, might be a sign of God's favour, possibly even that one was predestined for salvation. Other new branches of Christianity looked favourably on the accumulation of wealth. John Wesley (1703–1791), the eighteenth-century English cleric who founded Methodism, for example, urged his disciples to amass wealth and donate generously to charity.[2] These denominations of Christianity, which gained traction in Germany, Switzerland, France, England, Scotland and Holland, and subsequently spread to North America, as well as pre-Reformation ones such as the Cistercians, encouraged the emergence of cultural traits such as thrift and hard work that are commonly associated with economic growth.[3]

Protestantism in fact sowed the first seeds of modern thought about the relationship between cultural traits and economic growth. Most famously, in 1905 German sociologist Max Weber published his influential thesis *The Protestant Ethic and the Spirit of Capitalism*. He argued that Protestantism had contributed to the conviction that the ability to amass wealth in *this* world was a strong indication of the likelihood of reaching heaven, legitimising wealth as an end in itself, while recasting idleness as a source of shame. Accordingly, he argued that the Protestant ethic was the source of the 'spirit of capitalism' in Western Europe.

Weber's thesis was criticised for prioritising the power of ideas in the emergence of capitalism over the material forces underlined by Marx. Nonetheless, there is evidence to support the claim that the 'Protestant ethic' played a role in the emergence of cultural traits that are conducive for economic growth. During the nineteenth century, regions of Prussia that had relatively large Protestant populations did indeed enjoy higher levels of literacy and economic prosperity than their peers, and the Protestant inclination to invest in education has contributed to the long-term impact of this movement on economic prosperity.[4] Moreover, evidence from contemporary areas of the former Holy Roman Empire suggests that Protestantism is associated today with significantly higher likelihood of becoming an entrepreneur.[5]

Regardless of the importance of the Protestant ethic in the growth process, it is quite apparent that culture plays a key, sometimes critical role in the process of economic development.

The Power of Culture

Cultural traits – the shared values, norms, beliefs and preferences that prevail in a society and are transmitted across the generations – have often made a significant impact on a society's development process. In particular, aspects of culture that dispose populations towards or away from the maintenance of strong family ties, interpersonal trust, individualism, future orientation and investment in human capital have considerable long-term economic implications.[6]

The boundary between cultural and personal traits may often appear fuzzy. Some people might invest heavily in the education of their young because of the values of their social, ethnic or religious group, while others may be driven by personal traits, reflective of their life experiences, upbringing and family background. Nonetheless, one's values, beliefs and preferences are rarely independent of one's social and cultural context. And when variations in these norms correlate clearly with ethnic, religious or social groupings, it is plausible that they are, to a large extent, a manifestation of cultural rather than individual differences. In other words, it is the cultural component that is pertinent for the understanding of inequality *across groups*.

So how have cultural traits emerged and persisted and how have they affected the evolution of societies in the course of human history?

Judaism provides an example of a cultural trait that emerged rather spontaneously, endured because of its delayed unforeseen advantages and turned out to have long-lasting implications. Nearly 2,000 years ago, as part of the power struggle between rival movements within Judaism, several Jewish sages promoted universal literacy. The most famous advocates of this principle were Rabbi Shimon ben Shetach in the first century BCE and High Priest Joshua ben Gamla about a century later, who insisted that Jewish parents had a duty to acquire education for their sons. As noted in Chapter 5, this doctrine presented an immense challenge at a time when literacy rates were extremely low, few occupations required the ability to read or write, and most households could neither afford to forgo their sons' labour nor pay for their education.[7]

Cultural initiatives of this sort are a common feature of human societies but rarely do they survive long enough to contribute to meaningful cultural changes over the long term.[8] But in this case, a series of events conspired to keep this cultural change very much alive. In the aftermath of the Great Revolt against the Roman Empire, which erupted in Judaea in 66 CE, the Romans destroyed Jerusalem and the Jewish Temple. Several of the main branches of Judaism died out, including the Sadducees – the priestly elite – and the Zealots who fought for Jewish independence, while the Pharisees, the relatively moderate faction that emphasised the study of Jewish texts over ritual worship in the Temple, became the dominant group in the Jewish world. The scholarly Pharisees encouraged mass access to education and later imposed cultural sanctions on families who failed to send their sons to school, inadvertently inducing poorer households to abandon Judaism.

Hoping to strengthen the surviving remnants of his defeated people, Rabbi Judah ha-Nasi, the head of the Jewish community in Roman-occupied Judaea at the turn of the third century CE, also emphasised the importance of reading the Bible and practising its commandments. And over the centuries, the expulsion of the Jews from their homeland and the emergence of laws in the diaspora that banned them from land ownership made the acquisition of human capital, an inherently mobile asset, an especially attractive and worthwhile investment. The subsequent urbanisation of the Muslim world and medieval Europe increased the demand for an educated workforce, further enhancing the benefits of this cultural norm and accelerating the Jews' long-run trend away from agriculture-based occupations towards commercial and education-intensive urban professions.

Like biological mutations, the initial appearance of a cultural change may be 'random', but its survival or extinction is not accidental.[9] The norm of literacy and book-learning might never have appeared in either the Jewish or Protestant communities without the decree of the Jewish sages and the preaching of Luther; but it is nearly certain it would never have taken root in the way that it did were it not for the advantages – in this case commercial and economic – bestowed on those who embraced it, advantages that the early advocates of Bible study neither envisioned nor invoked.

Different societies in different places at different times have inevitably developed different norms in order to adapt to the particular ecologies they inhabit. Over time and across civilisations, thinkers and leaders have proposed countless initiatives to reform norms, values and beliefs. Yet it is mostly when either geographical and climatic characteristics, the disease environment, or technological, commercial and social conditions have reinforced the benefits of these novel cultural traits that they have persisted and generated significant cultural change.

Humans have developed traditions and norms that regulate, for example, diet, property rights, social cohesion, family structure and gender role. Individuals within these societies often consider these traditions to be based on timeless and essential truths, commonly adhering to and perpetuating them as such, without necessarily knowing their original purposes or understanding the adaptive reasons for their existence.[10] This psychological tendency to adhere to existing cultural norms without challenging their foundations has conferred a survival advantage. Societies with hardly any scientific knowledge of human biology, group consciousness or the ecological factors that affect their habitats have been able to thrive in complex and precarious environments, behaving as if they did possess such knowledge, thanks to accumulated wisdom of generations of trial and error, passed on in the form of ancient traditions, timeless beliefs and universal rules. For example, by inheriting dietary laws that were developed in response to poor sanitation or limited ability to distinguish poisonous from nourishing wild plants, new generations would be spared the potentially deadly process of learning and adapting to these conditions for themselves.

The great diversity of cultures across the world is an outcome of each society's adaptation to its unique ecological niche and historical circumstances.[11] This process, therefore, has *not* generated a hierarchy of norms across the globe. Nevertheless, as the founder of the field of cultural anthropology Franz Boas argued, the one trait most cultures have in common is the misguided and sometimes destructive conviction that their own norms are the proper ones, universally. This tendency may have contributed to the emergence of racism as a cultural trait in many societies. The portrayal of other people and cultures as inferior, or even subhuman, was often invoked by conquerors and colonial powers as moral legitimation for exploitation, slavery and genocide, and contributed to the tremendous disparity between colonial powers and the people they colonised.[12]

Unsurprisingly, many of the norms that persist are ones conducive to the long-term prosperity of those who adhere to them. These traits include a greater tendency towards wider cooperation, which emerged in regions where geographical characteristics necessitated the development of public agricultural infrastructure, such as terraces and irrigation systems; the adoption of more future-oriented behaviours, which evolved in agricultural communities where the benefits of the harvest are enjoyed for a significant while after the investment of planting; and greater trust in strangers, which arose in regions where climatic volatility necessitated risk-sharing. These traits emerged at various times in different places, but they all lasted and spread because they benefited the society as a whole.

But then a dramatic transformation occurred in one region of the world that galvanised these growth-enhancing traits, leading to 'a culture of growth'.

A Culture of Growth

For most of human history, individuals who questioned the norms, beliefs and preferences they inherited from their ancestors would have struggled to devise alternatives that were more efficient. Cultural wisdom and tradition were venerated because they had aided survival, and since few individuals had a deep understanding of *how* they contributed to their well-being, it would have been evolutionarily risky to question their validity. As such, most human societies in history have resisted rapid cultural changes, such as those that accompany major technological, philosophical and scientific advancements. Instead, cultures tend to emphasise the prudence of their ancient ancestors, revering the distant past with a mix of nostalgia and idealism. For instance, a tenet of Orthodox Judaism is the 'decline of generations': the belief that past generations were wiser and closer to God, and that the profound and well-argued interpretations of the Bible by the Jewish sages millennia ago are hard to match.

However, there came a point when technological change reached such a pace that the advantages of conservatism began to wane, and from that point onward the reverence for ancient wisdom gradually declined. *The Battle of the Books*, a satirical work by the Anglo-Irish writer Jonathan Swift published in 1704, contains a particularly colourful description of the spirit of this age, in which new and old books come to life in a library and fight one another. This was a metaphor for a quarrel that had started with the emergence of humanism during the Renaissance, gathered force over the seventeenth century and was shaking the European continent at the time. On one side were the 'Moderns', who argued that time and values had changed and it was feasible to progress beyond the classical thinking of Greece and Rome. On the other side were the 'Ancients', who maintained that the wisdom of the classical thinkers was eternal and universal and that modern philosophers and writers ought to confine themselves primarily to its salvation, restoration and imitation.

This quarrel marked a unique moment in history: the first time that forward-looking philosophers started to gain the upper hand over their rivals. Thus wrote Immanuel Kant in his 1784 essay 'What is Enlightenment?':

> Enlightenment is man's emergence from his self-imposed nonage. Nonage is the inability to use one's own understanding without another's guidance. This nonage is self-imposed if its cause lies not in lack of understanding but in indecision and lack of courage to use one's own mind without another's guidance. Dare to know! (*Sapere aude.*) 'Have the courage to use your own understanding,' is therefore the motto of the Enlightenment.[13]

The Enlightenment called on human beings to trust themselves and have the resolution to reject antiquated cultural traditions. It encouraged the development of a more sceptical, empirical and flexible approach towards the world, in the hope of creating a new culture founded not on a faith in the traditions of the past but on the belief that a better world could be built through scientific, technological and institutional progress. This outlook, suited as it was to rapid adaptation to a changing environment, has been described recently by the economic historian Joel Mokyr as 'a culture of growth'.[14]

As the pace of technological and social change dramatically increased, individuals and societies who were in a position to adopt this ethos thrived. This was a radical paradigm shift from previous periods when the pace of progress was slower and so the ethos of the Enlightenment was often *less* advantageous than reverence for the wisdom of the ancients and adherence to tradition.

Yet, it is in the nature and purpose of culture to preserve and persist, not to reject the past and celebrate change, and this inherent tension meant that for most societies, a rapid transformation was either challenging or infeasible.

Cultural Inertia

According to the *thrifty gene hypothesis*, an evolutionary adaptation permitted our distant ancestors to survive periods of food scarcity through the build-up of fat reserves. Today, however, in contemporary societies where food is abundant, this same adaptation has become a key contributor to the global obesity epidemic and a leading cause of morbidity and mortality.[15] The persistence of this trait in spite of its modern *dis*advantage reflects the fact that biological traits have typically evolved at a slower pace than the human habitat.

Cultural traits are, of course, distinct from biological traits. Unlike genes, they are transmitted horizontally among peers and not only vertically across generations. This social transmission occurs through learning, imitation, education and taboo, meaning that cultural characteristics may evolve far more rapidly than our genome does. Nonetheless, cultural traits have also evolved less rapidly than living conditions, and unlike institutional changes, they rarely undergo rapid transformation even in the face of major shifts in the surroundings.

The impact of cultural inertia on economic development can be seen in the different trajectories of northern and southern Italy. Since 1871, Italy has been a unitary republic, governed by a single set of political, legal and economic institutions. In contrast to Korea, there is no international border separating Italy's northern region from its southern one. Yet, the two parts of Italy differ considerably: in much of the south, income per capita is only two-thirds of the level in the affluent north.

In 1958 the American political scientist Edward Banfield advanced an influential thesis that attributed southern Italy's lower level of prosperity to stronger family ties in the region.[16] He argued that more intense family ties diminished trust outside of one's kinship group, weakened cooperation in pursuit of a common public goal, and thereby reduced the level of economic prosperity in the region. In line with his thesis, recent evidence suggests that kinship ties do indeed differ significantly across Italian regions, as they do more generally across countries. Likewise, tighter nuclear family bonds do tend to adversely affect levels of social trust, political participation, the status of women in the workforce and geographic mobility.[17] And since, as the Nobel Prize–winning American economist Kenneth Arrow noted, business deals often rely on trust while its absence harms trade, lower levels of trust outside of the family setting might have diminished the level of economic development in southern Italy compared to the north.[18]

But how did these differences in trust levels and family ties emerge in the first place? Nearly thirty years after Banfield's study, the American public policy researcher Robert Putnam released an equally influential book that offered an explanation for these puzzling variations. A thousand years ago, southern Italy was governed by Norman kings who imposed a feudal economic order, whereas northern cities that enjoyed relative freedom after casting off the yoke of the Holy Roman Empire developed more democratic institutions.[19] Historically, therefore, citizens in northern Italy had played an active role in political affairs, contributed to communal activities, and had greater levels of trust in their peers, whereas those in the south had grown accustomed to having limited voice in the hierarchical political system. According to Putnam, for that reason northern Italy nurtured a culture conducive to democracy, while swathes of southern Italy retained institutions reminiscent of the old feudal order and were dominated by the Mafia.

Putnam argued that democracy is critically nourished by *social capital* – cultural traits that foster trust and civic engagement in politics. Indeed, modern-day inhabitants of Italian cities that achieved independence relatively early in the Middle Ages exhibit higher levels of democratic and civil commitment, greater trust, and higher levels of economic prosperity.[20] Social capital has also contributed to greater openness to the instruments of contemporary finance and thus to economic prosperity. Residents of northern Italy, which is characterised by higher levels of social capital, reflected in higher voter turnout and blood donation rates, for example, have a greater tendency to hold their wealth in banks, accept credit, invest in stocks and obtain loans. Intriguingly, social capital has a long-term, persistent impact: Italians who migrate to other parts of Italy are still influenced by the cultural heritage of their ancestral regions.

The Italian divide illustrates the powerful influence of cultural attributes associated with social capital. It indicates that they persist over centuries, thereby bringing the effect of institutional changes from the ancient past to bear on social and political developments in the present. The fingerprints of the long-term historical impact of culture are visible in other regions, too. The Habsburg Empire governed a vast expanse of Central and Eastern Europe from the mid-fifteenth to early twentieth centuries and was known for the efficiency of its institutions. Parts of Eastern Europe once ruled by the Habsburgs *still* enjoy greater trust in governing institutions and lower levels of corruption than adjacent regions (even within the same country) that were formerly ruled by the Ottoman or the Holy Roman Empires.[21]

The enduring legacy of the slave trade in Africa provides a particularly sobering example of the persistence of social capital – or the lack of it. Slavery existed in parts of Africa before the fifteenth century, but with the advent of the transatlantic trade in enslaved Africans, abductions and inter-ethnic conflicts greatly increased in West Africa as local chiefs responded to the immense demand from European slave traders. These traumatising practices fomented a precautionary distrust of Europeans and strangers but also of neighbours and relatives. Indeed, based on a survey conducted by the Afrobarometer across sub-Saharan African countries, there appears to be a substantial gap in levels of inter-personal trust between areas affected by the slave trade and those that were spared, more than a century after that trade came to an end.[22]

Yet, the persistence of cultural traits is perhaps most clearly observable among migrants and their descendants. As you would expect, adaptation to a sudden change in environmental conditions and governing institutions can be a lengthy process. Among migrants into Europe and North America, attitudes towards women's role in the workforce and children's independence, for example, converge quite rapidly with those that prevail in the settled local population; however, when it comes to religious beliefs and moral values, even fourth-generation immigrants to these areas tend to maintain part of their traditional native culture.[23] This adaptation gap may reflect the fact that some cultural values do not have a significant impact on economic prosperity and so the incentive for rapid cultural adaptation is limited; in these circumstances, individuals are more likely to preserve their parental values and traditions.

In summary, cultural traits emerge from myriad factors, predominantly as an adaptive response to our habitat. Adjustments in that environment, whether in the form of new institutions, technology, the arrival of new crops, trade or migration, have had a major impact on the emergence and endurance of new cultural traits. When a shift in cultural characteristics has led to economic success, that change seems to have taken place more quickly. But since on the whole cultures evolve more slowly than technology, especially in the past few centuries, it is likely that in some societies cultural traits have been and may still be a barrier to development.

Culture and Prosperity

Culture has contributed to the growth process and economic prosperity in various ways. It has played a major role in how we raise our children, affecting human capital formation and ultimately the onset of the demographic transition. It has shaped the degree of trust we have in each other as well as in political and financial institutions, fostering social capital and cooperation. It has formed our inclination towards future-oriented behaviour, affecting saving, human capital formation and technological adoption, and it has affected the way we have perceived transformative ideas and paradigm shifts.

Indeed, just as political and economic institutions have influenced cultural values – enhancing or diminishing our tendency to trust strangers, invest in education, or cooperate with others – culture has also exerted its own influence on those institutions in return.[24] In North America, for example, various European immigrant groups established institutions that were aligned with the cultural values they held dear in their homelands.[25] The Quakers, whose culture valued personal and religious liberties, supported the formation of institutions that limited the role of government, prioritised individual freedom, separated church and state, and levied relatively low taxes. The Puritans, who valued literacy for the sake of spiritual independence, as well as social cohesion, founded institutions that promoted public education, communal involvement, and strict law and order, all supported by higher taxation. Meanwhile, immigrants from Scotland and Ireland, who favoured a limited role of government in personal affairs, established institutions that defended individual liberties, used ad hoc courts ('frontier justice') to settle disputes, supported the right to bear arms, and maintained low taxes. These cultural values are apparent in different segments of American society – and the types of institution they favour – to this day.

Over the course of human history, individuals across most societies have treated technological, scientific and philosophical changes with suspicion, safeguarding their governing institutions and existing power structures. This is no coincidence; as we have seen, it is a consequence of the critical role that intergenerationally stable values, beliefs and preferences have played in survival and prosperity in uncertain environments. However, a few centuries ago, societies in Western Europe *did* experience a cultural shift, one that accelerated the speed of the great cogs of human history, and helped bring about the modern era of sustained economic growth. They arrived at the conviction that scientific, technological and institutional development held the keys to a better world. In other words, they believed that developments of this sort *were progress*.

Crucially these societies adopted cultural traits such as a greater tendency towards investment in human capital and gender equality, which would become the central drivers of the Demographic Transition and the onset of the sustained growth regime. Furthermore, in time they came to embrace the growth-enhancing values of individualism and secularism: a belief that the individual should have the right to shape their own destiny, without social or even religious constraints. These cultural transformations were also instrumental in establishing political and economic institutions that were conducive to *further* technological progress. And as the pace of technological and social change intensified, these new cultural norms and institutional structures became even more advantageous. Thus, a virtuous cycle arose. Growth-enhancing cultural norms accelerated the pace of technological progress and the transition from stagnation to growth, while the great cogs of history encouraged the evolution of cultural traits that were adapted to the intensifying growth process.

Yet, a major puzzle remains unresolved: why did the cultures and institutions that were particularly conducive to technological development emerge in certain societies and not others? The technological development of both the Song Dynasty and the Abbasid Caliphate were spectacular, but ultimately their pace of development waned, while in the West it has so far persisted thanks to the emergence of growth-enhancing institutions and cultural traits.

At some junctures in human history, the location of cultural and institutional transformations may appear rather arbitrary;

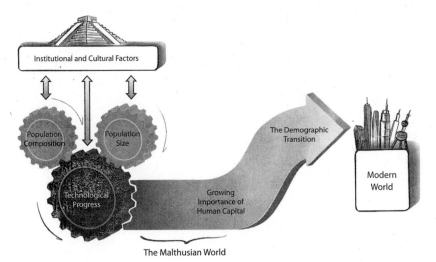

Institutions, Culture and the Cogs of Change

one can imagine a counterfactual history in which North Korea became a capitalist powerhouse while South Korea sank into communist poverty. However, in most circumstances, deep-rooted factors underpinned the emergence of cultural norms and institutional structures. These were geography and human diversity.

The Shadow of Geography

Prior to the Industrial Revolution, livestock was the basis of farming in much of the world. Animals served not only as a vital source of food but provided fibre for textiles and means of transportation. In Eurasia, cattle were integral to the Agricultural Revolution. In South America's Andes mountains, llamas and alpacas were beasts of burden as well as sources of wool and meat. In the Arabian, Sahara and Gobi deserts, camels not only bore nomads across the wilderness, but they also provided fur and milk during these journeys, and on the Tibetan mountains, yaks were used for ploughing and transporting cargo as well as for their hair, hides and milk. Livestock enabled societies to boost their agricultural output and consequently to expand their populations and intensify their technological progress.

One region of Planet Earth remained, however, essentially devoid of livestock: a wide strip of land stretching from the east coast of Africa to the west, hemmed in by the Sahara Desert to the north and the Kalahari Desert to the south. The absence of livestock in this territory appears to be one of the central reasons why, historically, this region has been relatively sparsely populated and why its residents have not enjoyed the same technological advances and political institutions seen in other regions. What caused this absence? The answer lies with an unassuming fly.[1]

The tsetse fly, which thrives in the humidity and warm temperatures of Central Africa, feeds on the blood of humans and animals. It is the main vector of the deadly parasite that causes sleeping sickness (African trypanosomiasis) in humans, as well as similar diseases in goats, sheep, pigs, horses and other livestock. The parasite kills some of the animals it infects and diminishes the milk production and energies of those that survive, making it impractical for societies to rely on them. Recent research based on anthropological evidence compiled in 1967 from nearly four hundred pre-colonial ethnic groups across this region of Africa suggests that the presence of the tsetse fly had a dramatic adverse effect on the adoption of animal husbandry and livestock-based farming techniques, such as ploughing.[2] In fact, it inflicted such considerable damage on domesticated livestock that the regions it plagued have remained less developed than other nearby regions ever since the transition to agriculture.[3] And because the tsetse fly lives only in certain geographical conditions, these are ultimately geographical characteristics that determined the absence of livestock from Central Africa and thus the economic development of the region thereafter.

The tsetse fly is not the only insect to have disrupted economic development in Africa. The Anopheles mosquito, which thrives in limited climatic conditions and transmits malaria to humans, has also inflicted a heavy toll on the continent. Populations in malaria-affected regions of sub-Saharan Africa, South East Asia and South America are subject to high infant mortality rates, and children who survive the disease often suffer lasting cognitive deficits.[4] Moreover, the likelihood of loss compels parents to increase the number of children they bear, reducing their ability to invest in their children's human capital and undermining women's education and labour force participation.[5] In recent decades, medical breakthroughs have diminished the adverse effects of other epidemics on economic growth, but in the absence of an effective malaria vaccine, this disease will continue to hinder the accumulation of human capital and the growth process in regions where it is prevalent.

Other aspects of geography have also affected economic development, independently of disease-bearing insects. Before the invention of the railways and air transport, proximity to the sea and navigable rivers was a key advantage for trade, technological diffusion and access to the bounty of the sea, and so had a major impact on the development process and state formation.[6] While some of the world's forty-four landlocked countries are economically prosperous, such as Austria and Switzerland, most remain impoverished. Similarly, especially rugged terrain or volatile local climates have typically had a direct detrimental effect on development.

Geography also determines the availability of natural resources such as fossil fuels and natural minerals. These have tended to provide a sizeable windfall in the short run but are often considered a 'resource curse' in the longer run, as they divert resources from human-capital intensive sectors and promote non-productive rent-seeking activities. Some have argued that plentiful coal mines provided Britain with a head start in the development of steam engine technologies and thus contributed to the early onset of its Industrial Revolution, but it remains the case that other countries with large quantities of coal, such as China, did not industrialise until much later. Intriguingly, during the Malthusian epoch, the suitability of land for agriculture was a boon, contributing to population density and technological advancement. In the modern era, however, having a comparative advantage in agriculture has tended to stymie the development of other more lucrative sectors and is negatively associated with prosperity.[7]

Yet, beyond these direct effects – on agricultural and labour productivity, on technological adoption, on trade and the availability of natural resources – many of geography's critical influences have been indirect: in the way it has fostered competition, shaped institutions and given rise to some key cultural traits.

Landscape Fragmentation and the Rise of Europe

Geography's ability to foster competition could account for the rise of Europe and its ability to leapfrog over other civilisations such as China – the so-called *European Miracle*.

The most fertile regions of China were unified as far back as 221 BCE. They have used a uniform system of writing and a single dominant language for the past 2,000 years, and have remained under central control for most of that time. In contrast, Europe has long been fragmented between a large number of states, a mosaic of countries and languages.[8] This political fragmentation, it is argued, fostered intense competition between European nations, which in turn appears to have facilitated and stimulated institutional, technological and scientific development.[9] As the Scottish Enlightenment philosopher David Hume wrote in 1742:

> Nothing is more favourable to the rise of politeness and learning, than a number of neighbouring and independent states, connected together by commerce and policy. The emulation, which naturally arises among those neighbouring states, is an obvious source of improvement: But what I would chiefly insist on is the stop which such limited territories give both to power and to authority.[10]

In centralised civilisations such as China and the Ottoman Empire, governments had the power to impede technological or cultural developments that threatened the interests of elites. In Europe, by contrast, inventors and entrepreneurs who encountered resistance could move to neighbouring states, where other monarchs might be hesitant to pass up technological, commercial or organisational revolutions that could ultimately determine their fate.

The funding of Christopher Columbus's voyages to the Americas illuminates the nature of this competition. Columbus initially petitioned King João II of Portugal to finance a journey to the west but was refused because the king believed that strengthening Portugal's route south and east around Africa was the more prudent investment. Columbus then tried his luck fundraising in Genoa and Venice to no avail. He sent his brother to check whether England's King Henry VII might foot the bill for the expedition, while he approached Queen Isabella I of Castile and her husband King Ferdinand II of Aragon. As Spain was already behind in the race to secure direct shipping lanes to the east, Columbus ultimately persuaded the royal couple to fund his voyage west, as a circuitous route to India. Not only did they provide the financing, but they also incentivised the commercial success of the journey by granting Columbus permission to reap some of the prospective profits.

The contrast between the Europeans' voyages of exploration and pillage, fuelled by competition, and the more modest maritime adventures of the Chinese dynasties further illustrates the impact of political competition. In the early fifteenth century, the Chinese imperial fleet sailed to Southern Asia and Africa using ships significantly larger than anything Columbus would use. But after the pro-navy factions were defeated in the internal power struggles that engulfed the Chinese imperial court in the middle of the century, China dismantled its own dockyards and ships, and forbade potentially lucrative long-distance voyages across the ocean.

The delayed introduction of the printing press in the Ottoman Empire provides another striking example of the ruinous effects of a lack of competition on technological change. In 1485, according to some accounts, the Ottoman sultan issued an edict banning the movable-type printing press in Arabic script, an attempt to alleviate the fears of the influential religious establishment that it would lose its monopoly on the dissemination of religious wisdom and, to a lesser extent, those of the scribes who would suffer from the competition.[11] Only in 1727, after centuries of using outdated printing technology, did the Ottomans permit the first Arabic-characters printing house to open. Even that was subjected to strict supervision and only a few hundred books were published in limited print runs by

Ottoman printing houses in the subsequent century.[12] This barrier may be one of the reasons that literacy rates in the Ottoman Empire languished at a mere 2 to 3 per cent of the total population at the beginning of the eighteenth century.[13]

Competition in Europe contributed to a culture of innovation and institutional adaptation, the Protestant Reformation being a prime example. Entrepreneurs pitched their initiatives across borders, and engineers, physicists, architects and skilled craftsmen migrated across the European continent in search of economic opportunities.[14] While the Muslim caliphates under the Abbasids (750–1258), and China under the Song Dynasty (960–1279), experienced periods of innovation, and intellectual advances in mathematics, astronomy and engineering, these trends ultimately did not last. In Europe, from the Renaissance onward, these cultural changes have so far endured, helping to place the European continent and its cultural cousin in North America at the forefront of technological progress for half a millennium, unrivalled until only very recently. In our present globalised era, the competition that fuels innovation is of course no longer intra-European but inter-continental – Europe versus North America versus South East Asia.

But where did this political fragmentation come from? Why was Europe decentralised and characterised by competition among relatively small powers, while extensive regions of Asia were controlled by monolithic mega-empires? One theory, advanced by the German American historian Karl Wittfogel, known as the *hydraulic hypothesis*, suggests that these differences may have resulted from the fact that European agriculture depended largely on rainfall, while the regions around the great rivers of China freed themselves from that dependency by developing a complex network of dams and canals, whose operation required a considerable degree of political centralisation.[15]

Other theories appeal directly to the landscapes of these regions. Fearsome leaders such as Julius Caesar, Charlemagne and Napoleon seized large portions of Europe, but their success in maintaining control of the continent paled in comparison to that of their contemporaries in China, partly because of their respective geographies: while the Yangtze and Yellow rivers provided Chinese emperors with transport links between their fertile heartlands, the great rivers of Europe – the Rhine and Danube – were much smaller and only partially allowed aspiring hegemons to travel rapidly between different sections of the continent. Moreover, the Pyrenees, Alps and Carpathian mountains presented major physical hurdles to ambitious European conquerors, as did the Baltic Sea and the English Channel, providing many European polities, including Britain, France, Spain, Switzerland, Italy and the Scandinavian states, with natural buffers to invasion. China's mountain ranges, in contrast, offered little protection from centralised imperial rule.[16]

Europe's fractal shoreline provides another geographical explanation for its decentralisation. The European coast is characterised by myriad bays and peninsulas, such as those of Greece, Italy, Spain and Scandinavia. The inhabitants of these regions were able to defend their territories from invaders and to keep commercial shipping lanes open even during times of war.[17] This fractal shoreline also encouraged the development of advanced technologies for maritime trade, laying the foundations for a future explosion of commerce and wealth.[18] The East Asian coastline had no such peninsulas, apart from Korea, which did indeed develop an independent culture.

With the benefit of hindsight, it becomes clear that China's *geographical connectivity*, which led to political centralisation, was beneficial in the Middle Ages, providing the region with an economic and technological head start. But it ended up having an adverse effect on the eve of the Industrial Revolution, when competition and cultural fluidity were instrumental in precipitating and taking advantage of this technological paradigm shift.[19]

These conflicting effects of geographical connectedness suggest that societies in various stages of economic development may benefit from different degrees of connectivity. When the potential pace of technological progress is relatively low, high geographical unity, as existed in China, despite its adverse effect on competition and innovation, allows centralised regimes to govern enormous empires efficiently and foster economic growth by establishing the rule of law and investing in public goods. But when technological progress accelerates, lower levels of connectivity, despite their adverse effect on social cohesiveness, facilitate competition and innovations and foster prosperity. In other words, as the great cogs of human history accelerated and technological progress picked up speed, the optimal degree of geographical connectivity for growth diminished, contributing to the reversal of fortunes between the two civilisations.

That said, since China has now made the transition to modern growth, in the absence of a major new technological paradigm shift and given the scale of the Chinese economy, its geographical connectivity, political centralisation and social cohesiveness may yet bring China back to the global forefront of prosperity.

Origins of Extractive Institutions

Geographical conditions have had a critical influence on the nature of the institutions that were formed in different colonies and persist to the present, as seen in Chapter 8.

The tropical climate and the volcanic soil in Central America and the Caribbean, as well as the agroclimatic conditions in other regions of Latin America and the US South, made these areas ideal for the cultivation of crops for which large plantations and a massive labour force were most efficient.[20] These geographical characteristics led during the colonial era to a high concentration of land ownership and the rampantly extractive and exploitative institutions of slavery and coerced labour. The effect was not short-lived. Once these colonies achieved independence, local elites tended to maintain these growth-retarding extractive institutions so as to benefit from the persistence of economic and political disparities.[21]

Moreover, the fertile areas of Central and South America that gave rise to the most technologically advanced pre-Columbian civilisations were the ones where colonial powers formed extractive institutions in order to administrate the exploitation of their immense indigenous populations.[22] The emergence of these institutions and their persistence in the post-colonial era can also be ascribed to geography's indirect influence, since population was denser where the land and climate had allowed for nutritious and reliable agriculture. They contributed to a slower development path, turning some of these prosperous regions into the least affluent in the Americas.

In a similar way, geography affected the viability of asymmetric trade during the colonial era, thus entrenching the extractive institutions that fuelled it and to which it gave rise. Less developed regions in Africa and the Americas endowed with raw materials and fertile soil were targeted in this trade, fuelling the most extractive institution of all, the slave trade. As discussed in Chapter 7, the gains from this asymmetric trade expedited the colonial powers' transition to the modern era of perpetual growth, while slowing this transition across the developing world.[23] In particular, the effects of slavery on the economic development of Africa have lasted well beyond the colonial era.[24] African countries whose populations were most affected by enslavement and forced migration have less developed economies to this day.[25] For this same reason, rugged terrain, which typically hinders trade and economic prosperity, had a long-lasting beneficial effect on economic development in the region because it provided protection from slave hunters.[26]

But deeper than geography's indirect effects on competition and institutions are the effects it has had on the evolution of cultural traits.

Geographical Roots of Cultural Traits

Future-Oriented Mindset

A future-oriented mindset, or long-term orientation, is one of the most important cultural traits for economic prosperity. It affects our propensity to save, acquire education, and advance or adopt novel technologies – and according to work by Dutch social psychologist Geert Hofstede it differs significantly between countries.[27] In light of the contribution of this trait to human and physical capital formation, technological advancement and economic growth, scholars consider it to be a fundamental determinant of the wealth of nations.

The origin of this cultural trait might be traced to the geographical environment in which it evolved. Consider a society during the Malthusian epoch whose members are contemplating two possible strategies for the use of their land. The consumption strategy is to exploit the entire land for gathering, fishing and hunting, so as to satisfy the daily consumption needs of the group. This strategy guarantees a modest, yet relatively stable, year-round food supply. The investment strategy, by contrast, is to forgo some of current consumption by planting crops on part of the territory. This strategy requires some degree of long-term orientation since it involves sacrificing short-term consumption for the sake of consumption in the future.

Over the course of history, the investment strategy would have been more profitable in regions where crops generated a higher yield, and so in these places one would expect a larger portion of the available territory to be devoted to cultivation. Societies located in these fruitful regions have indeed enjoyed higher levels of income and, in the Malthusian era, higher reproductive success. This would have vindicated their strategy, reinforcing their favourable attitude towards long-term orientation, which will have been transmitted intergenerationally and become more prevalent in those societies. Thus, variation in crop yield could be the origin of the different levels of future-oriented behaviour observed in different regions of the world.

It is certainly the case that crop returns are distributed unevenly within and between continents (Fig. 17). In particular, in the pre-1500 period, the dominating crops in Europe (barley) and Asia (rice) yielded almost twice as many potential daily calories (per acre) as the corresponding crop in sub-Saharan

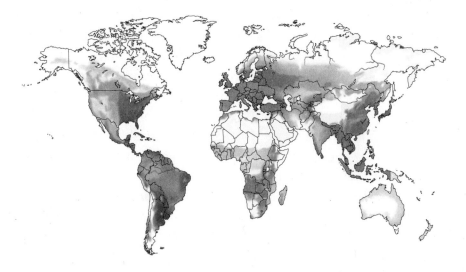

Figure 17. Potential Caloric Return of Native Crops before 1500 CE

This figure depicts the worldwide distribution of daily potential caloric yields, over the period from planting to harvesting, for crops that were native to a location before 1500 CE. Higher values of potential caloric yield are indicated by darker shadings.[28]

Africa (peas), while requiring only two-thirds of the cultivation period from planting to harvesting.

Empirical evidence suggests that, within each continent, countries whose populations originated in areas with higher potential return on crop cultivation do tend to be more long-term-oriented, even taking into account other geographical, cultural and historical factors.[29] Moreover, analysis based on polls conducted by the European Social Survey (2002–14) and the World Values Survey (1981–2014) suggests that people who come from regions with higher potential return to crop cultivation are predisposed to be more future-oriented.[30]

As ever, these findings might be driven by reverse causality. This correlation could reflect the fact that societies with greater long-term orientation are the ones that *choose* to cultivate crops that require longer-term investment. However, the correlation is with *potential* caloric return, which is inferred entirely from agroclimatic characteristics, rather than with the actual crops that were grown in a region; the fact that such characteristics are (largely) unaffected by human choice implies that reverse causality is not at play. At the same time, the fact that the potential crop yield is (unsurprisingly) highly correlated with the *actual* one suggests that crop yield is indeed the mechanism that triggered the evolution of this cultural trait.

Alternatively, it could be that societies who are more long-term-oriented end up *migrating* to regions suited to long-term, high-yield crops. However, evidence suggests that the adoption of high-yield crops such as maize and the potato from the Americas following the Columbian Exchange had a significant effect on the long-term orientation of the already settled Old World populations.[31] This indicates that crop yields have at least partly shaped future-oriented behaviour through a process of cultural adaptation rather than selective migration.

Importantly, studies of second-generation migrants that currently reside in Europe and the United States show that their degree of long-term orientation correlates with potential crop yields in their parental homelands rather than in the countries where they were born and raised. In other words, the effect of crop yield (or its underlying agroclimatic characteristics) on long-term orientation in these instances is not the direct effect of geography, but is rather culturally embodied and intergenerationally transmitted.[32]

Yield is not the only aspect of crops that translates geographic conditions into cultural traits. The type of cultivation they require can also do so. Evidence from Chinese regions suggests that the suitability of land for the cultivation of rice – which requires large-scale and therefore shared irrigation systems – has contributed to more collectivist, interdependent culture, whereas land that is suitable for the cultivation of wheat, which requires a lower degree of cooperation, has contributed to the emergence of more individualistic cultures.[33] Likewise, comparison between countries suggests that land suited to more labour-intensive crops is also associated with the emergence of more collectivist cultures.[34]

Gender Roles

One of the key drivers of the transition from stagnation to growth was the greater number of women entering the paid workforce. Industrialisation was a primary cause, and the resulting decline in the gender wage gap incentivised smaller families and hastened the demographic transition. But the prevailing attitude of different societies towards gender roles was also – and continues to be – an important factor, fostering women's arrival in the workplace and the development process in some places and hindering it in others.

Once again, the possible origin of a cultural trait with crucial implications for economic development can be traced to geographic conditions. In 1970, the Danish economist Ester Boserup hypothesised that variations in present-day attitudes towards the role of women in the workforce were a product of methods of cultivation in the pre-industrial era. Her argument was that, owing to differences in the nature of the soil and the prevailing crops across regions, farmers in some areas tilled their fields with hoes and rakes, whereas in others they used ploughs harnessed to horses or oxen. Since using a plough and controlling the animals that pull it requires massive upper-body strength, men have had a significant physiological advantage over women in ploughing and women in these regions have been limited to housework during the course of human history. It was largely the suitability of land for the use of the plough, Boserup argued, that led to the division of labour along gender lines.

Evidence from agricultural societies across the world supports Boserup's argument. Areas that used the plough have consistently had a greater division of labour within the household: men have been predominantly engaged in agriculture, whereas women have been mainly confined to housework. In regions that made use of hoes and rakes, meanwhile, men and women have tended to share the farm work – from land preparation to sowing and harvesting, as well as other tasks, such as ferrying water, milking cows, or collecting firewood – although most household work has remained predominantly in the domain of women.

As such, it appears that the plough gave rise to a division of labour not just in ploughing but in a whole range of activities. Analysis based on polls conducted by the World Values Survey in the years 2004–11 suggests that a range of present-day gender biases are associated with the adoption of the plough. This may partly explain why in regions that historically used the plough earlier and more intensely, such as Southern Europe, the Middle East and Central Asia, there are fewer women in the workforce, company boardrooms and the political arena.[35]

The impact of the plough on attitudes towards women is also evident among children of immigrants currently residing in Europe and the United States. Second-generation migrants from countries that used the plough hold fewer egalitarian views on women than those who migrated from areas that did not use the plough, and women among them tend to have a lower participation rate in the workforce, despite facing the same economic incentives and opportunities. The fact that these second-generation migrants are affected by their ancestral geographic environments suggests that these attitudes towards gender roles have been transmitted intergenerationally, and that this historical legacy endures even when families migrate to places with different institutions and education systems (although, as noted earlier, views on women entering the workforce tend to converge more rapidly with those of the dominant culture than other cultural traits).[36]

Loss Aversion

The Nobel Prize laureate Daniel Kahneman and cognitive psychologist Amos Tversky uncovered a common tendency among humans to attach greater weight to a loss than to a gain of equal or comparable size.[37] 'Loss aversion', as they term it, is an important determinant of the level of entrepreneurial activity in a population, which is in turn a significant factor in the driving of economic growth in the modern world.

The origin of this cultural trait might also be traced to the influence of the geographic and specifically the climatic environment. For most of history, human productivity – or 'earnings' – barely supported a subsistence level of consumption. For farmers, hunters and shepherds in the Malthusian era, adverse climatic conditions, such as droughts, often led to famine and even extinction. Meanwhile, favourable circumstances that produced plentiful crops brought about only temporary increases in their well-being and reproductive success. From an evolutionary viewpoint, therefore, it would be prudent to guard against catastrophic losses caused by adverse fluctuations in climate even at the expense of an overall potential gain.

Could our tendency to attribute greater importance to losses than to comparable gains be a cultural trait born from an ancient adaptation to the threat of extinction? The fact that loss aversion varies discernibly between populations that originate from regions with different climatic conditions suggests so.

Consider two imaginary continents: the volatile 'Volatilia' and the uniform 'Uniformia'. Both continents experience weather swings that impair crop production, although volatility is significantly more extreme on Volatilia. The continents also differ in the regional variations of their weather patterns. When Uniformia suffers a particularly cold year, every region on the continent is equally frigid. In harsh years on Volatilia, by contrast, most regions experience extreme temperatures, but some still experience favourable climatic conditions. Thus, in Volatilia, inhabitants of certain areas escape weather-inflicted damage even in exceptionally difficult years, while in Uniformia, severe weather conditions affect the entire population and threaten mass extinction.

Both continents are home to multiple societies. At first, some cultures on each of the continents are intensely loss-averse while others have more neutral attitudes towards losses. The loss-averse cultures adopt farming strategies that produce crop yields that are on average smaller but are also less vulnerable to climatic fluctuations. They can guarantee basic living conditions for their families regardless of weather conditions, so their population size remains stable over time. The loss-neutral cultures, in contrast, adopt farming strategies that generate higher average expected yields but are more vulnerable to adverse climate conditions. Under favourable climatic conditions, the loss-neutral cultures reap surplus harvests, allowing their families to grow; however, when the weather deteriorates, they reap smaller harvests than needed to survive, exposing their families to the risk of total annihilation.

Eventually both continents will experience exceptionally harsh weather. In Uniformia, a severe weather event will necessarily affect the entire population and may wipe out the loss-neutral societies that made risky decisions, per their inclination. Since the whole of Uniformia experiences identical weather conditions, all loss-neutral cultures will suffer a similar fate, and none will survive. In Volatilia, however, where regional weather patterns differ across the continent, some loss-neutral societies will be spared the extremely adverse climatic conditions, and at least some of those will experience long periods of plenty, bountiful crop yields and population growth. These few fortunate loss-neutral societies will expand at a faster rate than their loss-averse neighbours, and gradually the composition of Volatilia's population will change as loss-neutral characteristics become more prevalent in the overall population. Regions of Planet Earth that resemble Volatilia, therefore, can be expected to contain a lower proportion of the loss-averse type, while regions that resemble Uniformia can be projected to have a greater proportion.[38]

Experimental evidence, as well as polls conducted by the European Social Survey (2002–14), the World Values Survey (1981–2014) and the General Social Survey (1972–2018), provides estimates of the variation in the degree of loss aversion within and between countries. When combined with climate data from the past 1,500 years, and accounting for possible confounding factors from geography, culture and history, the evidence suggests that volatile climatic conditions have indeed contributed to the emergence of cultures with relatively low levels of loss aversion, while regions where climatic fluctuations are relatively uniform have contributed to more loss-averse cultures.[39]

Again, of course, this association between climatic volatility and loss aversion may reflect the fact that loss-averse individuals and societies are more likely to settle in less volatile environments. However, as seen earlier, the adoption of new crops in the course of the Columbian Exchange with different growing seasons and thus different levels of vulnerability to climatic volatility allows us to test this possibility. The evidence suggests that the volatility associated with these new crops had a significant effect on the degree of loss neutrality among the already settled populations in the Old World. This implies that climate is indeed at work.

And again, empirical analysis based on surveys of European- and American-born children of migrants finds that their degree of loss aversion correlates with the climatic conditions of their *parental* countries of origin, not their own. This underscores that the effect of climate volatility on loss aversion is not direct but is rather culturally embodied and intergenerationally transmitted, via traits moulded over centuries of adaptation.[40]

Co-Evolution of Cultural and Linguistic Traits

The Inuit, who live near the North Pole, and the Sámi, who live in the Arctic north of Norway, Sweden and Finland, are said to have numerous ways to describe different types of snow. Not surprisingly, ethnic groups further south, where snow is rarer, have not developed such a rich vocabulary to describe it.[41] Similarly, societies with greater exposure to sunlight are apparently more likely to speak languages that lump 'green' and 'blue' together, due to their diminished ability to distinguish the two colours, whereas those nearby lakes are more likely to have a distinct word for 'blue'.[42]

Languages are shaped by countless forces. It is wholly plausible that among those influences are the environmental, geographical, cultural and institutional characteristics of the regions where they evolve. Like cultures and institutions, linguistic traits are transmitted across generations. Languages are also unceasingly being altered and modified in order to communicate the ever-changing nature of the human experience. Inevitably, the most efficient and useful linguistic traits that have emerged in the course of the history of each linguistic group are the ones that have spread and prevailed.[43] According to the *linguistic niche hypothesis*, languages have evolved in response to social and environmental pressures.[44] Simply put, having additional words to describe various types of snow must have aided communication among the Inuit and the Sámi, and that is plausibly the reason those words emerged, evolved and survived.

Languages have not just facilitated communication in an increasingly complex world, they have also affected their speakers' mindset – the way they think, perceive and relate to one another and the world as a whole. In this way, languages have the potential to reinforce existing cultural attitudes.[45] The co-evolution of three key pairs of cultural and linguistic traits, each rooted in the geography of the language's home region, each having a significant impact on the process of development, illustrates this pattern.[46]

The first cultural-linguistic pair concerns attitudes towards gender roles. In regions such as Southern Europe, where the suitability of land for the use of the plough led to a starker division of labour according to gender, languages with gender-based grammatical distinctions, as in the Romance languages, have tended to emerge. In places less suited to the use of the plough, by contrast, gender-neutral languages have tended to arise. It is plausible that grammatical gender may have therefore entrenched and preserved gender biases and the sexual division of labour, adversely affecting female human capital formation, labour-force participation and overall economic development.[47]

The second pair concerns attitudes towards social hierarchies. In regions of high ecological diversity – where a mountainous region abuts desert on one side and ocean on the other, for instance – populations in distinct ecologies have typically developed specialised skills and goods, fostering trade between these communities. This in turn has led to the emergence of institutions designed to facilitate that trade, via the provision of infrastructure and the protection and enforcement of property rights.[48] The presence of such institutions and governing authorities contributed to the development of more hierarchical societies as well as to the appearance of *politeness distinctions* – linguistic structures that underline and accentuate those social hierarchies. In German, for example, one traditionally addresses older people and strangers using the polite form 'Sie', while children, friends and relatives are addressed using 'du'. Many other languages feature similar distinctions, such as between 'tú' and 'usted' in Spanish. These linguistic structures may have facilitated smooth interaction between people of different social standing, and language being the powerful force that it is has likely entrenched and perpetuated those social hierarchies, adversely affecting individualism and entrepreneurial spirit, while enhancing social cohesiveness.[49]

The third pair reflects attitudes towards the future. As we have seen, climatic and geographical conditions that were conducive to calorie-rich crops tended to foster a more future-oriented mindset. In such places, the periphrastic future tense – the use of auxiliary words, such as 'shall', 'will' or 'going to' in English, to indicate intentions, aspirations and future planning – tended to emerge. Some linguists argue that the periphrastic future tense reflects greater inclination towards longer-term thinking and determination concerning future action.[50] Indeed, societies that use this construct are characterised by higher long-term orientation; their people tend to save more, have higher levels of education, smoke less, suffer lower prevalence of obesity, and enjoy a higher level of income per capita.[51]

Roots of Comparative Development

We have seen how geography has affected development in various ways: through the prevalence of disease and natural resources, by enhancing competition and technological innovation, but also by fostering institutional, cultural and even linguistic traits that reinforce one another. Soil characteristics conducive for large plantations gave rise to the emergence of extractive intuitions – as well as a reinforcing cultural trait of racism that provided the distorted moral justification for exploitation and slavery. Geographic characteristics conducive for higher return from crop cultivation led to the emergence of the cultural trait of a more future-oriented mindset – as well as, plausibly, institutions that reinforced those traits by protecting property rights and enforcing contracts. Suitability of soil for the use of the plough has had a significant and lasting effect on cultural attitudes towards gender equality and may also have contributed to institutional gender discrimination.

Geographical characteristics are therefore some of the *ultimate* forces that set the evolution of culture, institutions and productivity in motion. They are among the deep-rooted factors affecting the great cogs that drive the journey of humanity, hastening the emergence of growth in some places and delaying it in others. In conjunction with cultural and institutional characteristics, they have contributed to the timing and the location of the technological outburst of the Industrial Revolution and ultimately to the onset of the Demographic Transition. They reveal some of the roots of the disparity in the wealth of nations today and so provide the clues to how we might address it.

But they also present a conundrum. If geography's influence is so deep-rooted, and if Europe was perhaps predestined to play host to the Industrial Revolution, how come Europe, and

Northern and Western Europe in particular, was a comparative economic backwater for most of human history? Put another way, why did the first major civilisations arise not in Europe but in Mesopotamia? Resolving these critical questions will require another step back in our journey to explore how geography affected the far earlier Neolithic Revolution.

The Legacy of the Agricultural Revolution

In 1989, after several years of drought, the water level of the Sea of Galilee in northern Israel dropped drastically, exposing the ruins of a small, 23,000-year-old village. Archaeologists found the vestiges of six relatively well-preserved brush huts, flint, bone and wooden tools and beads, as well as human skeleton. At first glance, this appeared to be a typical hunter-gatherer settlement, similar to others discovered around the world. But as the archaeologists dug deeper, they uncovered evidence of surprisingly advanced technology, such as sickles for harvesting crops and a grindstone for crushing grain, the likes of which had previously been unearthed only from much later periods. The most extraordinary discovery was the remains of the earliest small-scale plant cultivation. The evidence from 'Ohalo II' pointed to a prolonged period during which the village's inhabitants sowed and harvested wheat and barley, some 11,000 years before the accepted date of the dawn of the Neolithic Revolution and the transition to agriculture.[1]

The village appears to have burned down and been abandoned after several generations, although the region as a whole remained at the forefront of technological progress for millennia. The first evidence of wide-scale agriculture comes in fact from archaeological sites nearby, such as Tel Jericho in the Jordan Valley and Tel Aswad near Damascus.

Just as the British enjoyed a technological head start in the aftermath of the Industrial Revolution, civilisations that developed agriculture earlier experienced a similar head start over the rest of the world in the millennia following the Neolithic Revolution. Their relatively advanced levels of agricultural technology allowed them to support larger and denser populations, which catalysed further technological development and the emergence of the earliest human civilisations.

Why did the Neolithic Revolution first occur in this region and not elsewhere? And why were its effects so long-lasting?

Roots and Impacts of the Neolithic Revolution

Jared Diamond has advanced a powerful thesis that links the uneven development across the globe to regional variation in the timing of the onset of the Agricultural Revolution. In particular, he provides an intriguing resolution to the question why historically the most powerful civilisations on Earth arose on the Eurasian land mass, rather than in sub-Saharan Africa, the Americas or Oceania.[2]

Diamond has attributed the earlier emergence of the Neolithic Revolution in Eurasia to its biodiversity as well as the orientation of its continents. Specifically, he has argued that the earliest onset of the Agricultural Revolution nearly 12,000 years ago in the Fertile Crescent was due to its abundance in a wide range of domesticable species of plants and animals. A significant portion of the large-seeded, wild cereals on Planet Earth were first cultivated in the Fertile Crescent. Indeed, the founding crops of human agriculture, including wheat, barley, flax, chickpeas, lentils and peas, as well as fruit trees and various animal species, such as sheep, goats and pigs, were first domesticated in this fertile region. Meanwhile, biodiversity elsewhere in the Eurasia land mass contributed to the independent emergence of agriculture about 10,000 years ago in South East Asia.

There were numerous attempts made to cultivate wild animals and plants in other parts of the world, but their biological resistance to adaptation prevented or delayed the process. Wild grains in the Fertile Crescent were attractive and relatively simple to domesticate, since they spread through self-pollination, were already rich in protein, and were suitable for long-term storage. In contrast, the cultivation of the distant ancestor of maize, a radically different wild plant known as teosinte that grew in Meso-America, required a lengthy selective breeding process in order to bring about the necessary fundamental physical change. As a result, the inhabitants of Meso-America domesticated maize thousands of years after those of the Fertile Crescent domesticated wheat and barley. Similar difficulties hampered the domestication of other crops and trees, and still do for instance in the case of the oak tree; acorns were an important food source for Native Americans who instead developed a method to remove their bitter tannins.

The availability of animals for domestication was even more limited and differed greatly between continents. By the time of the Agricultural Revolution, animals in Africa and Eurasia had been living alongside different hominid species for millions of years, unceasingly adapting to their increasingly sophisticated hunting strategies. In Oceania and the Americas, however, the human species arrived at a much later stage of its development, and the large game there had insufficient time to adapt to their relatively advanced hunting techniques. Most of the big mammals in these regions were driven to extinction shortly after the first hunter-gatherers arrived and did not survive into the era in which societies started domesticating wild animals.

The earlier transition of Eurasia to the agricultural era is also attributed by Diamond to a second geographical factor, touched on in Chapter 1 – the East–West orientation of the Eurasian land mass. Since Eurasia stretches predominantly along this horizontal axis, large areas of it lie along similar lines of latitude and thus enjoy comparable climatic conditions, which during the Agricultural Revolution enabled the dispersal of plants, animals and agricultural practices across a vast territory.

New agricultural technologies and recently domesticated grains could spread extensively and rapidly without encountering major geographical obstacles. By contrast, the land masses of Africa and the Americas stretch predominantly along a North–South axis. Although Meso-America and some regions of Africa experienced a relatively early transition to agriculture, the diffusion of domesticable crops and agricultural practices from region to region was slower within these continents since they encountered major differences in climate and soil, as well as geographic obstacles such as the Sahara Desert and the tropical rainforests of Central America.

The faster diffusion of agricultural technologies as well as domesticated animals and plants contributed to the substantial technological head start of Eurasian civilisations. And once they acquired it, the advantages compounded. Technological innovation in the form of irrigation and cultivation methods generated higher agricultural yields, which led to greater population density. The rise in population density enabled specialisation: a family or community could dedicate its efforts to growing a particular crop, for example, because it could trade its produce with nearby families who grew different ones. This division of labour facilitated the development of more efficient methods of production and the emergence of a non-food-producing class, which spurred knowledge creation and further technological progress. With each advance leading to another, civilisations across the Fertile Crescent went on to construct the world's first cities and architectural wonders, to process bronze and later steel and to develop writing systems. They also devised growth-enhancing institutions that advanced the concept of property rights and the rule of law, supporting the effective use of resources and furthering technological progress yet again.[3]

The path forward was often countered by a significant head wind. The rise in population density and domestication of animals increased humans' exposure to viruses and bacteria. Some of the most catastrophic illnesses in history – smallpox, malaria, measles, cholera, pneumonia and influenza – are variants of diseases that originated predominantly in animals and spread to the human population in farming and shepherding societies. In the short run, these diseases triggered epidemics and high mortality rates. In the long run, though, populations that experienced the Neolithic Revolution earlier evolved stronger immunities to these infectious diseases.[4] This adaptation ultimately facilitated their transition to the harsh disease environment of towns and cities, and when they came into contact or conflict with populations that experienced the transition to agriculture much later, it provided them with a devastating advantage.

In the history of human warfare, the victors have often been those bearing the most lethal pathogens. In the sixteenth century, the Spanish attacked the two mightiest empires in the Americas – the Aztec, in modern-day Mexico, and the Inca, in and around Peru. The Spanish came ashore with smallpox, influenza, typhus and measles – diseases that had not previously reached the Americas – killing countless Aztecs, including possibly their penultimate king, Cuitláhuac. Hernán Cortés's conquistadors, shielded by their immune systems, and equipped with superior technology, were able to bring the most powerful empire in Meso-America to surrender.

The microbes they imported often spread more quickly than the invaders themselves; they annihilated the Inca population before the Spanish even set foot in the Andes. According to most accounts, the Incan emperor Huayna Capac was felled in 1524 by smallpox or measles which had struck his empire, and the resulting war of succession that unfolded between his sons enabled a small Spanish force with superior arms led by Francisco Pizarro to conquer the Inca Empire. In North America, the Pacific islands, Southern Africa and Australia, large swathes of the indigenous populations were similarly wiped out shortly after the first Europeans laid anchor and sneezed, spreading germs that had sailed with them from Europe.

On every continent, early agricultural civilisations typically used their larger populations and greater technological power either to displace hunter-gatherers, pushing some to remote corners while destroying others, or to integrate them.[5] In some encounters, hunter-gatherers adopted agriculture and changed their subsistence strategy more spontaneously.[6] In fact, when Europeans arrived on their shores, some of Central and South America's indigenous populations had already transitioned to agriculture thousands of years previously. But it was nevertheless much too late. The Europeans' head start led to a dramatic technological gulf and the indigenous populations had no match for Europeans' weapons nor the means to prevent the destruction of their civilisations.

The European conquest of the Americas is perhaps the most conspicuous example of the spread of a civilisation that had embraced agriculture relatively early. But of course there are much earlier ones, including the spread of Neolithic farmers into the European continent some 8,000–9,000 years ago. Following the onset of the Neolithic Revolution in the Fertile Crescent, prehistoric farmers built mighty communities around the Nile, Euphrates and Tigris rivers, displacing existing nomadic tribes. As their advantages increased, farmers began migrating from Anatolia (in modern-day Turkey) into Europe, displacing some hunter-gatherer tribes and converting others into agricultural societies. Intriguingly, despite migration into and out of Europe ever since, a significant component of the ancestry of modern-day Europeans originates from these Anatolian farmers.[7]

In East Asia, the Neolithic Revolution began in northern China 10,000 years ago. As farmers flocked south, linguistic evidence suggests that they, too, displaced the vast majority of the hunter-gatherer tribes in their way, as well as less developed agricultural societies that had been later to the Neolithic Revolution. Nearly 6,000 years ago, farmers migrated from southeast China and settled the island of Taiwan. According to most accounts, these migrants and their descendants – the Austronesians – used their sailing technology to make the journey between islands to the Philippines and Indonesia and then to cross much larger seas and oceans to reach Hawaii and Easter Island in the east, New Zealand in the south, and Madagascar in the west. Indigenous populations that survived the Austronesian onslaught were typically located in regions that had already adopted wide-scale agriculture, or where land cultivation was infeasible because of the nature of the terrain. On several islands, the Austronesians caused such damage to the local ecology that farming was no longer viable and they were forced to revert to fishing, hunting and gathering.[8]

In sub-Saharan Africa, farmers from the Bantu ethnic group spread out from their ancestral homeland in the border territory between present-day Nigeria and Cameroon as early as 5,000 years ago. Using their numerical advantage and iron tools, the *Bantu Expansion* displaced and integrated local hunter-gatherer groups such as the Pygmies and Khoisan, who managed to survive mainly in areas that were less suitable for the types of crops on which the Bantu depended.[9]

For almost 10,000 years, nearly everywhere, and at every time period, the same pattern repeated itself. Societies of farmers and shepherds that underwent the Neolithic Revolution earlier spread out and displaced established hunter-gatherer tribes and other cultures that had embraced agriculture later. But while the transition to sedentary agriculture was a necessary condition for the rise of technologically sophisticated civilisations, history suggests that it was not in itself a sufficient one. The islanders on New Guinea, for example, developed agriculture around the same period as the Egyptians in the Nile Delta, but while Ancient Egypt became one of the world's first empires governed by a structured political hierarchy, the increase in agricultural productivity in New Guinea left its highland population fragmented, subject to endemic tribal warfare, and without consolidation of power beyond the tribal level.[10]

What accounts for this perplexing pattern? Once again, geography and, specifically, the type of crops that were native in different regions provide a possible explanation.

The Grains of Civilisation

In the immediate aftermath of the transition to agriculture, most societies maintained the basic tribal frameworks that had prevailed beforehand. In societies of no more than a few hundred members, nearly every individual would have been familiar with, and often related to, most other members of their tribe. The small scale and cohesiveness of these societies facilitated cooperation and mitigated disputes. Typically, each community was headed by a single influential tribal leader, who enforced a basic set of rules and managed public activities that required unity. Leadership was generally merit-based rather than inherited, so tribal aristocracies rarely emerged. As tribes did not raise taxes on any meaningful scale, they were generally not engaged in the construction of major public infrastructure, such as irrigation canals, fortifications or temples, nor could they accommodate members of the tribe who did not contribute in some way to their agricultural or pastoral activities.

As population density rose, however, new frameworks tended to emerge. Commonly, the next stage in the political development of agricultural societies was the chiefdom – a hierarchical society consisting of a number of villages or communities governed by a supreme chief.[11] Chiefdoms first appeared in the Fertile Crescent. As societies in the region grew larger, it became essential for individuals to collaborate on a regular basis outside of their kinship group. To facilitate wide-scale cooperation, these more complex societies were characterised by persistent and often hereditary political leadership, social stratification and centralised decision-making. With significant disparities in wealth, authority and status came class divisions and a ruling class, consisting of a hereditary nobility, whose interest lay in maintaining the social hierarchy and unequal distribution of wealth. These distinctions in status were reinforced and maintained by cultural norms, beliefs and practices, often religious in nature. Crucially, these hierarchical societies tended to raise taxes or tithes to support the elite and pay for the provision of public infrastructure.

Ever since the appearance of chiefdoms, the difference between tyrannical and benevolent regimes has hinged largely on their use of tax revenues. Tyrants generally raid the public purse for personal gain, safeguarding their status and perpetuating inequality, while enriching a narrow elite. More benevolent rulers used tax revenues for the provision of public goods, such as irrigation, infrastructure, fortification and defence against bandits and invaders. But whether benevolent or tyrannical, the inescapable condition for their existence was their capacity to raise taxes. Without it, they would have struggled to build a polity containing more than a few thousand people.

During the agricultural stage of development, taxes were largely paid in crops. The feasibility and efficiency of tax collection depended, therefore, on the types of crops that were prevalent in the region, how easy it was to transport and store them,[12] and the ability to assess harvest sizes.[13] In more developed ancient civilisations, agriculture was based predominantly on grains, rather than on tubers and roots such as cassava, sweet potatoes and yams. This was no coincidence. Grains could be much more easily measured, transported, stored and therefore taxed.[14] And in fact, historical evidence suggests that regions with soil suitable for harvesting grain were more likely to produce complex hierarchical societies. In contrast, regions where harvests consisted of tubers and roots were characterised by simpler social organisation, similar to that of societies of shepherds and nomads.[15] Local rulers in these regions struggled to levy taxes, and even areas that underwent the Neolithic Revolution relatively early did not develop into more hierarchical societies – city states, nations and empires.

Structured polities were able to fund armies, provide public services, impose law and order, invest in human capital and enforce commercial contracts, all of which fostered technological progress and economic growth. Thus, the suitability of soil for either grains or tubers meaningfully influenced the formation of states, knowledge creation and technological progress, which in turn affected the speed at which the great cogs of human history turned.

And yet, if the contribution of biodiversity and crop type to the transition to agriculture and a technological head start was indeed among the ultimate causes of global inequalities today, then why is it that many places where the Neolithic Revolution and state formation occurred early, thanks to these geographic conditions, are relatively poor in the current era (Fig. 18)?

The cradle of the Neolithic Revolution and the early human civilisations – the Fertile Crescent – is not at the forefront of economic prosperity in the present day. Per capita incomes in China and in India are lower than in Korea and Japan, which underwent the Neolithic Revolution thousands of years later. Turkey and South-East Europe are poorer than Britain and the

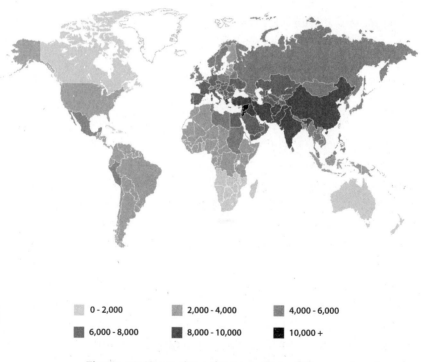

0 - 2,000   2,000 - 4,000   4,000 - 6,000

6,000 - 8,000   8,000 - 10,000   10,000 +

**Figure 18. Years since the Inception of the
Neolithic Revolution across the World**[16]

Nordic states, despite experiencing the Neolithic Revolution thousands of years earlier.

How was their head start lost?

Ceding the Head Start

For thousands of years, the parts of the world that had experienced the Neolithic Revolution earlier and enjoyed the advantage of taxable grains were indeed those with higher population densities and more advanced technologies.[17] However, empirical evidence shows that while the timing of the Neolithic Revolution had a significant effect on productivity in the pre-industrial era, that effect has dissipated in the period since 1500 and has a limited impact on per capita incomes in the modern era.[18] In other words, as the years went by, the advantages of the early onset of agriculture waned to the extent that they cannot in themselves account for disparities in the wealth of nations today. Why have those beneficial effects faded over the last five hundred years? What changed over this period?

The first regions to experience the Neolithic Revolution enjoyed two major benefits – higher agricultural productivity and a technological head start – placing these first-comers at the forefront of the world's economic development. However, by the dawn of the sixteenth century, as innovative activities shifted from the rural to the urban environment, the economic importance of the agricultural sector – farming – began its gradual decline, while the human-capital-intensive and technologically based urban sector began to flourish. An earlier onset of the Neolithic Revolution therefore started to generate conflicting effects. On the one hand, the technological head start continued to stimulate advancement in both the rural and the urban sectors. But on the other, the comparative advantage in agriculture led societies to specialise in this sector specifically, slowing down urbanisation and the rapid technological progress that went with it, and delaying human capital formation and the onset of the demographic transition.

As the importance of the urban sector to the development of new technologies intensified, the adverse effect of comparative advantage in the production of agricultural goods deepened and the technological advantages of an earlier onset of the Neolithic Revolution gradually faded away. Moreover, as urban and maritime nations developed technologies and financial instruments that better enabled global trade and the beginning of the colonial era, the unfavourable effects of specialisation in the agricultural sector was further reinforced, mitigating the head start even more.[19]

Ultimately, then, the technological head start was counterbalanced by the relative *dis*advantage of agricultural specialisation, and thus the timing of the Neolithic Revolution had a limited impact on economic development in the modern era. While this differential timing is critical to our understanding of the historical variation in the process of development across the globe, other forces are critical for understanding the Mystery of Inequality today.

Geography's Decree

Some scholars have attributed the European technological ascent to *critical junctures* in the course of human history: institutional and cultural transformations, such as those that occurred in the aftermath of the Black Death, the collapse of the Roman Empire, or the Age of Enlightenment.[20] They maintain that these transformations are at the root of modern-day wealth inequalities, and that attempts to identify deeper geographical factors are driven by the wisdom of hindsight.

Abrupt institutional and cultural changes that cannot be traced to deeper origins have undoubtedly played a role in the development of societies, as exemplified by the divergence of North and South Korea in recent decades. Indeed, random or accidental developments could have produced a delay centuries long in the invention of the printing press, prompted the Chinese imperial navy to explore the Americas, sparked the Industrial Revolution in Holland rather than Britain, or thwarted the Meiji Restoration in nineteenth-century Japan.

But while sudden institutional and cultural shifts have affected the growth process over the course of decades or centuries, they are very unlikely to have been at the core of the progression of the journey of humanity as a whole, or the ultimate factors that governed the divergence in the wealth of nations. Dramatic or sizeable as they may loom in our imaginations, they are mostly relatively modest, and largely temporary and regional, when viewed from a perspective of thousands, tens of thousands or hundreds of thousands of years.

The mere appearance of abrupt cultural or institutional transformations conducive to development is in fact secondary to their ability to proliferate and stand the test of time, and in this context their interaction with geographical forces has been critical. Whether the emergence and endurance of the cultural and institutional factors that hastened the 'Rise of Europe' were due to its geographical fragmentation – which promoted political competition and cultural fluidity – its high-yield crops that encouraged future-oriented mindset and long-term investment, or any other forces, the main source of modern-day disparities is far from a historical accident. Still, the evolution of institutions and culture, as well as the Neolithic Revolution, have been key determinants of the *pace* of this process as a whole and its differential patterns across countries and regions.

Undeniably, at the dawn of the Neolithic Revolution, one would not have been able to anticipate the outbreak of the Graeco-Persian wars, but given the wide array of domesticable plants and animals in the region, one could feasibly have foreseen that the eastern Mediterranean was conducive to a high population density; that advanced civilisations would eventually emerge in this region; and that conflicts between these societies were likely to occur. The emergence of early civilisations in the

12

Out of Africa

In the first half of the twentieth century, while cannons roared in Europe, the United States experienced one of the largest waves of internal migration in history. During this Great Migration, six million African Americans bade farewell to the poor rural villages of the American South and relocated to rapidly expanding cities, some in the south, but mostly in the north, the Midwest and the west. They were pursuing the growing opportunities for work in industry, particularly in the weapons factories that fed the American war machine during the world wars, while fleeing the oppression of the South. After the horror and degradation of enslavement and discrimination, which African Americans had endured for more than three hundred years, this wave of migration led to a dramatic increase in their interaction with Americans of European descent as urban neighbours.

The integration of these two groups was plagued, and some would say thwarted, by prejudice, racism and inequality, much of which persists to this day. And yet, from this fusion of peoples and traditions emerged one of the most eclectic developments in twentieth-century culture: rock and roll. As the American writer and music critic Robert Palmer argued, 'Rock 'n' roll was an inevitable outgrowth of the social and musical interactions across the racial divide in the South and Southwest.'[1]

Though the precise origins of rock and roll remain a subject of debate, as do the specific features that distinguish it from other styles of popular music, it is largely indisputable that cross-cultural encounters were a, if not the, critical impetus behind it. Americans of African and European ancestries combined a wide range of instruments and diverse traditions of rhythms, musical scales and ensembles to unleash a cultural explosion the likes of which the world had rarely experienced before. Despite the endemic racism of the time, young white Americans gravitated towards the sounds of African American musicians such as Fats Domino and Chuck Berry, as well as white singers, such as Elvis Presley.

The emergence of rock and roll, like that of samba in Brazil, and son cubano in Cuba, is a vivid example of how diversity can ultimately spur cultural, technological and economic progress. As science writer Matt Ridley observed in his book *The Rational Optimist*, technological progress occurs 'when ideas have sex'.[2] Like biological breeding, the mating of ideas also benefits from a broader pool of individuals, since diversity enhances the prospects for fruitful cross-pollination. Had they been surrounded only by others playing similar instruments in analogous rhythms, both European American and African American musicians would no doubt have advanced their own musical traditions, but would surely have been less likely to create an entirely new genre. Yet, the intense interaction between these two musical traditions sparked something entirely novel.

Rock and roll may be one of the loudest and most hip-gyrating examples of the creative effects of societal diversity, but there are countless others. In diverse societies, the fruits of collaboration and cross-fertilisation between individuals from different ethnic, cultural, national and geographical backgrounds – not to mention age groups, educational disciplines and personality types – stretch from new types of cuisine, fashion, literature, art and philosophy to breakthroughs in science, medicine and technology.

But too often diversity has also been the source of immense strife, prompting violent conflict. While some Americans of African and European descent collaborated and generated new musical fusions, in June 1943 an altercation between white and African American youths in a Detroit park deteriorated into riots across the city. For three days, thousands of young Americans clashed across the barricades, until President Roosevelt dispatched 6,000 federal troops to place Detroit under curfew. Thirty-four people were killed, twenty-five of them Black, and more than four hundred were injured in this social unrest. The same year, New York City was engulfed by turmoil after a police officer shot an African American soldier, Robert Bandy, and Los Angeles witnessed street riots in the wake of racially motivated attacks by Americans of European descent on Mexican immigrants.

Ethnic and racial conflict has been a recurring theme in the history of the United States since its genesis. Violent clashes between immigrants from different countries of origin, between new immigrants and settled populations, and between religious groups, such as Protestants and Catholics, have been a constant, blighting feature of the American experiment, as well as many other societies across the globe.

As the experience of the United States exemplifies, societal diversity can engender opposing forces, with conflicting implications for development. On the one hand, it can spur cultural cross-pollination, enhance creativity and inspire openness towards new ideas, all of which foster technological progress. On the other hand, diversity has the potential to diminish trust levels, provoke conflict, and hinder or erode the kind of social coherence necessary for proper investment in public goods, such as education and health care. An increase in societal diversity may therefore exert opposing effects on economic prosperity as well – enhancing creativity while reducing cohesiveness.

Indeed, there is an abundance of evidence of these conflicting economic effects. For instance, immigration is typically credited with having a positive impact on productivity and wages,[3] firms with greater ethnic diversity among their managerial team tend to be more innovative and profitable,[4] and diversity at school enhances a range of students' socio-economic outcomes.[5] Ethnic fractionalisation, on the other hand, has been found to be correlated with political instability, social conflict, the scale of the underground economy, underinvestment in education and infrastructure, and a lack of the kind of cooperation needed to avert environmental damage. Multicultural societies that successfully mitigate or avoid these outcomes are ones that expend significant effort and resources on promoting tolerance and coexistence.[6] In particular, the growth hurdles that have been faced by the most diverse and ethnically fractionalised region on Earth – sub-Saharan Africa – have been partly attributed to the adverse effect of its ethnic diversity on social cohesiveness, as manifested in the intensity of ethnic conflicts, and the insufficient provision of education, health services and infrastructure.[7]

Since diversity can both stimulate and hinder productivity, in the absence of measures that mitigate the adverse effects of high societal diversity on cohesiveness, relatively low or high levels of diversity may diminish economic prosperity, while an intermediate level of diversity may foster it. In particular, as long as the beneficial impact of increased diversity on innovativeness is diminishing (as society becomes increasingly diverse), and provided that the beneficial effects of increased homogeneity on social cohesiveness are diminishing (as society becomes increasingly homogenous), an intermediate level of diversity will be conducive for economic development.

In order to explore the impact that these conflicting forces have had on the journey of humanity, we will need first to uncover the causes of the variation in human diversity across the planet, reverting to its earliest origins: the exodus of *Homo sapiens* from Africa tens of thousands of years ago.

Origins of Human Diversity

Ever since the emergence of *Homo sapiens* in Africa, 300,000 years ago, diversity has facilitated humans' adaptation to the diverse environments across the African continent. For most of this period, successful adaptation generated progressively better hunters and gatherers, which enabled a rise in the food supply and a significant increase in the size of the human population. Eventually, living space and natural resources available per person declined and sometime as early as 60,000 to 90,000 years ago, *Homo sapiens* embarked on a large-scale exodus out of the African continent in search of additional fertile living grounds. Due to the serial nature of this migratory process, it was inherently associated with a reduction in the diversity of populations that settled at greater migratory distances from Africa; the further away from Africa humans moved, the lower the degree of cultural, linguistic, behavioural and physical diversity in their societies.

This phenomenon reflects the *serial founder effect*.[8] Imagine an island that is home to five main breeds of parrot – blue, yellow, black, green and red – equally well adapted for survival on this island. When the island is hit by a typhoon, a few parrots are swept away to a deserted, far-flung isle. This small subgroup is unlikely to contain parrots from all five of the original breeds. These parrots might be mostly red, yellow and blue, for instance, and their chicks – which will soon fill the new island – will inherit their colours. The colony that will develop on the new island will therefore be less diverse than the original population. If a very small flock of parrots then migrates from the second island to a third, that group is likely to be even less diverse than those in each of the previous colonies. Thus, as long as the parrots migrate from each parental island more rapidly than the pace of potential mutations on the island, the further away the parrots migrate (sequentially) from the original island, the less diverse their population will be.

Human migration out of Africa followed a comparable pattern. An initial group left Africa and settled in fertile regions nearby, carrying only a subset of the diversity that existed in their parental African population. Once the initial migratory group had grown to the extent that its new environment could no longer support any additional expansion, a less diverse subgroup departed in search of other virgin territory and settled in habitats further away. During this human dispersal out of Africa and the peopling of the continents, this process repeated itself: as populations grew, new subgroups containing only some of the diversity in their parental colony left again in a quest for greener pastures. Although some groups switched course, as will become apparent, the thrust of these migratory patterns was such that groups who left Africa and reached Western Asia were less diverse than the original human population in Africa, and their descendants who continued migrating east to Central Asia, and ultimately to Oceania and the Americas, or north-west to Europe were progressively even less diverse than those who remained behind.

This expansion of anatomically modern humans from the cradle of humankind in Africa has imparted a deep and indelible mark on the worldwide variation in the degree of diversity – cultural, linguistic, behavioural and physical – across populations (Fig. 19).[9]

This decline in the *overall* level of population diversity with migratory distance from Africa is partly reflected in the reduction in genetic diversity among indigenous ethnic groups at greater migratory distance from Africa. Based on a comparable measure of this type of diversity for 267 distinct populations, most of which can be associated with specific indigenous ethnic groups and their geographical homeland,[10] it is apparent that the most diverse indigenous ethnic groups are those closest to East Africa, whereas the least diverse are the indigenous communities of Central and South America, whose overland

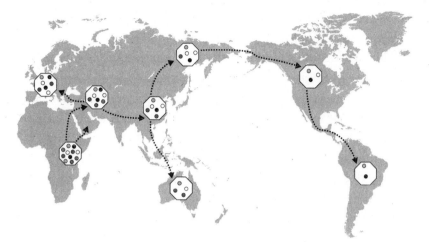

**Figure 19. The Impact of the Migration Out of Africa
on Human Diversity**

The dashed arrows represent approximate migration paths,
and the small circles represent variants of a hypothetical societal trait.
With each outward migration event, the departing population
carries with it only a subset of the diversity of its parental colony.

migratory distance from Africa is the longest (Fig. 20). This
negative correlation between diversity and migratory distance
from East Africa is a pattern that is observed not only across
continents. It is present *within continents* as well.

Broader evidence for the diminishing levels of diversity among
indigenous groups at greater migratory distance from Africa comes
from the fields of physical and cognitive anthropology. Studies of
particular features of body shape – for example, the bone structure pertaining to particular dental attributes, pelvic traits and
the shape of the birth canal – as well as cultural distinctions, such
as the differences between the fundamental units of speech ('pho-
nemes') in different languages, also confirm the existence of a
serial founder effect originating in East Africa; again, the greater

the migratory distance from East Africa, the lower the diversity in these physical and cultural characteristics.[12]

Of course, a proper exploration of the impact of the overall level of population diversity in all its multifaceted forms on the economic prosperity of nations would require a far more comprehensive measure than geneticists and anthropologists provide. In addition, it would need to be independent of the population's degree of economic development so as to be used to assess the *causal* effect of diversity on the wealth of nations. What might such a measure look like?

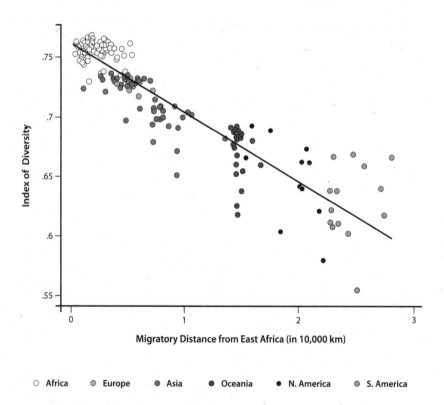

Figure 20. Migratory Distance from East Africa and Diversity among Geographically Indigenous Ethnic Groups[11]

Measuring Diversity

Conventional measures of population diversity tend to capture only the proportional representation of the ethnic or linguistic groups in a population.[13] These measures suffer therefore from two major deficiencies. One is that some ethnic and linguistic groups are more closely related than others. A society that consists of an equal proportion of Danish people and Swedish people may not be as diverse as a society that is composed of equal fractions of Danish and Japanese. The other is that ethnic and linguistic groups are not internally homogenous. A nation composed entirely of Japanese people would not necessarily be as diverse as a nation composed entirely of Danish people. In fact, diversity *within* an ethnic group is typically an order of magnitude larger than the diversity *between* groups.[14]

A comprehensive measure of the overall diversity of a national population ought therefore to capture at least two additional aspects of diversity. First, diversity *within* each ethnic or subnational group, such as within the Irish or the Scottish population in the US. Second, the degree of diversity *between* any pair of ethnic or subnational groups, capturing, for example, the relative cultural proximity of the Irish and Scottish populations of the US in comparision to its Irish and Mexican populations.

In view of the tight negative correlation between migratory distance from East Africa and diversity in observable traits, these *migratory distances* can be used as a proxy for the historical level of diversity in each geographical location on Planet Earth. We can therefore construct an index of *predicted* overall diversity for each national population today, based on the migratory distance from Africa of their ancestral populations, taking into account (i) the relative size of each ancestral subgroup within the country; (ii) the diversity of each of these subgroups as predicted by the distance that *their* ancestors travelled over the course of their migration from East Africa; and (iii) the degree of pairwise diversity between each of these subgroups, as predicted by the migratory distances between the geographical homelands of the ancestral populations of each pair.

This statistical measure of predicted diversity has two major virtues. First, prehistorical migratory distance from East Africa is clearly independent of current levels of economic prosperity and thus the measure permits the estimation of the *causal* effect of diversity on living standards. Second, as highlighted above, mounting evidence from the fields of physical and cognitive anthropology suggests that migratory distance from Africa has had an important effect on diversity in a range of traits that are expressed physically and behaviourally; reassuringly, therefore, the kind of diversity our measure predicts could affect societal outcomes. Moreover, if the index measures diversity inaccurately (in a random fashion) – because of a failure to properly account for internal migration within each of the continents, for example – statistical theory suggests that this would tend to lead us to reject, rather than to confirm, the hypothesised impact of diversity on economic prosperity. In other words, if we are erring, we are erring on the side of caution.

Finally, it is important to clarify that our measure of diversity is a *societal* characteristic. It measures the breadth of variety of human traits within a society regardless of what those traits are or how they may differ between societies. It therefore does not and cannot be used to imply that some traits are more conducive than others for economic success. Rather, it captures the potential impact of the *diversity* in human traits, within a society, on economic prosperity. In fact, accounting for confounding geographical and historical factors, it appears that migratory distance from Africa per se has *no* impact on the average level of traits such as height and weight across the globe. It predominantly affects the extent of the deviation of individuals in the population from this average level.

Armed with this powerful measure of the overall diversity of each population, we can at last explore whether the exodus out of Africa that occurred tens of thousands of years ago, and its impact on human diversity, might have had an astoundingly long-lasting effect on current living standards across the globe.

Diversity and Prosperity

Living conditions in the course of history have indeed been influenced significantly by levels of diversity and therefore by the migration of *Homo sapiens* out of Africa.[15] Migratory distances of the *ancestral* populations of each country, or ethnic group, from the cradle of humankind in East Africa have generated a persistent 'hump-shaped' influence on development outcomes, reflecting a fundamental trade-off between the beneficial and the detrimental effects of diversity on productivity at the societal level.

This 'hump-shaped' effect of diversity on economic productivity, whether captured by past levels of population density or urbanisation rates, or current levels of per capita income or night-light intensity (based on satellite imagery), is both stark and consistent across countries (Fig. 21) and ethnic groups (Fig. 22). Moreover, these hump-shaped patterns remain qualitatively unchanged over the 12,000 years since the Neolithic Revolution. Thus, in the absence of policies that mitigate the cost of diversity in heterogeneous nations and enhance the level of diversity in homogenous ones, *intermediate* levels of diversity have been most conducive to economic prosperity.

In fact, this hump-shaped effect is *unique* to the impact of ancestral migratory distance from Africa. Alternative distances, unrelated to the exodus of *Homo sapiens* from Africa and to human diversity, do not generate similar hump-shaped patterns. In particular, aerial distance from East Africa, as opposed to migratory distance, is uncorrelated with economic prosperity, which is reassuring, since prehistoric humans migrated out of Africa by foot rather than by airplane. Furthermore, migratory distances from 'placebo origins' – other focal points on Planet Earth from which *Homo sapiens* has clearly not emerged – London, Tokyo or Mexico City – do not have any effect on economic prosperity. Nor is this relationship driven by geographic proximity to leading technological frontiers in the distant past, such as the Fertile Crescent.

Separate bodies of evidence confirm the proposed mechanism behind this intriguing result: namely, that societal diversity has indeed exerted conflicting effects on economic well-being. On the one hand, by widening the spectrum of individual values, beliefs and preferences in social interactions, the findings suggest that diversity has diminished interpersonal trust, eroded social cohesion, increased the incidence of civil conflicts, and introduced inefficiencies in the provision of public goods, thus adversely affecting economic performance.[16] On the other hand, greater societal diversity has fostered economic development by widening the spectrum of individual traits, such as skills and approaches to problem-solving, thus fostering specialisation, stimulating the cross-fertilisation of ideas in innovative activities, and facilitating more rapid adaptation to changing technological environments.[19]

Furthermore, the 'sweet spot' level at which diversity is most conducive for economic prosperity has increased in the past centuries. This pattern is consistent with the hypothesis that diversity is increasingly beneficial in the rapidly changing technological environments that have been characteristic of advanced stages of development.[20] This growing importance of diversity in the development process sheds new light on the causes of China's and Europe's reversal of fortunes. In the year 1500 CE, the level of diversity most conducive to development existed among nations such as Japan, Korea and China. Evidently their relative homogeneity fostered social cohesion more than it stifled innovation and was ideal in the pre-1500 era, when technological progress was slower and the benefits of diversity therefore more limited. Indeed, China prospered greatly in the pre-industrial era. But as technological progress accelerated over the subsequent five

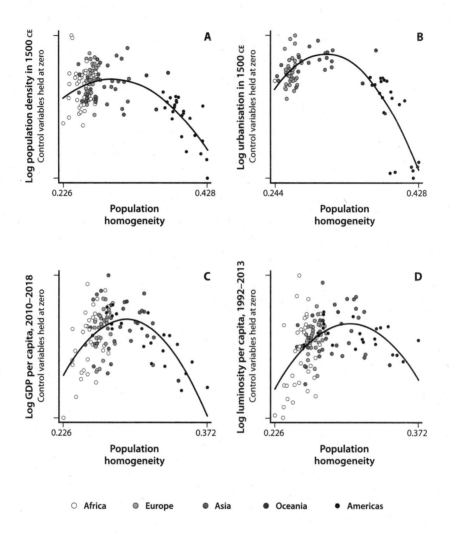

Figure 21. The Impact of Human Diversity on Economic Development across Countries: Past and Present[17]

The top panels depict the impact of predicted population homogeneity on economic development in 1500 CE, as reflected by either population density (Panel A) or urbanisation rate (Panel B). The bottom panels depict the impact of predicted ancestry-adjusted homogeneity on economic development in the contemporary era, as reflected by either income per capita during the 2010–18 time period (Panel C) or luminosity per capita during the 1992–2013 time period (Panel D).

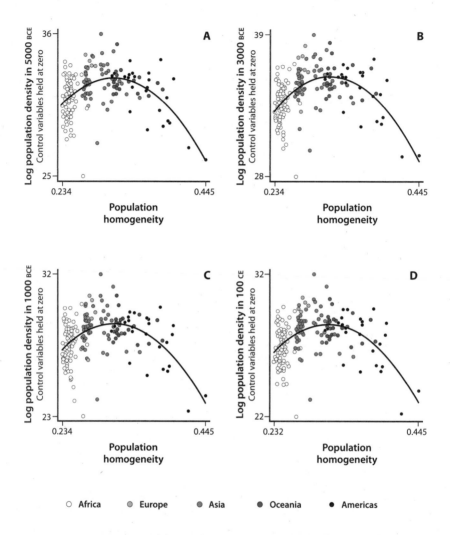

**Figure 22. The Impact of Human Diversity
on Economic Development across Ethnic Groups**[18]

This figure depicts the impact of *observed* population homogeneity
of geographically indigenous ethnic groups, as predicted by migratory
distance from Africa, on long-run historical economic development,
as reflected by population density in 5000 BCE (Panel A), 3000 BCE (Panel B),
1000 BCE (Panel C) and 100 CE (Panel D).

centuries, the relative homogeneity of China appears to have delayed its transition to the modern era of economic growth, transferring economic dominance to the more diverse socie- ties of Europe and subsequently North America. The level of diversity most advantageous for economic development in the modern era is now closer to the current level of diversity in the United States.[21]

Human diversity is of course just one of the factors that have affected economic fortunes, and proximity to the 'sweet spot' of population diversity does not ensure prosperity. Nevertheless, accounting for geographical, institutional and cultural charac- teristics, diversity retains a considerable effect on the economic development of countries, regions and ethnic groups in the pre- sent, just as in the past.[22] The significance of these effects is particularly extraordinary given the aeons that have passed since *Homo sapiens* first stepped out of Africa – and it can be quantified. About a quarter of the unexplained variation in prosperity between nations, as reflected in average income per capita during 2010–18, can be attributed to societal diversity. By comparison, using the same methods, geoclimatic character- istics account for about two-fifths of the variation, the disease environment for about one-seventh, ethnocultural factors account for one-fifth, and political institutions account for about one-tenth.[23]

Yet, despite human diversity being such a powerful determinant of prosperity, the fate of nations is not carved in stone. Quite the contrary: by understanding the nature of that power we can design appropriate policies to foster the benefits of diver- sity while mitigating its adverse effects. If Bolivia – which has one of the least diverse populations – would foster cultural diversity, its per capita income could increase as much as five- fold. In contrast, if Ethiopia – one of the world's most diverse countries – were to adopt policies to enhance social cohesion and tolerance of difference, it could double its current income per capita.[24]

More generally, much could be achieved through education

policies aimed at making best use of the levels of diversity that already exist, with highly diverse societies seeking to promote tolerance and respect for difference, and highly homogeneous ones encouraging openness to new ideas, scepticism and a willingness to challenge the status quo. In fact, any measures that successfully enhanced pluralism, tolerance and respect for difference would further elevate the level of diversity that is conducive to national productivity. And given the likelihood that technological progress will intensify in the coming decades, the advantages of diversity in societies that are able to foster social cohesiveness and mitigate its costs are only set to grow.

The Grip of the Past

The impact of human diversity on economic development may be the most striking example of how modern variations in the wealth of nations are rooted in complex factors originating in the ancient past. In fact, readers in urban pockets of the developed world with large migrant populations might find it surprising that the distribution of human diversity has persisted for quite so long across large segments of the planet. Institutional and cultural differences between countries have diminished in the modern era, as developing countries have tended to adopt the advantageous political and economic institutions of developed nations, and individuals have sought to emulate beneficial cultural norms. Likewise, some adverse effects of geography, such as disease prevalence or lack of access to the sea, have been mitigated by technological progress. And yet, largely due to the inherent attachment of individuals to their homelands and their native cultures, as well as the presence of legal barriers to international migration, human diversity in some regions in the modern era has changed at a much slower pace.

Thus, in the absence of proper inducements – educational, institutional or cultural – highly diverse societies are likely to struggle to achieve the trust and social cohesion levels needed for economic prosperity, while homogeneous ones will fail to benefit sufficiently from the intellectual cross-pollination on which technological and commercial progress rely. The income gap between nations may therefore endure despite the convergence of institutional and cultural traits across them. Such is the grip of the past.

Since the first bands of *Homo sapiens* walked out of Africa millennia ago, their societal characteristics and the distinct natural environments they settled have been dissimilar, and the effects of those dissimilarities have persisted over time. Some were blessed at the outset with human diversity levels and geographical attributes that were conducive for economic development, while others faced less favourable initial conditions that have been detrimental to their growth process ever since. Favourable initial conditions contributed to technological progress and led to the adoption of growth-enhancing institutional and cultural characteristics – inclusive political institutions, social capital and future-oriented mindset – further stimulating technological progress, and the pace of the transition from stagnation to growth. Unfavourable endowments, by contrast, dictated slower trajectories, reinforced by the adoption of institutions and cultural characteristics that hindered growth.

Although throughout our history institutions and cultures have been greatly influenced by geographic characteristics and human diversity, they have also remained susceptible to abrupt historical fluctuations that occasionally sway the fates of nations. As in the case of North and South Korea, living standards may differ sharply even between countries that share both their geography and population diversity. In these infrequent instances, cultures and institutions could be the leading forces behind the observed gaps across some nations.

However, the long arc of human history reveals that geographical characteristics and population diversity, formed partly during the migration of *Homo sapiens* from Africa tens of thousands of years ago, are predominantly the deepest factors behind global inequalities, while cultural and institutional adaptation have often dictated the speed at which development progressed in societies across the globe. In some regions, growth-enhancing geography and diversity led to the rapid adaptation of cultural traits and institutional features to their surroundings, and the acceleration of technological progress. Centuries later, this process triggered an outburst of demand for human capital, a sudden drop in birth rates and thus an earlier transition to the modern era of growth. Elsewhere, this interaction set societies on a slower journey, delaying their escape from the jaws of the Malthusian beast. Thus emerged the extreme global disparities of the modern world.

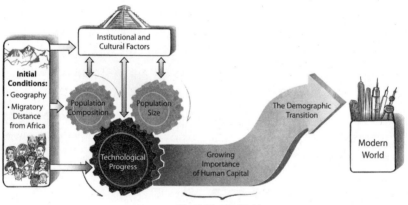

Ultimate Roots of Comparative Development

Coda: Unravelling the Mystery of Inequality

In the years that followed World War II, several facilities resembling military airbases were built on the small island of Tanna in the Pacific Ocean. These sites had planes, runways and watchtowers, as well as headquarters and canteens – but none of them was real. The aircraft were made of hollow tree trunks, the runways were insufficient to facilitate landings and take-offs, the reed watchtowers housed monitoring devices carved out of wood, and only flaming torches provided light. Although no planes had ever landed in these fabricated airfields, some of the islanders imitated air traffic controllers while others conducted military parades, carrying sticks instead of rifles.

The war had made a profound impression on the indigenous peoples of Tanna and other Melanesian islands across the Pacific. They had witnessed the might of the industrial powers of Japan and the United States, whose planes whizzed across the skies above their homes, whose ships fired at each other in the surrounding ocean, and whose troops set up bases on their islands. One phenomenon that made a particularly lasting impression on the islanders was the bountiful cargo that these strangers brought with them: crates of canned food, medicine, clothes, and a variety of equipment that the Tanna islanders had rarely encountered. When the war ended and the troops returned home, the source of this bounty dried up, and these islanders, unfamiliar with the modern manufacturing process and seeking to ascertain the provenance of this wealth, reproduced some of the features and practices that accompanied it, hoping ultimately that the cargo – perceived physical and spiritual wealth, equality, and political autonomy – might return to bless their islands again.[1]

Too often, Western policy recommendations for the development of poorer nations are not that different from these 'renewing rituals' of the Tanna islanders. They involve a superficial imitation of institutions that correlate with economic prosperity in developed countries, without a proper consideration of the underlying conditions that allow them to generate wealth – circumstances that may not exist in the poorer countries. In particular, the conventional wisdom has been that poverty in the developing world is predominantly the result of improper economic and governmental policies and it can therefore be eradicated through the application of a universal set of structural reforms. This presumption has been based on a fundamental misconception, since it ignores the critical impact of deep-rooted factors on the efficacy of such policies. An effective strategy would grapple instead with these primary factors as they are the ones that have invariably hindered the growth process and they often differ radically from one country to another.

One conspicuous example of this misguided approach is the Washington Consensus – a set of policy recommendations for developing countries focused on trade liberalisation, the privatisation of government-owned enterprises, greater protections for property rights, deregulation, broadening the tax base and reducing marginal tax rates. Despite intense efforts by the World Bank and the International Monetary Fund to implement Washington Consensus–inspired reforms in the 1990s, they have had limited success in producing the desired results.[2] Privatisation of industry, trade liberalisation and secure property rights might be growth-conducive policies for countries that have already developed the social and cultural prerequisites for economic growth, but in environments where these foundations are absent, where social cohesion is tenuous and corruption well entrenched, such universal reforms have often been fruitless.

No reforms, however efficient they may be, will transform impoverished nations into advanced economies overnight because much of the gulf between developed and developing economies is rooted in millennia-long processes. Institutional, cultural, geographical and societal characteristics that emerged in the distant past have propelled civilisations through their distinct historical routes and fostered the divergence in the wealth of nations. Incontestably, cultures and institutions conducive to economic prosperity can be gradually adopted and formed. Barriers erected by aspects of geography and diversity can be mitigated. But any such interventions that ignore the particular characteristics that have emerged over the course of each country's journey are unlikely to reduce inequality and may instead provoke frustration, turmoil and prolong stagnation.

At the outer layer of the roots of inequality are the asymmetric effects of globalisation and colonisation. These processes intensified the pace of industrialisation and development in Western European nations, while delaying the escape of less-developed societies from their poverty trap. The persistence of extractive colonial institutions in some regions of the world, designed to perpetuate existing economic and political inequalities, exacerbated this gap in the wealth of nations even further.

Nevertheless, these forces of domination, exploitation and asymmetric trade during the colonial age were predicated on uneven development prior to the colonial era. Pre-existing regional differences in political and economic institutions, as well as in prevailing cultural norms, had a governing influence on the pace of development and the timing of the transition from stagnation to growth.

Institutional reforms at critical junctures in the course of human history as well as the emergence of distinct cultural characteristics have occasionally placed societies on diverging growth trajectories over time. Nevertheless, random events – dramatic and substantial as they loom in our minds – have played a transitory and largely limited role in the progression of humanity as a whole and they are very unlikely to be the dominating factors behind the divergence in economic prosperity between countries and regions in the past few centuries. It is not a coincidence that the first great civilisations arose in fertile lands around major rivers, such as the Euphrates, Tigris, Nile, Yangtze and Ganges. No random historical, institutional and cultural developments could have triggered the formation of major ancient cities far from sources of water, or developed revolutionary agricultural technologies in the heart of the frost-bitten forests of Siberia or in the middle of the Sahara Desert.

At the inner layer, deeper factors rooted in geography and the distant past often underpinned the emergence of growth-enhancing cultural characteristics and political institutions in some regions of the world and growth-hindering ones in others. In places, such as Central America, the suitability of land for large plantations fostered the emergence and persistence of extractive political institutions characterised by exploitation, slavery and inequity. In others, such as sub-Saharan Africa, the disease environment contributed to lower agricultural and labour productivity and delayed the adoption of more advanced agricultural technologies, diminishing population density, political centralisation and long-run prosperity. In more fortunate regions, by contrast, favourable soil and climatic characteristics triggered the evolution of cultural traits conducive for development – greater inclination towards cooperation, trust, gender equality and a stronger future-oriented mindset.

An appreciation of the long-lasting impact of geographical characteristics led us 12,000 years back in time to the dawn of the Agricultural Revolution. During this period, biodiversity, the availability of domesticable species of plants and animals, and the orientation of the continents fostered an earlier transition from hunter-gatherer tribes to sedentary agricultural communities in some places and a later transition in others. Indeed, regions in Eurasia where the Neolithic Revolution took place earlier enjoyed a technological head start that persisted during the entire pre-industrial era. Importantly, however, the beneficial forces associated with this earlier transition to agriculture dissipated in the industrial era and ultimately have played a limited role in forging the extensive inequality across the globe today; societies who made the transition to agriculture earliest were not destined to become the most prosperous nations in the present, as their agricultural specialisation eventually hindered the process of urbanisation and mitigated their technological head start.

Ultimately, the quest for some of the deepest roots of modern-day prosperity led us further back to where it all began: the initial steps of the human species out of Africa, tens of thousands of years ago. The degree of diversity within each society, as determined partly by the course of that exodus, has had a long-lasting effect on economic prosperity over the entire course of human history – with those who enjoyed the sweet spot of innovation-inducing cross-fertilisation and social cohesiveness benefiting most.

In recent decades, the rapid diffusion of development among poorer countries has promoted the adoption of growth-enhancing cultural and institutional characteristics in all regions of the world and contributed to the growth of developing nations. Modern transportation, medical and information technologies have diminished the adverse effects of geography on economic development, and the intensification of technological progress has further enhanced the potential benefits of diversity for prosperity. If these trends were combined with policies that enabled diverse societies to achieve greater social cohesion and homogeneous ones to benefit from intellectual cross-pollination, then we could begin to address contemporary wealth inequalities at their very roots.

Today on Tanna Island, one can find a real airport; primary schools are available for most children; islanders own mobile phones; and streams of tourists, attracted by the Mount Yasur volcano and traditional culture, provide vital revenues to the local economy. While income per capita in the nation of Vanuatu to

Afterword

I am unaware of the fate of the squirrel that scuttled outside my window at Brown University when I began writing this book. I would like to believe that it survived the harsh New England winter and thrived in the manner of its species. I am confident, however, that if it reappeared for another peek, the sight of a peculiar individual devoting his energies to the final draft of this manuscript instead of foraging food and chasing prey would still be incomprehensible. It would surely struggle to envision a life not governed solely by the pursuit of survival and reproduction. And yet, for our species, such an existence is fading into memory.

This book has explored the unique forces that permitted humanity to journey from stagnation to growth, and then to inequality, a path that squirrels – or any other species residing on Planet Earth – may never take. Recognising that attempts to describe the entire course of the history of the human species are likely to be overwhelmed by fascinating details that may obscure the holistic view, I have strived to focus on the fundamental forces that have swept humanity along its voyage.

Ever since the development of the first stone-cutting tool, technological progress fostered the growth and the adaptation of the human population to its changing environment. In turn, these changes generated further technological progress across time and space – in every age, in every region, and in each and every civilisation. Nevertheless, one central aspect of all societies remained largely unaffected: living standards. Technological advancements failed to generate long-term betterment in the material well-being of the population. Like all other species, humanity was caught in a poverty trap. Technological progress unfailingly generated a larger population, mandating that the bounty of progress had to be divided among growing numbers of souls. Innovations engendered economic prosperity for a few generations, but ultimately, population growth brought living conditions back towards subsistence levels.

For millennia, the wheels of change – the reinforcing interplay between technological progress and the size and composition of the human population – turned at an ever-increasing pace until, eventually, a tipping point was reached, unleashing the rapid technological progress of the Industrial Revolution. The increasing demand for educated workers who could navigate this rapidly changing technological environment, combined with a decline in the gender wage gap, provided parents with a greater incentive to invest in the education of their existing children instead of giving birth to additional ones, triggering a fertility decline. The Demographic Transition shattered the Malthusian poverty trap, living standards improved without being swiftly counterbalanced by a population boom, and thus began a long-term rise in human prosperity.

Alongside this spectacular technological progress and the immense improvement in living standards, the human species experienced major catastrophes: the devastating effects of the Spanish flu pandemic, the Great Depression, political extremism, and the atrocities of World War I and II. While these calamities rained destruction on countless individuals, the living standards of humanity as a whole, seen through a wider lens, swiftly recovered from each of these tragedies. In the short run, the growth process has been highly vulnerable to massive swings, as the world has witnessed recently during the Covid-19 pandemic. But history shows that, shattering and dreadful as they are, these events have had limited long-term impact on the grand arc of human development. The relentless march of humanity has so far been unstoppable.

Nonetheless, while billions of people have been liberated from the vulnerability to hunger, disease and climatic volatility, a new peril looms over the horizon: the alarming impact of human-caused environmental degradation and climate change, originating during the Industrial Revolution. Will global warming be viewed in a few decades as the historical event that derailed humanity from its relentless march? Intriguingly, the parallel impact that industrialisation had on innovation, human capital formation and fertility decline may well hold the key to the mitigation of its adverse effects on climate change and the potential trade-off between economic growth and environmental preservation. The rapid decline in population growth, the increase in human capital formation and the capacity for innovativeness that have been sweeping the globe in the past century provide grounds for optimism regarding our species' ability to avert the most devastating consequences of global warming.

Since the dawn of the nineteenth century, living conditions have taken an unparalleled leap forward by every conceivable measure, as reflected in the rapid expansion of access to education, health infrastructure and technologies, forces that have radically transformed the lives of billions of people across the world. Nevertheless, our escape from the epoch of stagnation has occurred at different times across the globe. Western European countries and regions of North America experienced the remarkable leap in living conditions in the immediate aftermath of the Industrial Revolution, whereas in most regions of Asia, Africa and Latin America the transition did not take place until the latter half of the twentieth century – spurring vast disparities in wealth and well-being. But there are grounds for optimism here, as well. Admittedly, regional differences in institutions, culture, geography and diversity will not disappear entirely; we know how lasting these factors can be. Over time, though, cultural and technological diffusion as well as diversity-related policies could bridge some of these gaps and mitigate the impact of these deep-rooted factors. It should not be long before the Malthusian forces fade from our collective memory and humanity as a whole embarks on a new phase in its journey.

Highlighting the incredible progress of the past two centuries should not diminish the significance of the misery and injustice that continue to affect a large portion of humanity, nor the urgency of our responsibility to address them. Rather, my hope is that an understanding of the origins of this inequality will empower us with better approaches to the alleviation of poverty and contribute to the prosperity of humanity as a whole. Recognising our roots will permit us to participate in the design of our futures. The uplifting realisation that the great cogs of human history have continued whirring apace in recent decades, contributing to the global diffusion of economic prosperity, should sharpen our appetite to seize what is within our grasp.

For as long as humans have been self-reflective, thinkers have wondered about the rise and fall of nations and the origins of wealth and inequality. Now, thanks to long-term perspectives born from decades of investigation, as well as an empirically based unifying framework of analysis, we have the tools to understand the journey of humanity in its entirety, and to resolve its central mysteries. My hope is that our understanding of the origins of wealth and global inequality will guide us in the design of policies that facilitate prosperity over the world and allow readers to envision – and strive for – the even more bountiful future that lies ahead, as the human species continues its journey into uncharted territories.

Acknowledgements

This book is devoted to an intellectual endeavour conceived and developed by the author over the course of three decades.

The research underneath the various layers of the book has benefited from the author's research collaborations with Quamrul Ashraf, Gregory Casey, Raphaël Franck, Marc Klemp, Stelios Michalopoulos, Omer Moav, Andrew Mountford, Ömer Özak, Harl Ryder, Assaf Sarid, Viacheslav Savitskiy, Daniel Tsiddon, Dietrich Vollrath, David Weil and Joseph Zeira, as well as from fruitful discussions over the years with researchers across the globe, in particular Daron Acemoglu, Alberto Alesina, Sascha Becker, Roland Bénabou, Alberto Bisin, Matteo Cervellati, Carl-Johan Dalgaard, David de la Croix, Klaus Desmet, Matthias Doepke, Steven Durlauf, James Fenske, Moshe Hazan, Andreas Irmen, Ross Levine, Joel Mokyr, Nathan Nunn, Louis Putterman, Jim Robinson, Uwe Sunde, Enrico Spolaore, Holger Strulik, Joachim Voth, Romain Wacziarg and Fabrizio Zilibotti.

Segments of the book and its underlying theoretical framework were the subject of the author's Doctor Honoris Causa Lecture (Université catholique de Louvain, 2021), Doctor Honoris Causa Lecture (Poznań University for Economics and Business, 2019), the Copernican Lecture (Torun, 2019), the Ricardo Lecture (Denmark, 2019), the Bogen Lecture (Hebrew University, 2019), the Zeuthen Lectures (Copenhagen, 2016), the Berglas Lecture (Tel Aviv University, 2015), the Maddison

Lecture (Groningen, 2012), the Kuznets Lecture (Yale University, 2009), the Klein Lecture (Osaka, 2008), the Opening Lectures of the German Economic Association (Augsburg, 2016) and the Israeli Economic Association (Jerusalem, 2003), as well as keynote lectures in the Meeting of the European Public Choice Society (Jerusalem, 2019), NBER, Macroeconomics Across Time and Space (Philadelphia, 2018), the Association for the Study of Religion, Economics & Culture (Copenhagen, 2016), the Long Shadow of History (Munich, 2014), 9th IZA Annual Migration Meeting (Bonn, 2012), BETA-Workshop in Historical Economics (Strasbourg 2012), Fourth International Conference on Migration and Development (Harvard University, 2011), Korean Economic Association (Seoul, 2008), Early Economic Developments (Copenhagen, 2006), DEGIT Annual Meeting (Rome, 2000; Vienna, 2001; Mexico City, 2005), Annual T2M Conferences (Paris, 2000).

In addition, the theoretical foundations of the book were the focus of the author's lecture series at Kiel (2015), St Gallen (2012–15), the Summer Schools of Economic Growth (Warwick, 2011–13; Naples, 2012; Jerusalem, 2008), Bar-Ilan University (2012), Ben-Gurion University (2012), Luxembourg (2012), Porto (2012), Science Po (2012), Danish Doctoral Programme (Copenhagen, 2008), the International Monetary Fund Training Programme (2006 and 2008), the Centre for Economic Policy Research Summer Workshop (Florence, 2007), Zurich (2003) and the Dutch Joint Doctoral Programme (2000).

I have benefited from my collaboration with Ori Katz in the writing of an earlier version of this book that was released in Hebrew in March 2020, and was wonderfully translated into English by Eylon Levy. In the past two years, the structure, the scope, the style and the content of this earlier version has been entirely transformed and augmented. This process has greatly benefited from the careful reading and insightful comments by Guillaume Blanc, Gregory Casey, Amaury Dehoux, Raphaël Franck, Martin Fiszbein, Mariko Klasing, Marc Klemp, Julia

Lynn, María Medellín Esguerra, Petros Milionis, Diego Ramos-Toro, Balazs Zelity, Ally Zhu and, especially, Erica Durante.

I am grateful for my literary agent, Jennifer Joel, whose invaluable comments and extensive editing greatly contributed to the quality of the book and its broader appeal. I am indebted to Will Hammond (Penguin Random House, Vintage) and John Parsley (Penguin Random House, Dutton), who have further transformed the scope of the book and its wider appeal. In particular, the thorough and instrumental editing of Will Hammond, and his extensive and gracious debates over many of the subjects and the underlying research methodologies, have had a tremendous impact on the quality of the manuscript, and the presentation of the more technical aspects of the theory and the empirical methodologies.

References

Abram, Nerilie J., Helen V. McGregor, Jessica E. Tierney, Michael N. Evans, Nicholas P. McKay and Darrell S. Kaufman, 'Early onset of industrial-era warming across the oceans and continents', *Nature* 536, no. 7617 (2016): 411–18.

Abramovitz, Moses, and Paul A. David, *American macroeconomic growth in the era of knowledge-based progress: The long-run perspective*, Vol. 93, 1999.

Acemoglu, Daron, Davide Cantoni, Simon Johnson and James A. Robinson, 'The Consequences of Radical Reform: The French Revolution', *American Economic Review* 101, no. 7 (2011): 3286–307.

Acemoglu, Daron, Simon Johnson and James A. Robinson, 'Reversal of Fortune: Geography and institutions in the making of the modern world income distribution', *The Quarterly Journal of Economics* 117, no. 4 (2002): 1231–94.

Acemoglu, Daron, Simon Johnson and James A. Robinson, 'The Colonial Origins of Comparative Development: An empirical investigation', *American Economic Review* 91, no. 5 (2001): 1369–1401.

Acemoglu, Daron, and James A. Robinson, 'Why did the West extend the franchise? Democracy, inequality, and growth in historical perspective', *The Quarterly Journal of Economics* 115, no. 4 (2000): 1167–99.

Acemoglu, Daron, and James A. Robinson, *Why Nations Fail: The origins of power, prosperity, and poverty*, Crown Books, 2012.

Acsádi, György, János Nemeskéri and Kornél Balás, *History of human life span and mortality*, Budapest: Akadémiai Kiadó, 1970.

Aghion, Philippe, and Peter Howitt, 'A Model of Growth Through Creative Destruction', *Econometrica* 60, no. 2 (1992): 323–51.

Aidt, Toke S., and Raphaël Franck, 'Democratization under the Threat of Revolution: Evidence from the Great Reform Act of 1832', *Econometrica* 83, no. 2 (2015): 505–47.

Aiello, Leslie C., and Peter Wheeler, 'The expensive-tissue hypothesis: the brain and the digestive system in human and primate evolution', *Current Anthropology* 36, no. 2 (1995): 199–221.

Alesina, Alberto, Arnaud Devleeschauwer, William Easterly, Sergio Kurlat and Romain Wacziarg, 'Fractionalization', *Journal of Economic Growth* 8, no. 2 (2003): 155–94.

Alesina, Alberto, and Paola Giuliano, 'Culture and Institutions', *Journal of Economic Literature* 53, no. 4 (2015): 898–944.

Alesina, Alberto, and Paola Giuliano, 'The Power of the Family', *Journal of Economic Growth* 15, no. 2 (2010): 93–125.

Alesina, Alberto, Paola Giuliano and Nathan Nunn, 'On the Origins of Gender Roles: Women and the plough', *The Quarterly Journal of Economics* 128, no. 2 (2013): 469–530.

Alesina, Alberto, and Nicola Fuchs-Schündeln, 'Goodbye Lenin (or not?): The Effect of Communism on People's Preferences', *American Economic Review* 97, no. 4 (2007): 1507–28.

Allen, Robert C., 'Progress and Poverty in Early Modern Europe', *The Economic History Review* 56, no. 3 (2003): 403–43.

Allen, Robert C., 'Agriculture and the Origins of the State in Ancient Egypt', *Explorations in Economic History* 34, no. 2 (1997): 135–54.

Alsan, Marcella, 'The effect of the tsetse fly on African development', *American Economic Review* 105, no. 1 (2015): 382–410.

Andersen, Thomas Barnebeck, Jeanet Bentzen, Carl-Johan Dalgaard and Paul Sharp, 'Pre-reformation roots of the Protestant Ethic', *The Economic Journal* 127, no. 604 (2017): 1756–93.

Andersen, Thomas Barnebeck, Carl-Johan Dalgaard and Pablo Selaya, 'Climate and the Emergence of Global Income Differences', *The Review of Economic Studies* 83, no. 4 (2016): 1334–63.

Andrews, Kehinde, *The New Age of Empire: How Racism and Colonialism Still Rule the World*, Penguin UK, 2021.

Ang, James B., 'Agricultural legacy and individualistic culture', *Journal of Economic Growth* 24, no. 4 (2019): 397–425.

Angel, J. Lawrence, 'The Bases of Paleodemography', *American Journal of Physical Anthropology* 30, no. 3 (1969): 427–37.

Angrist, Joshua D., and Jörn-Steffen Pischke, *Mostly Harmless Econometrics*, Princeton University Press, 2008.

Aquinas, Thomas, *Summa Theologica*, Authentic Media Inc., 2012.

Arbatlı, Cemal Eren, Quamrul H. Ashraf, Oded Galor and Marc Klemp, 'Diversity and Conflict', *Econometrica* 88, no. 2 (2020): 727–97.

Arias, Elizabeth, 'United States Life Tables, 2012' (2016).

Arrow, Kenneth J., 'Gifts and Exchanges', *Philosophy & Public Affairs* (1972): 343–62.

Ashraf, Quamrul, and Oded Galor, 'Genetic diversity and the origins of cultural fragmentation', *American Economic Review* 103, no. 3 (2013): 528–33.

Ashraf, Quamrul, and Oded Galor, 'The "Out of Africa" hypothesis, human genetic diversity, and comparative economic development', *American Economic Review* 103, no. 1 (2013): 1–46.

Ashraf, Quamrul, and Oded Galor, 'Dynamics and stagnation in the Malthusian Epoch', *American Economic Review* 101, no. 5 (2011): 2003–41.

Ashraf, Quamrul, Oded Galor and Marc Klemp, 'Population Diversity and Differential Paths of Long-Run Development since the Neolithic Revolution' (2020).

Ashraf, Quamrul, Oded Galor and Marc Klemp, 'Ancient Origins of the Wealth of Nations', in *Handbook of Historical Economics*, Elsevier, 2021.

Ashraf, Quamrul, Oded Galor and Ömer Özak, 'Isolation and development', *Journal of the European Economic Association* 8, no. 2–3 (2010): 401–12.

Ashraf, Quamrul, and Stelios Michalopoulos, 'Climatic fluctuations and the diffusion of agriculture', *Review of Economics and Statistics* 97, no. 3 (2015): 589–609.

Atack, Jeremy, Fred Bateman, Michael Haines and Robert A. Margo, 'Did railroads induce or follow economic growth? Urbanization and population growth in the

American Midwest, 1850–1860', *Social Science History* 34, no. 2 (2010): 171–97.

Atkinson, Quentin D., 'Phonemic diversity supports a serial founder effect model of language expansion from Africa', *Science* 332, no. 6027 (2011): 346–9.

Bae, Christopher J., Katerina Douka and Michael D. Petraglia, 'On the origin of modern humans: Asian perspectives', *Science* 358, no. 6368 (2017).

Bairoch, Paul, 'International industrialization levels from 1750 to 1980', *Journal of European Economic History* 11, no. 2 (1982): 269–333.

Bairoch, Paul, 'Geographical structure and trade balance of European foreign trade from 1800 to 1970', *Journal of European Economic History* 3, no. 3 (1974): 557–608.

Banfield, Edward C., *The Moral Basis of a Backward Society*, Free Press, 1967.

Bar-Yosef, Ofer, 'The Natufian culture in the Levant, threshold to the origins of agriculture', *Evolutionary Anthropology: Issues, News, and Reviews* 6, no. 5 (1998): 159–77.

Bar-Yosef, Ofer, and François R. Valla, *Natufian foragers in the Levant: Terminal Pleistocene social changes in Western Asia*, Vol. 19, Berghahn Books, 2013.

Barlow, Nora (ed.), *The Autobiography of Charles Darwin 1809–1882*, Collins, 1958.

Barro, Robert J., 'Determinants of Democracy', *Journal of Political Economy* 107, no. S6 (1999): S158–83.

Barro, Robert J., 'Democracy and growth', *Journal of Economic Growth* 1, no. 1 (1996): 1–27.

Basu, Aparna, *The Growth of Education and Political Development in India, 1898–1920*, Oxford University Press, 1974.

Basu, Kaushik, 'Child labor: cause, consequence, and cure, with remarks on international labor standards', *Journal of Economic Literature* 37(3) (1999): 1083–119.

Baudin, Thomas, David de la Croix and Paula E. Gobbi, 'Fertility and Childlessness in the United States' *American Economic Review* 105, no. 6 (2015): 1852–82.

Bazzi, Samuel, Martin Fiszbein and Mesay Gebresilasse, 'Frontier culture: The roots and persistence of "rugged individualism" in the United States', *Econometrica* 88, no. 6 (2020): 2329–68.

Becerra-Valdivia, Lorena, and Thomas Higham, 'The timing and effect of the earliest human arrivals in North America', *Nature* 584, no. 7819 (2020): 93–97.

Becker, Gary S., and Nigel Tomes, 'Child Endowments and the Quantity and Quality of Children', *Journal of Political Economy* 84, no. 4, Part 2 (1976): S143–62.

Becker, Sascha O., Thiemo Fetzer and Dennis Novy, 'Who Voted for Brexit? A Comprehensive District-Level Analysis', *Economic Policy* 32, no. 92 (2017): 601–50.

Becker, Sascha O., Katrin Boeckh, Christa Hainz and Ludger Woessmann, 'The Empire is Dead, Long Live the Empire! Long-Run Persistence of Trust and Corruption in the Bureaucracy', *The Economic Journal* 126, no. 590 (2016): 40–74.

Becker, Sascha O., Francesco Cinnirella and Ludger Woessmann, 'The Trade-Off Between Fertility and Education: Evidence from Before the Demographic Transition', *Journal of Economic Growth* 15, no. 3 (2010): 177–204.

Becker, Sascha O., and Ludger Woessmann, 'Was Weber Wrong? A Human Capital Theory of Protestant Economic History', *The Quarterly Journal of Economics* 124, no. 2 (2009): 531–96.

Bellwood, Peter, James J. Fox and Darrell Tyron, *The Austronesians: historical and comparative perspectives*, ANU Press, 2006.

Benhabib, Jess, and Mark M. Spiegel, 'Human Capital and Technology Diffusion', *Handbook of Economic Growth* 1 (2005): 935–66.

Bennett, Matthew R. et al., 'Evidence of humans in North America during the Last Glacial Maximum', *Science* 373, no. 6562 (2021): 1528–1531.

Bentzen, Jeanet Sinding, Nicolai Kaarsen and Asger Moll Wingender, 'Irrigation and autocracy', *Journal of the European Economic Association* 15, no. 1 (2017): 1–53.

Betti, Lia, and Andrea Manica, 'Human variation in the shape of the birth canal is significant and geographically structured', *Proceedings of the Royal Society* B 285, no. 1889 (2018): 20181807.

Betti, Lia, Noreen von Cramon-Taubadel, Andrea Manica and Stephen J. Lycett, 'Global geometric morphometric analyses of the human pelvis reveal substantial neutral population history effects, even across sexes', *PloS One* 8, no. 2 (2013): e55909.

Betti, Lia, François Balloux, William Amos, Tsunehiko Hanihara and Andrea Manica, 'Distance from Africa, not climate, explains within-population phenotypic diversity in humans', *Proceedings of the Royal Society B: Biological Sciences* 276, no. 1658 (2009): 809–14.

Bignon, Vincent, and Cecilia García-Peñalosa, 'Protectionism and the education-fertility trade-off in late 19th century France' (2016).

Bisin, Alberto, and Thierry Verdier, 'The economics of cultural transmission and the dynamics of preferences', *Journal of Economic Theory* 97, no. 2 (2001): 298–319.

Bisin, Alberto, and Thierry Verdier, '"Beyond the melting pot": cultural transmission, marriage, and the evolution of ethnic and religious traits', *The Quarterly Journal of Economics* 115, no. 3 (2000): 955–88.

Blackmore, Susan, 'Evolution and Memes: The Human Brain as a Selective Imitation Device', *Cybernetics & Systems* 32, no. 1–2 (2001): 225–55.

Blayo, Yves, 'Mortality in France from 1740 to 1829', *Population* 30 (1975): 123–43.

Bleakley, Hoyt, 'Malaria eradication in the Americas: A retrospective analysis of child-hood exposure', *American Economic Journal: Applied Economics* 2, no. 2 (2010): 1–45.

Bleakley, Hoyt, 'Disease and Development: Evidence from hookworm eradication in the American South', *The Quarterly Journal of Economics* 122, no. 1 (2007): 73–117.

Bleakley, Hoyt, and Fabian Lange, 'Chronic Disease Burden and the Interaction of Education, Fertility, and Growth', *Review of Economics and Statistics* 91, no. 1 (2009): 52–65.

Bleasdale, Madeleine, Kristine K. Richter, Anneke Janzen et al., 'Ancient proteins provide evidence of dairy consumption in eastern Africa', *Nature Communication* 12, 632 (2021).

Bockstette, Valerie, Areendam Chanda, and Louis Putterman, 'States and markets: The advantage of an early start', *Journal of Economic Growth* 7, no. 4 (2002): 347–69.

Bolt, Jutta, Robert Inklaar, Herman de Jong and Jan Luiten van Zanden, 'Rebasing "Maddison": new income comparisons and the shape of long-run economic development', Maddison Project Database (2018).

Bolt, Jutta, and Jan Luiten van Zanden, 'The Maddison Project: collaborative research on historical national accounts', *The Economic History Review* 67, no. 3 (2014): 627–51, Maddison Project Database (2013).

Boserup, Ester, *Woman's Role in Economic Development*, St. Martin's Press, 1970.

Boserup, Ester, *The Conditions of Agricultural Growth: The economics of agrarian change under population pressure*, Aldine Publishing, 1965.

Bostoen, Koen, *The Bantu Expansion*, Oxford University Press, 2018.

Boyd, Robert, Peter J. Richerson and Joseph Henrich, 'The cultural niche: Why social learning is essential for human adaptation', *Proceedings of the National Academy of Sciences* 108, Supplement 2 (2011): 10918–25.

Botticini, Maristella, and Zvi Eckstein, *The Chosen Few: How Education Shaped Jewish History*, Vol. 42, Princeton University Press, 2014, pp. 70–1492.

Brown, John C., and Timothy W. Guinnane, 'Fertility Transition in a Rural, Catholic Population: Bavaria, 1880–1910', *Population Studies* 56, no. 1 (2002): 35–49.

Buggle, Johannes C., and Ruben Durante, 'Climate Risk, Cooperation and the Co-Evolution of Culture and Institutions', *The Economic Journal* 131, no. 637 (2021): 1947–87.

Buringh, Eltjo, and Jan Luiten van Zanden, 'Charting the "Rise of the West": Manuscripts and Printed Books in Europe, a long-term Perspective from the Sixth through Eighteenth Centuries', *The Journal of Economic History* 69, no. 2 (2009): 409–45.

Burnette, Joyce, 'An Investigation of the Female–Male Wage Gap During the Industrial Revolution in Britain', *The Economic History Review* 50, no. 2 (1997): 257–81.

Bybee, Joan L., and Östen Dahl, *The Creation of Tense and Aspect Systems in the Languages of the World*, John Benjamins, 1989.

Carneiro, Robert L., 'The Chiefdom: precursor of the state', *The Transition to Statehood in the New World* (1981): 37–79.

Casey, Gregory, and Oded Galor, 'Is faster economic growth compatible with reductions in carbon emissions? The role of diminished population growth', *Environmental Research Letters* 12, no. 1 (2017): 014003.

Cervellati, Matteo, and Uwe Sunde, 'Human capital formation, life expectancy, and the process of development', *American Economic Review* 95, no. 5 (2005): 1653–72.

Chandler, Tertius, *Four Thousand Years of Urban Growth: An Historical Census*, Mellen, 1987.

Charnov, Eric L., and S. K. Morgan Ernest, 'The offspring-size/clutch-size trade-off in mammals', *The American Naturalist* 167, no. 4 (2006): 578–82.

Chaudhuri, Kurti N., 'Foreign trade and balance of payments (1757–1947)', *The Cambridge Economic History of India* 2 (1983): 804–77.

Chen, M. Keith, 'The Effect of Language on Economic Behavior: Evidence from Savings Rates, Health Behaviors, and Retirement Assets', *American Economic Review* 103, no. 2 (2013): 690–731.

Chen, Shuo, and James Kai-sing Kung, 'Of Maize and Men: The Effect of a New World Crop on Population and Economic Growth in China', *Journal of Economic Growth* 21, no. 1 (2016): 71–99.

Chesnais, Jean-Claude, *The Demographic Transition: Stages, Patterns and Economic Implications*, Oxford University Press, 1992.

Cinnirella, Francesco, and Jochen Streb, 'The Role of Human Capital and Innovation in Prussian Economic Development', *Journal of Economic Growth* 22, no. 2 (2017): 193–227.

Cipolla, Carlo M., *Literacy and Development in the West*, Vol. 1027, Penguin, 1969.

Clark, Gregory, 'Microbes and Markets: Was the Black Death an Economic Revolution?', *The Journal of Economic History* 82, no. 2 (2016): 139–65.

Clark, Gregory, *A Farewell to Alms: A Brief Economic History of the World*, Vol. 25, Princeton University Press, 2008.

Clark, Gregory, and David Jacks, 'Coal and the Industrial Revolution, 1700–1869', *European Review of Economic History* 11, no. 1 (2007): 39–72.

Clark, Gregory, 'The Long March of History: Farm Wages, Population, and Economic Growth, England 1209–1869', *The Economic History Review* 60, no. 1 (2007): 97–135.

Clarkson, Chris, Zenobia Jacobs, Ben Marwick, Richard Fullagar, Lynley Wallis, Mike Smith, Richard G. Roberts et al., 'Human occupation of northern Australia by 65,000 years ago', *Nature* 547, no. 7663 (2017): 306–10.

Clutton-Brock, Tim H., and Paul H. Harvey, 'Primates, Brains and Ecology', *Journal of Zoology* 190, no. 3 (1980): 309–23.

Cohen, Mark Nathan, *Health and the Rise of Civilization*, Yale University Press, 1989.

Comin, Diego, William Easterly and Erick Gong, 'Was the Wealth of Nations Determined in 1000 BC?', *American Economic Journal: Macroeconomics* 2, no. 3 (2010): 65–97.

Cook, C. Justin, and Jason M. Fletcher, 'High-School Genetic Diversity and Later-Life Student Outcomes: Micro-Level Evidence from the Wisconsin Longitudinal Study', *Journal of Economic Growth* 23, no. 3 (2018): 307–39.

Cook, C. Justin., 'The Role of Lactase Persistence in Precolonial Development', *Journal of Economic Growth* 19, no. 4 (2014): 369–406.

Cosandey, David, *Le Secret de l'Occident*, Champs-Flammarion, 2007.

Crafts, Nicholas F. R., 'Duration of Marriage, Fertility and Women's Employment Opportunities in England and Wales in 1911', *Population Studies* 43, no. 2 (1989): 325–35.

Crafts, Nicholas F. R., and C. Knick Harley, 'Output Growth and the British Industrial Revolution: A Restatement of the Crafts–Harley view', *The Economic History Review* 45, no. 4 (1992): 703–30.

Crafts, Nicholas F. R., and Mark Thomas, 'Comparative advantage in UK manufacturing trade, 1910–1935', *The Economic Journal* 96, no. 383 (1986): 629–45.

Cubberley, Ellwood Patterson, *The History of Education: Educational Practice and Progress Considered as a Phase of the Development and Spread of Western Civilization*, Houghton Mifflin Company, 1920.

Dahl, Östen, and Viveka Velupillai, 'The Future Tense', from *The World Atlas of Language Structures Online*, edited by Matthew Dryer and Martin Haspelmath, Max Planck Institute for Evolutionary Anthropology, 2011.

Dalgaard, Carl-Johan, Anne Sofie Knudsen and Pablo Selaya, 'The bounty of the sea and long-run development', *Journal of Economic Growth* 25, no. 3 (2020): 259–95.

Dalgaard, Carl-Johan, Jakob B. Madsen, and Holger Strulik, 'Physiological Constraints and the Transition to Growth: Implications for Comparative Development', *Journal of Economic Growth* 26, no. 3 (2021): 241–289.

Dalgaard, Carl-Johan, and Holger Strulik, 'The Physiological Foundations of the Wealth of Nations', *Journal of Economic Growth* 20, no. 1 (2015): 37–73.

Darlington, Philip J., 'Group Selection, Altruism, Reinforcement, and Throwing in Human Evolution', *Proceedings of the National Academy of Sciences* 72, no. 9 (1975): 3748–52.

Dawkins, Richard, *The Selfish Gene*, Oxford University Press, 1976.

de la Croix, David, Eric B. Schneider and Jacob Weisdorf, 'Childlessness, celibacy and net fertility in pre-industrial England: the middle-class evolutionary advantage', *Journal of Economic Growth* 24, no. 3 (2019): 223–56.

de la Croix, David, Matthias Doepke and Joel Mokyr, 'Clans, guilds, and markets: Apprenticeship institutions and growth in the preindustrial economy', *The Quarterly Journal of Economics* 133, no. 1 (2018): 1–70.

De Pleijt, Alexandra, Alessandro Nuvolari and Jacob Weisdorf, 'Human capital formation during the first industrial revolution: Evidence from the use of steam engines', *Journal of the European Economic Association* 18, no. 2 (2020): 829–89.

De Pleijt, Alexandra, and Jan Luiten van Zanden, 'Two worlds of female labour: gender wage inequality in western Europe, 1300–1800', *The Economic History Review* (2018).

Delis, Manthos D., Chrysovalantis Gaganis, Iftekhar Hasan and Fotios Pasiouras, 'The effect of board directors from countries with different genetic diversity levels on corporate performance', *Management Science* 63, no. 1 (2017): 231–49.

Dell, Melissa, 'The Persistent Effects of Peru's Mining *Mita*', *Econometrica* 78, no. 6 (2010): 1863–1903.

Depetris-Chauvin, Emilio, and Ömer Özak, 'The origins of the division of labor in pre-modern times', *Journal of Economic Growth* (2021).

Desmet, Klaus, Ignacio Ortuño-Ortín and Romain Wacziarg, 'Culture, ethnicity, and diversity', *American Economic Review* 107, no. 9 (2017): 2479–2513.

Diamond, Jared, *Collapse: How Societies Choose to Succeed or Fail*, Viking Penguin, 2005.

Diamond, Jared M., 'Taiwan's gift to the world', *Nature* 403, no. 6771 (2000): 709–10.

Diamond, Jared, *Guns, Germs and Steel: The Fates of Human Societies*, Vintage, 1997.

Dickens, Charles, *The Adventures of Oliver Twist*, Ticknor and Fields, 1868.

Dittmar, Jeremiah E., 'Information Technology and Economic Change: The Impact of the Printing Press', *The Quarterly Journal of Economics* 126, no. 3 (2011): 1133–72.

Doepke, Matthias, and Fabrizio Zilibotti, 'Occupational choice and the spirit of capitalism', *The Quarterly Journal of Economics* 123, no. 2 (2008): 747–93.

Doepke, Matthias, and Fabrizio Zilibotti, 'The Macroeconomics of Child Labor Regulation', *American Economic Review* 95, no. 5 (2005): 1492–1524.

Dunbar, Robin I. M., 'The Social Brain Hypothesis', *Evolutionary Anthropology: Issues, News, and Reviews* 6, no. 5 (1998): 178–90.

Durlauf, Steven N., Paul A. Johnson and Jonathan R.W. Temple, 'Growth Econometrics', *Handbook of Economic Growth* 1 (2005): 555–677.

Durlauf, Steven N., and Danny T. Quah, 'The New Empirics of Economic Growth' *Handbook of Macroeconomics* 1 (1999): 235–308.

Easterly, William, *The Elusive Quest for Growth: Economists' Adventures and Misadventures in the Tropics*, MIT Press, 2001.

Easterly, William, and Ross Levine, 'The European Origins of Economic Development', *Journal of Economic Growth* 21, no. 3 (2016): 225–57.

Easterly, William, and Ross Levine, 'Africa's Growth Tragedy: Policies and Ethnic Divisions', *The Quarterly Journal of Economics* 112, no. 4 (1997): 1203–50.

Engerman, Stanley, and Kenneth Sokoloff, 'Factor Endowments, Institutions, and Differential Paths of Growth Among New World Economies: A View from Economic Historians of the United States', in *How Latin America Fell Behind: Essays on the Economic Histories of Brazil and Mexico, 1800–1914*, edited by Stephen Haber, 260–304, Stanford University Press, 1997.

Estevadeordal, Antoni, Brian Frantz and Alan M. Taylor, 'The rise and fall of world trade, 1870–1939', *The Quarterly Journal of Economics* 118, no. 2 (2003): 359–407.

Fanon, Frantz, *Black Skin, White Masks*, Grove Press, 2008.

Fanon, Frantz, *The Wretched of the Earth*, Grove/Atlantic, Inc., 2007.

Feldman, Michal, Eva Fernández-Domínguez, Luke Reynolds, Douglas Baird, Jessica Pearson, Israel Hershkovitz, Hila May et al., 'Late Pleistocene human genome suggests a local origin for the first farmers of central Anatolia', *Nature Communications* 10, no. 1 (2019): 1–10.

Feldman, Naomi E., and Karine Van der Beek, 'Skill Choice and Skill Complementarity in Eighteenth Century England', *Explorations in Economic History* 59 (2016): 94–113.

Fenske, James, 'Ecology, Trade, and States in Pre-Colonial Africa', *Journal of the European Economic Association* 12, no. 3 (2014): 612–40.

Fernihough, A., 'Human Capital and the Quantity–Quality Trade-Off During the Demographic Transition', *Journal of Economic Growth* 22, no. 1 (2017): 35–65.

Fewlass, Helen, Sahra Talamo, Lukas Wacker, Bernd Kromer, Thibaut Tuna, Yoann Fagault, Edouard Bard et al., 'A 14 C chronology for the Middle to Upper Paleolithic transition at Bacho Kiro Cave, Bulgaria', *Nature Ecology & Evolution* (2020): 1–8.

Findlay, Ronald, and Kevin H. O'Rourke, *Commodity Market Integration, 1500–2000*, University of Chicago Press, 2007.

Fischer, David Hackett, *Albion's Seed: Four British Folkways in America*, Oxford University Press, 1989.

Flora, Peter, Franz Kraus and Winfried Pfenning, *State, Economy, and Society in Western Europe 1815–1975: The growth of industrial societies and capitalist economies*, Vol. 2. St James Press, 1983.

Franck, Raphaël, and Oded Galor, 'Flowers of Evil or Evil of Flowers? Industrialization and Long-Run Development', *Journal of Monetary Economics* (2021).

Franck, Raphaël, and Oded Galor, 'Technology-skill Complementarity in Early Phases of Industrialization', *The Economic Journal* (2022).

Franck, Raphaël, and Ilia Rainer, 'Does the leader's ethnicity matter? Ethnic favoritism, education, and health in sub-Saharan Africa', *American Political Science Review* 106, no. 2 (2012): 294–325.

Fu, Qiaomei, Alissa Mittnik, Philip L. F. Johnson, Kirsten Bos, Martina Lari, Ruth Bollongino, Chengkai Sun et al., 'A revised timescale for human evolution based on ancient mitochondrial genomes', *Current Biology* 23, no. 7 (2013): 553–9.

Fukuyama, Francis, *The End of History and The Last Man*, Simon and Schuster, 2006.

Gallup, John Luke, Jeffrey D. Sachs and Andrew D. Mellinger, 'Geography and economic development', *International Regional Science Review* 22, no. 2 (1999): 179–232.

Galor, Oded, 'The Demographic Transition: causes and consequences', *Cliometrica* 6, no. 1 (2012): 1–28.

Galor, Oded, *Unified Growth Theory*, Princeton University Press, 2011.

Galor, Oded, *Discrete Dynamical Systems*, Springer, 2010.

Galor, Oded, 'The Lawrence R. Klein lecture – Comparative economic development: Insights from unified growth theory', *International Economic Review* 51, no. 1 (2010): 1–44.

Galor, Oded, 'From Stagnation to Growth: Unified Growth Theory', *Handbook of Economic Growth* 1 (2005): 171–293.

Galor, Oded, 'Convergence? Inferences from theoretical models', *The Economic Journal* 106, no. 437 (1996): 1056–69.

Galor, Oded, 'A two-sector overlapping-generations model: A global characterization of the dynamical system', *Econometrica* 60, no. 6 (1992): 1351–86.

Galor, Oded, and Marc Klemp, 'Human Genealogy Reveals a Selective Advantage to Moderate Fecundity', *Nature Ecology & Evolution* 3, no. 5 (2019): 853–7.

Galor, Oded, and Marc Klemp, 'Roots of Autocracy', Working paper No. w23301, National Bureau of Economic Research, 2018.

Galor, Oded, and Andrew Mountford, 'Trading Population for Productivity: Theory and evidence', *The Review of Economic Studies* 75, no. 4 (2008): 1143–79.

Galor, Oded, and Andrew Mountford, 'Trade and the great divergence: the family connection', *American Economic Review* 96, no. 2 (2006): 299–303.

Galor, Oded, and Omer Moav, 'The neolithic origins of contemporary variations in life expectancy', SSRN 1012650 (2007).

Galor, Oded, and Omer Moav, 'Das Human-Kapital: A theory of the demise of the class structure', *The Review of Economic Studies* 73, no. 1 (2006): 85–117.

Galor, Oded, and Omer Moav, 'Natural selection and the evolution of life expectancy', (2005).

Galor, Oded, and Omer Moav, 'From Physical to Human Capital Accumulation: Inequality and the Process of Development', *The Review of Economic Studies* 71, no. 4 (2004): 1001–26.

Galor, Oded, and Omer Moav, 'Natural Selection and the Origin of Economic Growth', *The Quarterly Journal of Economics* 117, no. 4 (2002): 1133–91.

Galor, Oded, and Omer Moav, 'Ability-biased technological transition, wage inequality, and economic growth', *The Quarterly Journal of Economics* 115, no. 2 (2000): 469–97.

Galor, Oded, Omer Moav and Dietrich Vollrath, 'Inequality in Landownership, the Emergence of Human-Capital Promoting Institutions, and the Great Divergence', *The Review of Economic Studies* 76, no. 1 (2009): 143–79.

Galor, Oded, and Stelios Michalopoulos, 'Evolution and the Growth Process: Natural selection of entrepreneurial traits', *Journal of Economic Theory* 147, no. 2 (2012): 759–80.

Galor, Oded, and Ömer Özak, 'The Agricultural Origins of Time Preference', *American Economic Review* 106, no. 10 (2016): 3064–103.

Galor, Oded, Ömer Özak and Assaf Sarid, 'Geographical Roots of the Coevolution of Cultural and Linguistic Traits', SSRN 3284239 (2018).

Galor, Oded, Ömer Özak and Assaf Sarid, 'Linguistic Traits and Human Capital Formation', *AEA Papers and Proceedings*, Vol. 110 (2020), 309–13.

Galor, Oded, and Harl E. Ryder, 'Existence, uniqueness, and stability of equilibrium in an overlapping-generations model with productive capital', *Journal of Economic Theory* 49, no. 2 (1989): 360–75.

Galor, Oded, and Viacheslav Savitskiy, 'Climatic Roots of Loss Aversion', Working Papers 2018-1, Brown University, Department of Economics, 2018.

Galor, Oded, and Daniel Tsiddon, 'Technological progress, mobility, and economic growth', *American Economic Review* (1997): 363–82.

Galor, Oded, and Daniel Tsiddon, 'The distribution of human capital and economic growth', *Journal of Economic Growth* 2, no. 1 (1997): 93–124.

Galor, Oded, and David N. Weil, 'Population, Technology, and Growth: From Malthusian Stagnation to the Demographic Transition and Beyond', *American Economic Review* 90, no. 4 (2000): 806–28.

Galor Oded, and David N. Weil, 'The Gender Gap, Fertility, and Growth,' *American Economic Review* 86, no. 3 (1996): 374–87.

Galor, Oded, and Joseph Zeira, 'Income Distribution and Macroeconomics', *The Review of Economic Studies* 60, no. 1 (1993): 35–52.

Gates, Bill, *How to Avoid a Climate Disaster: The Solutions We Have and the Breakthroughs We Need*, Knopf, 2021.

Giavazzi, Francesco, Ivan Petkov and Fabio Schiantarelli, 'Culture: Persistence and Evolution', *Journal of Economic Growth* 24, no. 2 (2019): 117–54.

Gibbons, Ann, 'How farming shaped Europeans' immunity', *Science* 373, no. 6560 (2021): 1186.

Glaeser, Edward L., Rafael La Porta, Florencio Lopez-de-Silanes and Andrei Shleifer, 'Do Institutions Cause Growth?', *Journal of Economic Growth* 9, no. 3 (2004): 271–303.

Glaeser, Edward L., and Andrei Shleifer, 'Legal origins', *The Quarterly Journal of Economics* 117, no. 4 (2002): 1193–229.

Goldin, Claudia, 'America's graduation from high school: The evolution and spread of secondary schooling in the twentieth century', *The Journal of Economic History* 58, no. 2 (1998): 345–74.

Goldin, Claudia, 'Understanding the gender gap: An economic history of American women', No. gold90-1, National Bureau of Economic Research, 1990.

Goldin, C., 'Women's Employment and Technological Change: A Historical Perspective', *Computer Chips and Paper Clips: Technology and Women's Employment* 2 (1987): 185–222.

Goldin, Claudia, and Lawrence F. Katz, 'The legacy of US educational leadership: Notes on distribution and economic growth in the 20th century', *American Economic Review* 91, no. 2 (2001): 18–23.

González-Forero, Mauricio, and Andy Gardner, 'Inference of ecological and social drivers of human brain-size evolution', *Nature* 557, no. 7706 (2018): 554–7.

González-Fortes, Gloria, Eppie R. Jones, Emma Lightfoot, Clive Bonsall, Catalin Lazar, Aurora Grandal-d'Anglade, María Dolores Garralda et al., 'Paleogenomic evidence for multi-generational mixing between Neolithic farmers and Mesolithic hunter-gatherers in the lower Danube basin', *Current Biology* 27, no. 12 (2017): 1801–10.

Goody, Jack, *Technology, Tradition and the State in Africa*, Oxford University Press, 1971. Reprint, Routledge, 2018.

Gordon, Robert J., *The Rise and Fall of American Growth: The US standard of living since the civil war*, Vol. 70, Princeton University Press, 2017.

Gorodnichenko, Yuriy, and Gerard Roland, 'Culture, Institutions, and the Wealth of Nations', *Review of Economics and Statistics* 99, no. 3 (2017): 402–16.

Grande, James, and John Stevenson, *The Opinions of William Cobbett*, Routledge, 2017.

Green, Andy, *Education and State Formation: The Rise of Education Systems in England, France, and the USA*, St. Martin's Press, 1990, p. 295.

Greenwood, Jeremy, Ananth Seshadri and Mehmet Yorukoglu, 'Engines of liberation', *The Review of Economic Studies* 72, no. 1 (2005): 109–33.

Greif, Avner, 'Contract enforceability and economic institutions in early trade: The Maghribi Traders' Coalition', *American Economic Review* (1993): 525–48.

Grosman, Leore, 'The Natufian chronological scheme – New insights and their implications', *Natufian Foragers in the Levant: Terminal Pleistocene social changes in Western Asia*, Archaeological Series 19 (2013): 622–37.

Grossman, Gene M., and Elhanan Helpman, *Innovation and Growth in the Global Economy*, MIT Press, 1991.

Guinnane, Timothy W., 'The Historical Fertility Transition: A Guide for Economists', *Journal of Economic Literature* 49, no. 3 (2011): 589–614.

Guiso, Luigi, Paola Sapienza and Luigi Zingales, 'Does Culture Affect Economic Outcomes?', *Journal of Economic Perspectives* 20, no. 2 (2006): 23–48.

Guiso, Luigi, Paola Sapienza and Luigi Zingales, 'The Role of Social Capital in Financial Development', *American Economic Review* 94, no. 3 (2004): 526–56.

Gurven, Michael, and Hillard Kaplan, 'Longevity Among Hunter-Gatherers: A Cross-Cultural Examination', *Population and Development Review* 33, no. 2 (2007): 321–65.

Haidt, Jonathan, *The Righteous Mind: Why Good People Are Divided by Politics and Religion*, Vintage, 2012.

Hajnal, John, 'European marriage patterns in perspective', in D. V. Glass and D. E. C. Eversley (eds.), *Population in History*, Arnold, 1965.

Hanihara, Tsunehiko, 'Morphological variation of major human populations based on nonmetric dental traits', *American Journal of Physical Anthropology* 136, no. 2 (2008): 169–82.

Hanioğlu, M. Şükrü, *A Brief History of the Late Ottoman Empire*, Princeton University Press, 2010.

Harari, Yuval Noah, *Sapiens: A Brief History of Humankind*, Random House, 2014.

Harpending, Henry, and Alan Rogers, 'Genetic perspectives on human origins and differentiation', *Annual Review of Genomics and Human Genetics* 1, no. 1 (2000): 361–85.

Harper, John L., P. H. Lovell and K. G. Moore, 'The shapes and sizes of seeds', *Annual Review of Ecology and Systematics* 1, no. 1 (1970): 327–56.

Harvati, Katerina, Carolin Röding, Abel M. Bosman, Fotios A. Karakostis, Rainer Grün, Chris Stringer, Panagiotis Karkanas et al., 'Apidima Cave fossils provide earliest evidence of *Homo sapiens* in Eurasia', *Nature* 571, no. 7766 (2019): 500–4.

Hassan, Fekri A., 'Demographic archaeology', in *Advances in Archaeological Method and Theory*, Academic Press, 1981, pp. 225–79.

Hausmann, Ricardo, Dani Rodrik and Andrés Velasco, 'Growth Diagnostics', *The Washington Consensus Reconsidered: Towards a New Global Governance* (2008): 324–55.

Hausmann, Ricardo, Lant Pritchett and Dani Rodrik, 'Growth Accelerations', *Journal of Economic Growth* 10, no. 4 (2005): 303–29.

Hazan, Moshe, and Binyamin Berdugo, 'Child Labour, fertility, and Economic Growth', *The Economic Journal* 112, no. 482 (2002): 810–28.

Hazan, Moshe, David Weiss and Hosny Zoabi, 'Women's Liberation, Household Revolution, (2021).

Heckman, J. J., and J. R. Walker, 'The Relationship Between Wages and Income and the Timing and Spacing of Births: Evidence from Swedish Longitudinal Data', *Econometrica* (1990): 1411–41.

Henrich, Joseph, *The Secret of Our Success: How Culture is Driving Human Evolution, Domesticating our Species, and Making us Smarter*, Princeton University Press, 2017.

Herrmann, Esther, Josep Call, María Victoria Hernández-Lloreda, Brian Hare and Michael Tomasello, 'Humans have Evolved Specialized Skills of Social Cognition: The Cultural Intelligence Hypothesis', *Science* 317, no. 5843 (2007): 1360–6.

Hershkovitz, Israel, Gerhard W. Weber, Rolf Quam, Mathieu Duval, Rainer Grün, Leslie Kinsley, Avner Ayalon et al., 'The earliest modern humans outside Africa', *Science* 359, no. 6374 (2018): 456–9.

Hill, Christopher, *The Century of Revolution, 1603–1714*, W. W. Norton, 1966, p. 32.

Ho, Ping-ti, *Studies on the Population of China, 1368–1953*, Harvard University Press, 2013.

Hobbes, Thomas, *Leviathan, or, The Matter, Form, and Power of a Common-Wealth Ecclesiastical and Civil*, printed for Andrew Crooke, 1651.

Hoffman, Philip T., *Why Did Europe Conquer the World?*, Vol. 54, Princeton University Press, 2017.

Hofstede, Geert, Gert Jan Hofstede and Michael Minkov, *Cultures and Organizations: Software of the mind*, Vol. 2, McGraw-Hill, 2005.

Hopkins, Keith, 'On the Probable Age Structure of the Roman Population', *Population Studies* 20, no. 2 (1966): 245–64.

Hublin, Jean-Jacques, Nikolay Sirakov, Vera Aldeias, Shara Bailey, Edouard Bard, Vincent Delvigne, Elena Endarova et al., 'Initial Upper Palaeolithic *Homo sapiens* from Bacho Kiro Cave, Bulgaria', *Nature* 581 (2020): 1–4.

Hume, David, 'Essays, Moral, Political, and Literary', from *Essays and Treatises on Several Subjects*, Vol. 1, Bell & Bradfute, 1825, p. 112.

Hunt, Terry L., and Carl P. Lipo, 'Late Colonization of Easter Island', *Science* 311, no. 5767 (2006): 1603–6.

Jackson, Tim, *Prosperity Without Growth: Foundations for the economy of tomorrow*, Taylor & Francis, 2016.

Jacobs, Jane, *The Death and Life of Great American Cities*, Vintage, 2016.

Jedwab, Remi, Noel D. Johnson and Mark Koyama, 'Pandemics, Places, and Populations: Evidence from the Black Death', *CEPR Discussion Papers* DP13523 (2019).

Jelinek, Arthur J., 'The Tabun cave and Paleolithic man in the Levant', *Science* 216, no. 4553 (1982): 1369–75.

Jones, Charles I., 'R & D-based models of economic growth', *Journal of Political Economy* 103, no. 4 (1995): 759–84.

Jones, Eric, *The European Miracle: Environments, Economies and Geopolitics in the History of Europe and Asia*, Cambridge University Press, 2003.

Josserand, Mathilde, Emma Meeussen, Asifa Majid, and Dan Dediu, 'Environment and culture shape both the colour lexicon and the genetics of colour perception', *Scientific Reports* 11, no. 1 (2021): 1–11.

Kannisto, Väinö, Oiva Turpeinen and Mauri Nieminen, 'Finnish Life Tables since 1751', *Demographic Research* 1 (1999).

Kant, Immanuel, *Answering the Question: What is Enlightenment?*, 1784.

Katz, Ori, 'Railroads, Economic Development, and the Demographic Transition in the United States', University Library of Munich (2018).

Kendi, Ibram X., *Stamped from the Beginning: The definitive history of racist ideas in America*, Nation Books, 2016.

Kettlewell, H. Bernard D., 'Selection Experiments on Industrial Melanism in the Lepidoptera', *Heredity* 9, no. 3 (1955): 323–42.

Keynes, J. M., 'A Tract on Monetary Reform', in *The Collected Writings of John Maynard Keynes*, Macmillan Press, 1971.

Klasing, Mariko J., and Petros Milionis, 'The International Epidemiological Transition and the Education Gender Gap', *Journal of Economic Growth* 25, no. 1 (2020): 1–50.

Klemp, Marc P., 'Prices, Wages and Fertility in Pre-Industrial England', *Cliometrica* 6, no. 1 (2012): 63–77.

Klemp, Marc, and Jacob L. Weisdorf, 'Fecundity, Fertility and the Formation of Human Capital', *The Economic Journal* 129, no. 618 (2019): 925–60.

Kline, Michelle A., and Robert Boyd, 'Population Size Predicts Technological Complexity in Oceania', *Proceedings of the Royal Society B: Biological Sciences* 277, no. 1693 (2010): 2559–64.

Kremer, Michael, 'Population growth and technological change: One million BC to 1990', *The Quarterly Journal of Economics* 108, no. 3 (1993): 681–716.

Krupnik, Igor, and Ludger Müller-Wille, 'Franz Boas and Inuktitut terminology for ice and snow: From the emergence of the field to the "Great Eskimo Vocabulary Hoax"', in *SIKU: Knowing our ice*, Springer, Dordrecht, 2010, pp. 377–400.

Kuhn, Thomas S., *The Copernican Revolution: Planetary Astronomy in the Development of Western Thought*, Vol. 16, Harvard University Press, 1957.

Kuznets, Simon, 'Quantitative Aspects of the Economic Growth of Nations: X. Level and Structure of Foreign Trade: Long-Term Trends', *Economic Development and Cultural Change* 15, no. 2, Part 2 (1967): 1–140.

La Porta, Rafael, Florencio Lopez-de-Silanes, Andrei Shleifer and Robert W. Vishny, 'Legal Determinants of External Finance', *The Journal of Finance* 52, no. 3 (1997): 1131–50.

Lagerlöf, Nils-Petter, 'Gender Equality and Long-run Growth', *Journal of Economic Growth* 8, no. 4 (2003): 403–26.

Lagerlöf, Nils-Petter, 'The Galor–Weil model revisited: A quantitative exercise', *Review of Economic Dynamics* 9, no. 1 (2006): 116–42.

Lang, Graeme, 'State Systems and the Origins of Modern Science: A Comparison of Europe and China', *East-West Dialog* 2 (1997): 16–30.

Lazaridis, Iosif, Nick Patterson, Alissa Mittnik, Gabriel Renaud, Swapan Mallick, Karola Kirsanow, Peter H. Sudmant et al., 'Ancient human genomes suggest three ancestral populations for present-day Europeans', *Nature* 513, no. 7518 (2014): 409–13.

Lee, Neil, 'Migrant and Ethnic Diversity, Cities and Innovation: Firm Effects or City Effects?', *Journal of Economic Geography* 15, no. 4 (2015): 769–96.

Lipset, Seymour Martin, 'Some social requisites of democracy: Economic development and political legitimacy', *American Political Science Review* 53, no. 1 (1959): 69–105.

Litina, Anastasia, 'Natural land productivity, cooperation and comparative development', *Journal of Economic Growth* 21, no. 4 (2016): 351–408.

López, Saioa, Lucy Van Dorp and Garrett Hellenthal, 'Human dispersal out of Africa: A lasting debate', *Evolutionary Bioinformatics* 11 (2015): EBO-S33489.

Lucas, Adrienne M., 'The impact of malaria eradication on fertility', *Economic Development and Cultural Change* 61, no. 3 (2013): 607–31.

Lucas, Adrienne M., 'Malaria eradication and educational attainment: evidence from Paraguay and Sri Lanka', *American Economic Journal: Applied Economics* 2, no. 2 (2010): 46–71.

Lupyan, Gary, and Rick Dale, 'Language Structure is Partly Determined by Social Structure', *PLoS One* 5, no. 1 (2010).

Lucas, Robert E., *Lectures on Economic Growth*, Harvard University Press, 2002.

Lucas, Robert E., Jr, 'On the Mechanics of Economic Development', *Journal of Monetary Economics* 22, no. 1 (1988): 3–42.

MacArthur, Robert H., and Edward O. Wilson, *The Theory of Island Biogeography*, Vol. 1, Princeton University Press, 1970.

Madsen, Jakob B., Md. Rabiul Islam and Xueli Tang, 'Was the post-1870 Fertility Transition a Key Contributor to Growth in the West in the Twentieth Century?', *Journal of Economic Growth* 25, no. 4 (2020): 431–54.

Madsen, Jakob, and Holger Strulik, 'Testing Unified Growth Theory: Technological Progress and the Child Quantity–Quality Trade-off', (2020).

Madsen, Jakob B., Peter E. Robertson and Longfeng Ye, 'Malthus Was Right: Explaining a Millennium of Stagnation', *European Economic Review* 118 (2019): 51–68.

Magga, Ole Henrik, 'Diversity in Saami terminology for reindeer, snow, and ice', *International Social Science Journal* 58, no. 187 (2006): 25–34.

Maloney, William, and Felipe Valencia Caicedo, 'Engineering Growth: Innovative Capacity and Development in the Americas', no. 6339, CESifo Group Munich (2017).

Manica, Andrea, William Amos, François Balloux and Tsunehiko Hanihara, 'The Effect of Ancient Population Bottlenecks on Human Phenotypic Variation', *Nature* 448, no. 7151 (2007): 346–8.

Murtin, Fabrice, and Romain Wacziarg, 'The democratic transition', *Journal of Economic Growth* 19, no. 2 (2014): 141–81.

Mathieson, Iain, Iosif Lazaridis, Nadin Rohland, Swapan Mallick, Nick Patterson, Songül Alpaslan Roodenberg, Eadaoin Harney et al., 'Genome-Wide Patterns of Selection in 230 Ancient Eurasians', *Nature* 528, no. 7583 (2015): 499–503.

Matranga, Andrea, 'The Ant and the Grasshopper: Seasonality and the Invention of Agriculture' (2017).

Matthews, Robert Charles Oliver, Charles Hilliard Feinstein and John C. Odling-Smee, *British Economic Growth 1856–1973: The post-war period in historical perspective*, Oxford University Press, 1982.

Mayshar, Joram, Omer Moav and Zvika Neeman, 'Geography, Transparency, and Institutions', *American Political Science Review* 111, no. 3 (2017): 622–36.

Mayshar, Joram, Omer Moav and Luigi Pascali, 'Cereals, Appropriability and Hierarchy', *Journal of Political Economy* (2022).

McCloskey, Deirdre Nansen, 'The Industrial Revolution: A Survey', in *The Economic History of Britain Since 1700*, Vol. 1, edited by Roderick C. Floud and D. N. McCloskey, Cambridge University Press, 1981, pp. 103–27.

McEvedy, Colin, and Richard Jones, *Atlas of World Population History*, Penguin, 1978.

McNeill, W. H., 'The Introduction of the Potato into Ireland', *The Journal of Modern History* 21, no. 3 (1949): 218–22.

Meisenzahl, Ralf R., and Joel Mokyr, 'The Rate and Direction of Invention in the British Industrial Revolution: Incentives and Institutions', in *The Rate and Direction of Inventive Activity Revisited*, University of Chicago Press, 2011, pp. 443–79.

Mellars, Paul, 'Why did modern human populations disperse from Africa ca. 60,000 years ago? A new model', *Proceedings of the National Academy of Sciences* 103, no. 25 (2006): 9381–6.

Michalopoulos, Stelios, and Elias Papaioannou, 'Pre-colonial Ethnic Institutions and Contemporary African Development', *Econometrica* 81, no. 1 (2013): 113–52.

Miller, Geoffrey, *The Mating Mind: How sexual choice shaped the evolution of human nature*, Anchor, 2011.

Mischel, Walter, Ozlem Ayduk, Marc G. Berman, B. J. Casey, Ian H. Gotlib, John Jonides, Ethan Kross et al., '"Willpower" Over the Life Span: Decomposing Self-Regulation', *Social Cognitive and Affective Neuroscience* 6, no. 2 (2011): 252–6.

Mitch, David, *The Rise of Popular Literacy in Victorian England: The influence of private choice and public policy*, University of Pennsylvania Press, 1992.

Modelski, George, *World Cities: –3000 to 2000*, Faros 2000, 2003.

Mokyr, Joel, 'The intellectual origins of modern economic growth', *The Journal of Economic History* 65, no. 2 (2005): 285–351.

Mokyr, Joel, *A Culture of Growth: The origins of the modern economy*, Princeton University Press, 2016.

Mokyr, Joel, 'The New Economic History and the Industrial Revolution', in J. Mokyr (ed.), *The British Industrial Revolution: An Economic Perspective*, Westview Press, 1999, pp. 1–127.

Mokyr, Joel, *The Lever of Riches: Technological creativity and economic progress*, Oxford University Press, 1992.

Møller, Niels Framroze, and Paul Sharp, 'Malthus in cointegration space: evidence of a post-Malthusian pre-industrial England', *Journal of Economic Growth* 19, no. 1 (2014): 105–40.

Morelli, Giovanna, Yajun Song, Camila J. Mazzoni, Mark Eppinger, Philippe Rou-magnac, David M. Wagner, Mirjam Feldkamp et al., 'Yersinia pestis genome sequencing identifies patterns of global phylogenetic diversity', *Nature Genetics* 42, no. 12 (2010): 1140–3.

Moreno-Mayar, J. Víctor, Ben A. Potter, Lasse Vinner, Matthias Steinrücken, Simon Rasmussen, Jonathan Terhorst, John A. Kamm et al., 'Terminal Pleistocene Alaskan genome reveals first founding population of Native Americans', *Nature* 553, no. 7687 (2018): 203–7.

Morris, Ian, *Social Development*, Stanford University, 2010.

Morris, Ian, *Why the West Rules – For Now: The Patterns of History and What They Reveal About The Future*, Profile, 2010.

Murdock, George Peter, 'Ethnographic atlas: a summary', *Ethnology* 6, no. 2 (1967): 109–236.

Murphy, T. E., 'Old Habits Die Hard (Sometimes)', *Journal of Economic Growth* 20, no. 2 (2015): 177–222.

Nardinelli, Clark, 'Child Labor and the Factory Acts', *The Journal of Economic History* 40, no. 4 (1980): 739–55.

Neel, James V., 'Diabetes Mellitus: a "Thrifty" Genotype Rendered Detrimental by "Progress"?', *American Journal of Human Genetics* 14, no. 4 (1962): 353.

Nelson, Richard R., and Edmund S. Phelps, 'Investment in Humans, Technological Diffusion, and Economic Growth', *American Economic Review* 56, no. 1/2 (1966): 69–75.

North, Douglass C., and Robert Paul Thomas, 'The First Economic Revolution', *The Economic History Review* 30, no. 2 (1977): 229–41.

North, Douglass, *Institutions, Institutional Change, and Economic Performance*, Cambridge University Press, 1990.

Nunn, Nathan, 'The long-term effects of Africa's slave trades', *The Quarterly Journal of Economics* 123, no. 1 (2008): 139–76.

Nunn, Nathan, and Diego Puga, 'Ruggedness: The Blessing of Bad Geography in Africa', *Review of Economics and Statistics* 94, no. 1 (2012): 20–36.

Nunn, Nathan, and Leonard Wantchekon, 'The Slave Trade and the Origins of Mistrust in Africa', *American Economic Review* 101, no. 7 (2011): 3221–52.

Nunziata, Luca, and Lorenzo Rocco, 'The Protestant ethic and entrepreneurship: Evidence from religious minorities in the former Holy Roman Empire', *European Journal of Political Economy* 51 (2018): 27–43.

Nunziata, Luca, and Lorenzo Rocco, 'A tale of minorities: evidence on religious ethics and entrepreneurship', *Journal of Economic Growth* 21, no. 2 (2016): 189–224.

OECD (2017), Life expectancy at birth (indicator).

Ofek, Haim, *Second Nature: Economic Origins of Human Evolution*, Cambridge University Press, 2001.

Ó'Gráda, Cormac, *The Great Irish Famine*, no. 7, Cambridge University Press, 1995.

Ó'Gráda, Cormac, 'The population of Ireland 1700–1900: a survey', in *Annales de démographie historique*, Société de Demographie Historique, 1979, pp. 281–99.

Olsson, Ola, and Douglas A. Hibbs Jr, 'Biogeography and long-run economic development', *European Economic Review* 49, no. 4 (2005): 909–38.

O'Rourke, Kevin H., and Jeffrey G. Williamson, *Globalization and History: The evolution of a nineteenth-century Atlantic economy*, MIT Press, 1999.

Ottaviano, Gianmarco I. P., and Giovanni Peri, 'The Economic Value of Cultural Diversity: Evidence from US Cities', *Journal of Economic Geography* 6, no. 1 (2006): 9–44.

Palmer, Robert, 'Church of the Sonic Guitar', in *Present Tense: Rock & Roll and Culture*, edited by Anthony DeCurtis, Duke University Press, 1992, pp. 13–38.

Papaioannou, Elias, and Gregorios Siourounis, 'Democratisation and growth', *The Economic Journal* 118, no. 532 (2008): 1520–51.

Parker, Andrew R., 'On the Origin of Optics', *Optics & Laser Technology* 43, no. 2 (2011): 323–9.

Pascali, Luigi, 'The Wind of Change: Maritime Technology, Trade, and Economic Development', *American Economic Review* 107, no. 9 (2017): 2821–54.

Pemberton, Trevor J., Michael DeGiorgio and Noah A. Rosenberg, 'Population Structure in a Comprehensive Genomic Data Set on Human Microsatellite Variation', *G3: Genes, Genomes, Genetics* 3, no. 5 (2013): 891–907.

Persson, Torsten, and Guido Tabellini, 'Democracy and development: The devil in the details', *American Economic Review* 96, no. 2 (2006): 319–24.

Persson, Torsten, and Guido Tabellini, *Political Economics: Explaining economic policy*, MIT Press, 2002.

Pinker, Steven, 'Language as an Adaptation to the Cognitive Niche', *Studies in the Evolution of Language* 3 (2003): 16–37.

Pinker, Steven, *Enlightenment Now: The Case for Reason, Science, Humanism, and Progress*, Penguin, 2018.

Piketty, Thomas, *Capital in the Twenty-First Century*, Harvard University Press, 2018.

Pomeranz, Kenneth, *The Great Divergence: China, Europe, and the Making of the Modern World Economy*, Vol. 28, Princeton University Press, 2009.

Popper, Karl, *The Open Society and Its Enemies*, Routledge, 1945.

Poznik, G. David, Brenna M. Henn, Muh-Ching Yee, Elzbieta Sliwerska, Ghia M. Euskirchen, Alice A. Lin, Michael Snyder et al., 'Sequencing Y Chromosomes Resolves Discrepancy in Time to Common Ancestor of Males Versus Females', *Science* 341, no. 6145 (2013): 562–5.

Prugnolle, Franck, Andrea Manica and François Balloux, 'Geography predicts neutral genetic diversity of human populations', *Current Biology* 15, no. 5 (2005): R159–60.

Putnam, Robert D., Robert Leonardi and Raffaella Y. Nanetti, *Making Democracy Work: Civic traditions in modern Italy*, Princeton University Press, 1994.

Putterman, Louis, and David N. Weil, 'Post-1500 Population Flows and the Long-Run Determinants of Economic Growth and Inequality', *The Quarterly Journal of Economics* 125, no. 4 (2010): 1627–82.

Putterman, Louis, 'Agriculture, Diffusion and Development: Ripple Effects of the Neolithic Revolution', *Economica* 75, no. 300 (2008): 729–48.

Quataert, Donald, *The Ottoman Empire, 1700–1922*, Cambridge University Press, 2005.

Ramachandran, Sohini, Omkar Deshpande, Charles C. Roseman, Noah A. Rosenberg, Marcus W. Feldman and L. Luca Cavalli-Sforza, 'Support from the relationship of genetic and geographic distance in human populations for a serial founder effect originating in Africa', *Proceedings of the National Academy of Sciences* 102, no. 44 (2005): 15942–7.

Ramos-Toro, Diego, 'Social Cohesion and Carbon Emissions' (2017).

Richerson, Peter J., Robert Boyd and Joseph Henrich, 'Gene-Culture Coevolution in the Age of Genomics', *Proceedings of the National Academy of Sciences* 107, Supplement 2 (2010): 8985–92.

Ridley, Matt, 'The Rational Optimist: How Prosperity Evolves', *Brock Education: A Journal of Educational Research and Practice* 21, no. 2 (2012).

Roberts, Seán, and James Winters, 'Social Structure and Language Structure: The New Nomothetic Approach', *Psychology of Language and Communication* 16, no. 2 (2012): 89–112.

Rodrik, Dani, 'Goodbye Washington Consensus, Hello Washington Confusion? A Review of the World Bank's Economic Growth in the 1990s: Learning from a Decade of Reform', *Journal of Economic Literature* 44, no. 4 (2006): 973–87.

Roebroeks, Wil, and Paola Villa, 'On the earliest evidence for habitual use of fire in Europe', *Proceedings of the National Academy of Sciences* 108, no. 13 (2011): 5209–14.

Romer, Paul M., 'Endogenous Technological Change', *Journal of Political Economy* 98, no. 5, Part 2 (1990): S71–102.

Rosenberg, N., and M. Trajtenberg, 'A General-Purpose Technology at Work: The Corliss Steam Engine in the Late-Nineteenth-Century United States', *The Journal of Economic History* 64, no. 1 (2004): 61–99.

Roser, Max, Hannah Ritchie and Esteban Ortiz-Ospina, 'Life Expectancy', Our World in Data (2019).

Roser, Max, Hannah Ritchie and Esteban Ortiz-Ospina, 'World Population Growth', Our World in Data (2019).

Rubin, Jared, *Rulers, Religion, and Riches: Why the West Got Rich and the Middle East Did Not*, Cambridge University Press, 2017.

Sachs, Jeffrey D., 'Government, geography, and growth: The true drivers of economic development', *Foreign Affairs* 91, no. 5 (2012): 142–50.

Sachs, Jeffrey, and Pia Malaney, 'The Economic and Social Burden of Malaria', *Nature* 415, no. 6872 (2002): 680–5.

Schultz, T. P., 'Changing World Prices, Women's Wages, and the Fertility Transition: Sweden, 1860–1910', *Journal of Political Economy* 93, no. 6 (1985): 1126–54.

Scott, James C., *Against the Grain: A Deep History of the Earliest States*, Yale University Press, 2017.

Ségurel, Laure, and Céline Bon, 'On the evolution of lactase persistence in humans', *Annual Review of Genomics and Human Genetics* 18 (2017).

Shimelmitz, Ron, Iris Groman-Yaroslavski, Mina Weinstein-Evron and Danny Rosenberg, 'A Middle Pleistocene abrading tool from Tabun Cave, Israel: A search for the roots of abrading technology in human evolution', *Journal of Human Evolution* 150 (2020): 102909.

Shiue, Carol H., 'Human Capital and Fertility in Chinese Clans Before Modern Growth', *Journal of Economic Growth* 22, no. 4 (2017): 351–96.

Shoda, Yuichi, Walter Mischel and Philip K. Peake, 'Predicting Adolescent Cognitive and Self-Regulatory Competencies from Preschool Delay of Gratification: Identifying Diagnostic Conditions', *Developmental Psychology* 26, no. 6 (1990): 978.

Simon, Julian Lincoln, *The Economics of Population Growth*, Princeton University Press, 1977.

Skoglund, Pontus, Helena Malmström, Ayça Omrak, Maanasa Raghavan, Cristina Valdiosera, Torsten Günther, Per Hall et al., 'Genomic diversity and admixture differs for Stone-Age Scandinavian foragers and farmers', *Science* 344, no. 6185 (2014): 747–50.

Snir, Ainit, Dani Nadel, Iris Groman-Yaroslavski, Yoel Melamed, Marcelo Sternberg, Ofer Bar-Yosef and Ehud Weiss, 'The Origin of Cultivation and Proto-Weeds, Long before Neolithic Farming', *PLoS One* 10, no. 7 (2015).

Snyder, Timothy, *Black Earth: The Holocaust as History and Warning*, Tim Duggan Books, 2015.

Sokoloff, Kenneth L., and Stanley L. Engerman, 'Institutions, Factor Endowments, and Paths of Development in the New world', *Journal of Economic Perspectives* 14, no. 3 (2000): 217–32.

Spolaore, Enrico, and Romain Wacziarg, 'How Deep are the Roots of Economic Development?', *Journal of Economic Literature* 51, no. 2 (2013): 325–69.

Spolaore, Enrico, and Romain Wacziarg, 'The Diffusion of Development', *The Quarterly Journal of Economics* 124, no. 2 (2009): 469–529.

Squicciarini, Mara P., and Nico Voigtländer, 'Human Capital and Industrialization: Evidence from the Age of Enlightenment', *The Quarterly Journal of Economics* 130, no. 4 (2015): 1825–83.

Stahlberg, Dagmar, Friederike Braun, Lisa Irmen and Sabine Sczesny, 'Representation of the Sexes in Language', *Social Communication* (2007): 163–87.

Steinbauer, Friedrich, *Melanesian Cargo Cults: New salvation movements in the South Pacific*, University of Queensland Press, 1979.

Steward, Julian Haynes, *Theory of Culture Change: The methodology of multilinear evolution*, University of Illinois Press, 1972.

Talhelm, Thomas, Xiao Zhang, Shige Oishi, Chen Shimin, Dechao Duan, Xiaoli Lan and Shinobu Kitayama, 'Large-scale psychological differences within China explained by rice versus wheat agriculture', *Science* 344, no. 6184 (2014): 603–8.

Taylor, Walter W., 'Storage and the Neolithic Revolution', in *Estudios Dedicados al Professor Dr. Luis Pericot*, edited by Edwardo Ropillo, Universidad de Barcelona, Instituto de Arqueología y Prehistoria, 1973, pp. 193–7.

Testart, Alain, Richard G. Forbis, Brian Hayden, Tim Ingold, Stephen M. Perlman, David L. Pokotylo, Peter Rowley-Conwy and David E. Stuart, 'The Significance of Food Storage among Hunter-Gatherers: Residence Patterns, Population Densities, and Social Inequalities', *Current Anthropology* 23, no. 5 (1982): 523–37.

Tversky, Amos, and Daniel Kahneman, 'Loss Aversion in Riskless Choice: A Reference-Dependent Model', *The Quarterly Journal of Economics* 106, no. 4 (1991): 1039–61.

United Nations, World Population Prospects, 2017.

United Nations, Human Development Report, 2018.

United States Bureau of the Census, and United States, Congress House, *Historical Statistics of the United States, Colonial Times to 1970*, no. 93, US Department of Commerce, Bureau of the Census, 1975.

Vallin, Jacques, and France Meslé, *French Mortality Tables for XIXe and XXe Centuries and Projections for the Twenty First Century*, Données statistiques, no. 4, French Institute for Demographic Studies, 2001.

Vaquero, J. M. and Gallego, M. C., 'Two Early Observations of Aurora at Low Latitudes', *Annales Geophysicae* 19, no. 7 (2001): 809–11.

Vogl, Tom S., 'Differential fertility, human capital, and development', *The Review of Economic Studies* 83, no. 1 (2016): 365–401.

Voigtländer, Nico, and Hans-Joachim Voth, 'How the West "Invented" Fertility Restriction', *American Economic Review* 103, no. 6 (2013): 2227–64.

Voigtländer, Nico, and Hans-Joachim Voth, 'Why England? Demographic Factors, Structural Change and Physical Capital Accumulation During the Industrial Revolution', *Journal of Economic Growth* 11, no. 4 (2006): 319–61.

von Cramon-Taubadel, Noreen, and Stephen J. Lycett, 'Brief Communication: Human Cranial Variation Fits Iterative Founder Effect Model with African Origin', *American Journal of Physical Anthropology* 136, no. 1 (2008): 108–13.

Walker, Robert S., Michael Gurven, Oskar Burger and Marcus J. Hamilton, 'The trade-off between number and size of offspring in humans and other primates', *Proceedings of the Royal Society B: Biological Sciences* 275, no. 1636 (2008): 827–34.

Wallsten, Scott, 'Ringing in the 20th Century: The Effects of State Monopolies, Private Ownership, and Operating Licenses On Telecommunications in Europe, 1892–1914', SSRN, 2001.

Waters, Michael R., 'Late Pleistocene exploration and settlement of the Americas by modern humans', *Science* 365, no. 6449 (2019).

Wanamaker, M. H., 'Industrialization and Fertility in the Nineteenth Century: Evidence from South Carolina', *The Journal of Economic History* 72, no. 1 (2012): 168–96.

Weisdorf, Jacob L., 'From Foraging to Farming: Explaining the Neolithic Revolution', *Journal of Economic Surveys* 19, no. 4 (2005): 561–86.

Weiss, Ehud, Mordechai E. Kislev, Orit Simchoni, Dani Nadel and Hartmut Tschauner, 'Plant-Food Preparation Area on an Upper Paleolithic Brush Hut floor at Ohalo II, Israel', *Journal of Archaeological Science* 35, no. 8 (2008): 2400–14.

Wesley, John, 'Sermon 50: The Use of Money', in *The Sermons of John Wesley*, edited by Thomas Jackson, 1872.

West, Barbara A., *Encyclopedia of the Peoples of Asia and Oceania*, Infobase Publishing, 2010.

Westaway, Kira E., J. Louys, R. Due Awe, Michael J. Morwood, Gilbert J. Price, J-X. Zhao, Maxime Aubert et al., 'An Early Modern Human Presence in Sumatra 73,000–63,000 years ago', *Nature* 548, no. 7667 (2017): 322–5.

White, Leslie A., *The Evolution of Culture: The development of civilization to the fall of Rome*, McGraw-Hill, 1959.

Wiesenfeld, Stephen L., 'Sickle-cell Trait in Human Biological and Cultural Evolution: Development of Agriculture Causing Increased Malaria Is Bound to Gene-pool Changes Causing Malaria Reduction', *Science* 157, no. 3793 (1967): 1134–1140.

Wittfogel, K. A., *The Hydraulic Civilizations*, University of Chicago Press, 1956.

Woodham-Smith, Cecil, *The Great Hunger: Ireland 1845–9*, Penguin, 1962.

World Bank, World Development Indicators (WDI), 2017.

World Health Organization, *Life Expectancy Data by WHO Region*, 2016.

Worsley, Peter, 'The trumpet shall sound: a study of "cargo" cults in Melanesia', (1957).

Wrangham, Richard, and NancyLou Conklin-Brittain, 'Cooking as a biological trait', *Comparative Biochemistry and Physiology Part A: Molecular & Integrative Physiology* 136, no. 1 (2003): 35–46.

Wrigley, Edward Anthony, Ros S. Davies, James E. Oeppen and Roger S. Schofield, *English Population History from Family Reconstitution 1580–1837*, Cambridge University Press, 1997.

Wrigley, Edward Anthony, and Roger Schofield, *The Population History of England 1541–1871*, Cambridge University Press, 1981.

Endnotes

Mysteries of the Human Journey

1 Hobbes (1651). • 2 Data sources: Maddison Project Database (2010, 2013, 2018); Bolt and van Zanden (2014); Bolt et al. (2018); Roser et al. (2019): https://ourworldin-data.org/life-expectancy. • 3 Data sources: Bolt and van Zanden (2014); Bolt et al. (2018). • 4 Galor (2011). • 5 Some of these major events have been explored by Diamond (1997) and Harari (2014). • 6 Acemoglu and Robinson (2012); Alesina and Giuliano (2015). • 7 Data sources: Bolt et al. (2018). Western offshoots: Australia, Canada, New Zealand and the USA. • 8 Popper (1945). • 9 Pinker (2018).

Chapter 1: First Steps

1 Jelinek (1982). • 2 Roebroeks and Villa (2011); Shimelmitz et al. (2021). • 3 Parker (2011). • 4 Clutton-Brock et al. (1980); González-Forero and Gardner (2018). • 5 Dunbar (1998); Ofek (2001). • 6 Herrmann et al. (2007); Henrich (2017). • 7 Miller (2011). • 8 Aiello and Wheeler (1995); Wrangham (2003). • 9 Darlington (1975). • 10 Mellars (2006). • 11 Hershkovitz et al. (2018); Harvati et al. (2019). • 12 Bae et al. (2017). • 13 Poznik et al. (2013). • 14 Fu et al. (2013). • 15 López et al. (2015). • 16 Westaway et al. (2017). • 17 Clarkson et al. (2017). • 18 Hublin et al. (2020); Fewlass et al. (2020). • 19 Moreno-Mayar et al. (2018); Walters (2019); Becerra-Valdivia and Higham (2020); Bennett et al. (2021). • 20 Bar-Yosef (1998); Bar-Yosef and Valla (2013); Grossman (2013). • 21 Diamond (1997). • 22 Ibid. • 23 Haidt (2012). • 24 Modelski (2003); Morris (2010). • 25 Chandler (1987); Morris (2010); Modelski (2003); Vaquero and Gallego (2001). • 26 Ségurel and Bon (2017); Bleasdale et al. (2021). • 27 Ségurel and Bon (2017). • 28 Wiesenfeld (1967); Gibbons (2011).

Chapter 2: Lost in Stagnation

1 Diamond (1997); Comin, Easterly and Gong (2010); Ashraf and Galor (2011). • 2 Ashraf and Galor (2011); Dalgaard and Strulik (2015); Madsen et al. (2019). • 3 Ashraf and Galor (2011). • 4 Cohen (1989). • 5 Hunt and Lipo (2006). • 6 West (2010). • 7 Diamond (2005). • 8 Weisdorf (2005); Ashraf and Michalopoulos (2015);

Matranga (2019). • 9 Diamond (1997). • 10 Morelli et al. (2010). • 11 Jedwab et al. (2019). • 12 Photo © José Luiz Bernades Ribeiro / CC BY-SA 4.0 / Source: Wikimedia Commons • 13 Data sources: Clark (2007); Clark (2016); Wrigley et al. (1997). • 14 McNeill (1949); Fukayama (2006). • 15 Ó'Gráda (1979). • 16 Woodham-Smith (1962). • 17 Chen and Kung (2016). • 18 Ho (2013). • 19 Angrist and Pischke (2008). • 20 Ibid. • 20 Clark (2008). • 22 Angel (1969). • 23 Acsádi et al. (1970); Hassan (1981); Galor and Moav (2005). • 24 Hopkins (1966). • 25 Wrigley and Schofield (1981). • 26 Blayo (1975). • 27 Human Mortality Database, University of California, Berkeley (USA), and Max Planck Institute for Demographic Research (Germany). • 28 Kannisto et al. (1999). • 29 Data source: Bolt et al. (2018).

Chapter 3: The Storm Beneath the Surface

1 Copernicus, cited in Kuhn (1957). • 2 Galor (2011). • 3 Ibid.; Galor and Weil (2000); Galor and Moav (2002); Galor and Mountford (2008). • 4 Data sources: Hyde (History database of the Global Environment); Roser et al. (2019): https://ourworldindata.org/world-population-growth. • 5 Simon (1977); Kremer (1993). • 6 Kline and Boyd (2010). • 7 Richerson et al. (2011). • 8 Galor and Weil (2000); Lagerlöf (2006); • 9 Galor and Moav (2002). • 10 Barlow (1958). • 11 Kettlewell (1955). • 12 Mathieson et al. (2015). • 13 Bisin and Verdier (2000, 2001); Doepke and Zilibotti (2008); Galor and Michalopoulos (2012). • 14 MacArthur and Wilson (1970). • 15 Harper et al. (1970); Charnov and Morgan (2006); Walker et al. (2008). • 16 Galor and Klemp (2019). • 17 de la Croix et al. (2019).

Chapter 4: Full Steam

1 Dickens (1868). • 2 McCloskey (1981). • 3 Crafts and Harley (1992). • 4 Rosenberg and Trajtenberg (2004). • 5 Pascali (2017). • 6 *New York Herald* (1879). • 7 Allen (2003). • 8 Mokyr (1992). • 9 Dittmar (2011). • 10 Buringh and van Zanden (2009). • 11 Dittmar (2011). • 12 Data source: https://ourworldindata.org/literacy. • 13 Mitch (1992). • 14 Flora et al. (1983). • 15 Cipolla (1969). • 16 Green (1990). • 17 Flora et al. (1983). • 18 Cubberley (1920); Green (1990). • 19 Abramovitz and David (1999); Goldin and Katz (2001). • 20 Goldin (1988). • 21 Franck and Galor (2022). • 22 De Pleijt et al. (2020). • 23 Katz (2018). • 24 Atack et al. (2010). • 25 Nelson and Phelps (1966). • 26 Meisenzahl and Mokyr (2011). • 27 Feldman and van der Beek (2016); de la Croix et al. (2018). • 28 Nelson and Phelps (1966). • 29 Cinnirella and Streb (2017). • 30 Squicciarini and Voigtländer (2015). • 31 Maloney and Valencia Caicedo (2017). • 32 Benhabib and Spiegel (2005). • 33 Acemoglu and Robinson (2000); Aidt and Franck (2015). • 34 Galor and Moav (2006). • 35 Galor and Tsiddon (1997); Galor and Moav (2000). • 36 Green (1990). • 37 Ibid. • 38 Galor and Moav (2006). • 39 Galor et al. (2009). • 40 Ibid. • 41 Photo by Lewis Hine. Source: Library of Congress. Wikimedia Commons. • 42 Basu (1999). • 43 Hazan and Berdugo (2002); Doepke and Zilibotti (2005). • 44 Nardinelli (1980). • 45 Data source: https://ourworldindata.org/child-labor. • 46 Doepke and Zilibotti (2005). • 47 Pinker (2018).

Chapter 5: Metamorphosis

1 Data source: https://ourworldindata.org/fertility-rate. • 2 Jones and Tertlit (2009). • 3 Galor (2005); Cervellati and Sunde (2005); Voigtländer and Voth (2006). • 4 Data

source: Chesnais (1992). • 5 Grande and Stevenson (2017). • 6 Hanjal (1965); Guinnane (2011); Voigtländer and Voth (2013). • 7 Potts and Campbell (2002). • 8 Collier
(2010). • 9 Galor and Weil (2000); Becker and Tomes (1976). • 10 Botticini and Eckstein (2014). • 11 Galor (2012); Vogl (2016). • 12 Becker et al. (2010). • 13 Bleakley
and Lange (2009). • 14 Fernihough (2017); Murphy (2015); Andersen et al. (2016);
Vogl (2016). • 15 Klemp and Weisdorf (2019). • 16 Shiue (2017). • 17 Goldin (1990).
• 18 Cipolla (1969). • 19 Schultz (1985). • 20 Greenwood et al. (2005); Hazan et al.
(2021). • 21 Wrigley and Schofield (1989); Burnette (1997). • 22 Goldin (1990). • 23
Goldin (1987). • 24 Galor and Weil (1996), Lagerlof (2003); de la Croix et al. (2015).
• 25 Crafts (1989). • 26 Brown and Guinnane (2002). • 27 Wanamaker (2012). • 28
Schultz (1985); Heckman and Walker (1990).

Chapter 6: The Promised Land

1 Gordon (2017). • 2 Data sources: Wrigley and Schofield (1981); Arias (2016); Blayo
(1975); Vallin and Meslé (2001); United Nations (2017); Kannisto et al. (1999);
OECD (2017); Human Mortality Database, University of California, Berkeley (USA),
and Max Planck Institute for Demographic Research (Germany); World Health
Organization (2016). • 3 Bleakley (2010); Lucas (2010). • 4 Data source: United
States, Bureau of the Census, and United States. • 5 Wallsten (2001). • 6 Data sources:
Maddison Project Database (2020); Bolt and van Zandan (2020). • 7 Data source:
World Economic Outlook, 2018, IMF. • 8 Data source: Office for National Statistics
(ONS), UK. • 9 Data source: Bureau of Labor Statistics. • 10 Data source: World
Economic Outlook, IMF (2018). • 11 Franck and Galor (2020). • 12 Becker et al.
(2017). • 13 Franck and Galor (2020). • 14 Data source: WDI, World Bank. • 15 Ibid.
• 16 Keynes (1971). • 17 Abram et al. (2016). • 18 Jackson (2016). • 19 Casey and
Galor (2017). • 20 Gates (2021).

Chapter 7: Splendour and Misery

1 Data sources: WDI, World Bank (2017); United Nations (2018). • 2 GDP per capita
adjusted for purchasing power. Data sources: https://www.cdc.gov; https://www.cen-
sus.gov. • 3 Data source: WDI, World Bank (2017). • 4 Ibid. • 5 Romer (1990);
Aghion and Howitt (1992); Grossman and Helpman (1991); Jones (1995); Lucas
(1988, 2002). • 6 Data source: Bolt et al. (2018); Durlauf and Quah (1999); Duraluf
et al. (2005). • 7 Easterly (2001); Hausmann et al. (2005). • 8 Estavadeordal et al.
(2002). • 9 Findlay and O'Rourke (2001). • 10 Crafts and Thomas (1986); O'Rourke
and Williamson (1999); Pomeranz (2000); Andrews (2021). • 11 Mokyr (1989). • 12
Kuznets (1967). • 13 Galor and Mountford (2008). • 14 Ibid.; Bignon and García-
Peñalosa (2016). • 15 Bairoch (1982). • 16 Chaudhuri (1983). • 17 Bairoch (1974,
1982). • 18 Matthews et al. (1982). • 19 Basu (1974). • 20 Morris (2010).

Chapter 8: The Fingerprints of Institutions

1 Produced by NASA. Source: Wikimedia Commons. • 2 Data source: Maddison Project Database (2020); *The World Factbook* (2020). • 3 North (1990). • 4 Greif (1993).
• 5 Acemoglu and Robinson (2012). • 6 Hill (1966). • 7 Acemoglu and Robinson
(2012). • 8 Ibid. • 9 Mokyr (1992). • 10 Klemm (1964). • 11 Mokyr (1992). • 12
Murtin and Wacziarg (2004). • 13 Barro (1996); Persson and Tabellini (2006);

Papaioannou and Siourounis (2008). • 14 Lipset (1959); Barro (1999); Fukayama (2006). • 15 Dell (2010). • 16 Acemoglu et al. (2011). • 17 McEvedy and Jones (1978). • 18 Sokoloff and Engerman (2000). • 19 La Porta et al. (1997); Glaeser and Shleifer (2002). • 20 Galor et al. (2009). • 21 Engerman and Sokoloff (1997). • 22 Acemoglu et al. (2002). • 23 Acemoglu et al. (2001). • 24 Sachs (2012). • 25 Easterly and Levine (2016). • 26 Glaeser et al. (2004). • 27 Putterman and Weil (2010). • 28 Michalopoulos and Papaioannou (2013). • 29 Acemoglu and Robinson (2012). • 30 Fenske (2014); Galor and Klemp (2019). • 31 Data source: WDI, World Bank.

Chapter 9: *The Cultural Factor*

1 Mark 9:24; Timothy 6:10; Aquinas (1920); Matthew 5:5. • 2 Wesley (1872). • 3 Becker and Woessmann (2009); Andersen et al. (2017). • 4 Becker and Woessmann (2009). • 5 Nunziata and Rocco (2016, 2018). • 6 Guiso et al. (2006); Bazzi et al. (2020). • 7 Botticini and Eckstein (2014). • 8 Blackmore (2001). • 9 Dawkins (1976). • 10 Henrich (2017). • 11 White (1959); Steward (1972). • 12 Fanon (2007, 2008); Andrews (2021). • 13 Kant (1784). • 14 Mokyr (2016). • 15 Neel (1962). • 16 Banfield (1967). • 17 Alesina and Giuliano (2010). • 18 Arrow (1972). • 19 Putnam et al. (1994). • 20 Guiso at al. (2004). Trust is measured by the response to a question in a survey conducted by the European Social Survey over the years 2002–11: 'Would you say that most people can be trusted, or that you can't be too careful in dealing with people?' • 21 Becker et al. (2016). • 22 Nunn and Wantchekon (2011). • 23 Giavazzi et al. (2019). • 24 Gorodnichenko and Roland (2017). • 25 Fischer (1989).

Chapter 10: *The Shadow of Geography*

1 Goody (2018). • 2 Murdock (1967). • 3 Alsan (2015). • 4 Sachs (2002). • 5 Lucas (2010, 2013). • 6 Dalgaard et al. (2020). • 7 Ashraf and Galor (2013). • 8 Diamond (1997). • 9 Jones (2003). • 10 Hume (1825). • 11 Cosgel et al. (2012); Rubin (2017). • 12 Hanioğlu (2010). • 13 Quataert (2005). • 14 Mokyr (2016). • 15 Wittfogel (1956). • 16 Lang (1997). • 17 Cosandey (2007). • 18 Hoffman (2017). • 19 Ashraf et al. (2010); Ashraf and Galor (2011). • 20 Engerman and Sokoloff (1997). • 21 Acemoglu et al. (2002). • 22 Ibid. • 23 Galor and Mountford (2006, 2008). • 24 Kendi (2015). • 25 Nunn (2008). • 26 Nunn and Puga (2012). • 27 Hofstede et al. (2005). • 28 Galor and Ozak (2016). • 29 Ibid.; Data source for 'Long-Term Orientation across countries': https://hi.hofstede-insights.com/national-culture. • 30 Galor and Ozak (2016). • 31 Ibid. • 32 Ibid. • 33 Talhelm et al. (2014). • 34 Ang (2019). • 35 Alesina et al. (2013). • 36 Ibid. • 37 Tversky and Kahneman (1991). • 38 Galor and Savitskiy (2018). • 39 Ibid. • 40 Ibid. • 41 Magga (2006); Krupnik and Müller-Wille (2010). • 42 Josserand et al. (2021). • 43 Pinker (2003). • 44 Roberts and Winters (2012); Lupyan and Dale (2010). • 45 Richerson et al. (2010). • 46 Galor et al. (2018). • 47 Stahlberg et al. (2007); Galor et al. (2020). • 48 Fenske (2014). • 49 Galor et al. (2018). • 50 Bybee and Dahl (1989); Dahl and Velupillai (2011). • 51 Chen (2013); Galor (2016); Galor et al. (2019).

Chapter 11: *The Legacy of the Agricultural Revolution*

1 Weiss et al. (2008); Snir et al. (2015). • 2 Diamond (1997). • 3 North and Thomas (1977). • 4 Galor and Moav (2007); Gibbons (2021). • 5 Skoglund et al. (2014);

González-Fortes et al. (2017). • 6 Feldman et al. (2019). • 7 Lazaridis et al. (2014). • 8 Bellwood and Fox (2006). • 9 Bostoen (2018). • 10 Murdock (1967). • 11 Carneiro (1981). • 12 Taylor (1973); Testart et al. (1982); Allen (1997). • 13 Mayshar et al. (2017). • 14 Scott (2017). • 15 Mayshar et al. (2019). • 16 Data source: Putterman (2008). • 17 Ashraf and Galor (2011). • 18 Ashraf and Galor (2013). • 19 Galor and Mountford (2006, 2008). • 20 Acemoglu and Robinson (2012); Mokyr (2016); Hoffman (2017).

Chapter 12: Out of Africa

1 Palmer (1992). • 2 Ridley (2012). • 3 Ottaviano and Peri (2006); Lee (2015). • 4 Delis et al. (2017). • 5 Cook and Fletcher (2018). • 6 Alesina et al. (2003); Ramos-Toro (2017). • 7 Easterly and Levine (1997). • 8 Harpending and Rogers (2000); Ramachandran et al. (2005); Prugnolle et al. (2005); Manica et al. (2007); von Cramon-Taubadel and Lycett (2008); Hanihara (2008); Betti et al. (2009); Atkinson (2011); Betti et al. (2013); Betti and Manica (2018). • 9 Ibid. • 10 Pemberton et al. (2013). • 11 Data source: Pemberton et al. (2013). Figure source: Ashraf, Galor and Klemp (2021). • 12 Harpending and Rogers (2000); Ramachandran et al. (2005); Prugnolle et al. (2005); Manica et al. (2007); von Cramon-Taubadel and Lycett (2008); Hanihara (2008); Betti et al. (2009); Atkinson (2011); Betti et al. (2013); Betti and Manica (2018). • 13 Alesina et al. (2003). • 14 Pemberton (2013); Desmet et al. (2017). • 15 Ashraf and Galor (2013). • 16 Arbatlı et al. (2020); Ashraf et al. (2021). • 17 Ashraf et al. (2021). The observed hump-shaped relationship between population diversity and population density in the year 1500 (Fig. 23(a)) does not reflect a potential underestimation of the diversity of pre-colonial Amerindian societies, which are all placed to the right of the hump. The impact of diversity on productivity in general and on population density in 1500 in particular is established based on variations in diversity *within* each continent, and thus an underestimation of the *entire* American population, as may well have occurred, would have no bearing on the depicted pattern. In fact, the statistical method used is such that even if the native population of *each* ethnic group in the Americas was, say, 100 times larger, the impact of diversity as depicted in Fig. 23(a) would remain intact. • 18 Ibid. • 19 Cook and Fletcher (2018); Depetris-Chauvin and Özak (2021); Ashraf et al. (2021). • 20 Manica et al. (2007); von Cramon-Taubadel et al. (2008). • 21 Ashraf and Galor (2013). • 22 Ashraf et al. (2021). • 23 Ibid. • 24 Ashraf and Galor (2013).

Coda: Unravelling the Mystery of Inequality

1 Worsley (1967); Steinbauer (1979). • 2 Rodrik (2006); Hausmann et al. (2008).

Index